CAMBRIDGE

G000138031

EMPOWER

SECOND EDITION

STUDENT'S BOOK

WITH EBOOK

B1+

INTERMEDIATE

Adrian Doff, Craig Thaine
Herbert Puchta, Jeff Stranks, Peter Lewis-Jones
with Rachel Godfrey and Gareth Davies

CAMBRIDGE

EMPOWER SECOND EDITION is a six-level general English course for adult and young adult learners, taking students from beginner to advanced level (CEFR A1 to C1). *Empower* combines course content from Cambridge University Press with validated assessment from the experts at Cambridge Assessment English.

Empower's unique mix of engaging classroom materials and reliable assessment enables learners to make consistent and measurable progress.

Content you love.

Assessment you

can trust.

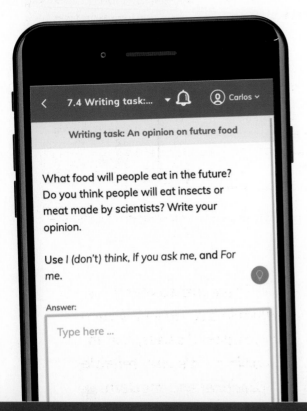

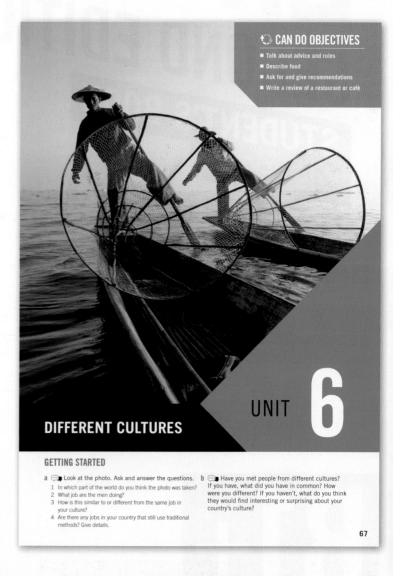

Better Learning with *Empower*

Better Learning is our simple approach where **insights** we've gained from research have helped shape **content** that drives **results** .

Learner engagement

1 Content that informs and motivates

Insights
Sustained motivation is key to successful language learning and skills development.

Content
Clear learning goals, thought-provoking images, texts and speaking activities, plus video content to arouse curiosity.

Results
Content that surprises, entertains and provokes an emotional response, helping teachers to deliver motivating and memorable lessons.

6A YOU SHOULD WEAR GOOD WALKING SHOES

Learn to talk about advice and rules
- **G** Modals of obligation
- **V** Compound nouns

1 SPEAKING AND READING

a Discuss the questions.
1 What do you think the phrase 'culture shock' means? What difficulties might culture shock cause?
2 Think of a country you would like to visit. How do you think it is different from your own country? Think about the words in the box.

cities and streets   customs   food
getting around   people

b Quickly read the article about CultureMee, an app for tourists travelling to other countries. Which of the things below does the app provide?
1 'insider tips' about the culture
2 information about main tourist sites
3 a history of the country
4 detailed descriptions of famous buildings
5 lists of recommended hotels and restaurants
6 tips about how to behave in the country
7 information about local attitudes and customs

CULTURE SHOCK? THERE'S AN APP TO DEAL WITH THAT

Many travel apps and guidebooks can help you to book a cheap homestay or an expensive hotel with a swimming pool, and they can tell you where to go windsurfing or what restaurants serve the best seafood. But what if you want information on how to greet people politely in Tokyo, how much to tip a taxi driver in Madrid or where to meet local people in Rio de Janeiro? Well, a new app for your smartphone can now do all that for you.

The app is called CultureMee, and it not only gives straightforward travel advice, but it also provides **insights** into the culture of the country you're visiting. It was set up by an Irish couple, John and Dee Lee, and has quickly grown in popularity. Thousands of people are already using the app, which now covers locations all over the world. It has also won several international awards.

The idea for the app came to them while they were on holiday in East Africa a few years ago. They had guidebooks that told them about places to visit, but they found it difficult to find out about what kind of plug they needed for their hair dryer or exactly what vaccinations they needed.

They realised that it would be very useful to have an app that could give people this kind of basic travel advice. They also wanted to help people understand the culture of any country they might visit, so this became an **integral** part of the app's content.

The couple decided not to take the conventional **approach to** culture, which is already a feature of standard guidebooks, but rather to focus on the everyday lives of people in the country. There are plenty

of apps available that can help you book holidays and places to stay, and that give you information about tourist sights and museums. However, John and Dee felt that most travel apps don't focus on ordinary people, so they decided to put this **at the heart of** what CultureMee does.

CultureMee offers a wide range of cultural content, including background information about the country and its history, details on contemporary culture and advice on dealing with culture shock. Users can access videos, produced by the couple themselves, that **supplement** the core content of the app. Many of these give tips on how to engage with local people and how to behave in an appropriate way. They are based on interviews with people who have visited the country, and who can talk **with authority** about it from a visitor's point of view. There are also interviews with local people who provide insights into how they view their own culture.

So, imagine that someone from the UK wants to travel to Thailand. They can select the appropriate culture video and hear a Thai person talking about Thai culture. They can also watch a video of a non-Thai person talking about how to get on with Thai people and understand their culture.

An essential aim of John and Dee's project is to create an online community of people who are interested in travel and culture. As the app becomes more popular, they hope this community will continue to augment* it with their own stories and viewpoints.

augment (v) to increase the size or value of something by adding to it

A screenshot from CultureMee

John and Dee Lee, founders of CultureMee

68

UNIT 6

c Read the article again. Decide if the sentences are true (T) or false (F). Find phrases in the text that tell you the answer.
1 The new app only gives cultural advice, not practical travel advice.
2 CultureMee has already been successful.
3 John and Dee's guidebook on East Africa didn't tell them everything they needed to know.
4 John and Dee decided to interview ordinary people who know about a country.
5 All the interviews are with people who come from the country they talk about.
6 They would like people who use the app to contribute to it and improve it.

d What do the words in **bold** mean in the context of the article? Choose a or b.
1 **insights**
 a knowledge of something
 b suggested places to visit
2 **integral**
 a additional, extra
 b central, essential
3 **approach to**
 a information about
 b way of looking at
4 **at the heart of**
 a feeling strongly about something
 b central to something
5 **supplement**
 a add to something
 b use instead of something
6 **with authority**
 a knowledgeable about something
 b having permission to talk about something

2 VOCABULARY Compound nouns

a Read the information below about compound nouns, then underline the compound nouns in the title and introduction to the article on p. 68.

Compound nouns combine two words. We write some compound nouns as one word (e.g., *lunchtime*) and others as two words (e.g., *living room*). They are usually formed by:
- noun + noun (e.g., *newspaper*)
- verb + *-ing* + noun (e.g., *washing machine*)
- noun + verb + *-ing* (e.g., *ice skating*)

b ▶06.01 Pronunciation Listen to the compound nouns from the article. Which part is stressed – the first or the second word? Practise saying the words.

c Complete the compound nouns with the words in the box.

baseball   book   insect   pack   screen   shop   tour   walking

1 _____ guide
2 sun_____
3 souvenir _____
4 _____ cap
5 back_____
6 guide_____
7 _____ shoes
8 _____ repellent

The Ruins of Tikal: Insider Tips

If you're in Guatemala, you really must go to Tikal. It's a huge ancient city, built by the Maya civilisation in the 5th century, and it's one of the world's most amazing sights.

You can hire an official ¹_____ to show you around, but it's better to take a good ²_____ with you – it will tell you everything you need to know about the ruins and allow you to look at them at your own pace. The sun is very strong, so don't forget to put ³_____ on your face and arms and wear a(n) ⁴_____. Also, there are mosquitoes in the area, so you should put on some ⁵_____ before you start. The ruins cover several square kilometres and you have to walk, so you should wear good ⁶_____. You can buy food at the site, but it's pretty expensive. I always carry a small ⁷_____ with my own food and plenty of water to drink. After your visit, you might want to stop off at the visitor centre near the entrance, where you can find a café and a(n) ⁸_____.

Special tip: Go at dawn to watch the sun rise over the ruins. It's an experience you'll never forget!

d Read the travel tips for Tikal in Guatemala. Complete the text with compound nouns from 2c.

e ≫ Communication 6A Student A: Go to p. 130. Student B: Go to p. 132.

3 LISTENING

a Look at the photos and the information about Kim, Will and Tasia. What cultural differences do you think they noticed when they lived overseas? Compare your ideas with other students.

Kim from England went to live in Brazil.

Will from the USA worked for a company in Nigeria.

Tasia from Greece went to live in the UK.

69

---

2 Personalised and relevant

Insights
Language learners benefit from frequent opportunities to personalise their responses.

Content
Personalisation tasks in every unit make the target language more meaningful to the individual learner.

Results
Personal responses make learning more memorable and inclusive, with all students participating in spontaneous spoken interaction.

There are so many adjectives to describe such a wonderful series, but in my opinion it's very reliable, practical and modern.

Zenaide Brianez, Director of Studies, Instituto da Língua Inglesa, Brazil

Measurable progress

1 Assessment you can trust

Insights
Tests developed and validated by Cambridge Assessment English, the world leaders in language assessment, to ensure they are accurate and meaningful.

Content
End-of-unit tests, mid- and end-of-course competency tests and personalised CEFR test report forms provide reliable information on progress with language skills.

Results
Teachers can see learners' progress at a glance, and learners can see measurable progress, which leads to greater motivation.

Results of an impact study showing % improvement of Reading levels, based on global *Empower* students' scores over one year.

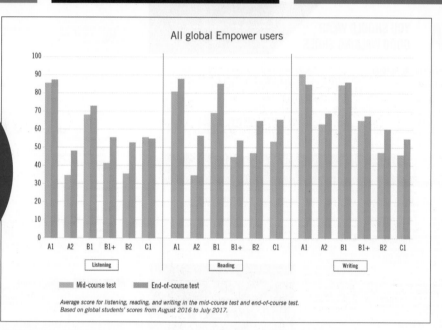

All global Empower users

Mid-course test   End-of-course test

Average score for listening, reading, and writing in the mid-course test and end-of-course test. Based on global students' scores from August 2016 to July 2017.

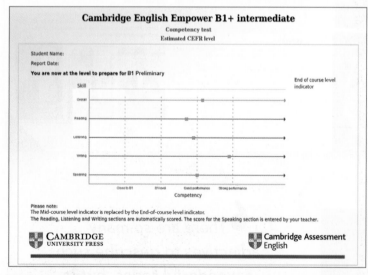

Cambridge English Empower B1+ intermediate
Competency test
Estimated CEFR level

Student Name:
Report Date:
You are now at the level to prepare for B1 Preliminary

Please note:
The Mid-course level indicator is replaced by the End-of-course level indicator.
The Reading, Listening and Writing sections are automatically scored. The score for the Speaking section is entered by your teacher.

CAMBRIDGE UNIVERSITY PRESS   Cambridge Assessment English

> *We started using the tests provided with Empower and our students started showing better results from this point until now.*

Kristina Ivanova, Director of Foreign Language Training Centre, ITMO University, Saint Petersburg, Russia

2 Evidence of impact

Insights
Schools and colleges need to show that they are evaluating the effectiveness of their language programmes.

Content
Empower (British English) impact studies have been carried out in various countries, including Russia, Brazil, Turkey and the UK, to provide evidence of positive impact and progress.

Results
Colleges and universities have demonstrated a significant improvement in language level between the mid- and end-of-course tests, as well as a high level of teacher satisfaction with *Empower*.

Manageable learning

1 Mobile friendly

Insights
Learners expect online content to be mobile friendly but also flexible and easy to use on any digital device.

Content
Empower provides easy access to Digital Workbook content that works on any device and includes practice activities with audio.

Results
Digital Workbook content is easy to access anywhere, and produces meaningful and actionable data so teachers can track their students' progress and adapt their lesson accordingly.

> " *I had been studying English for ten years before university and I didn't succeed. But now with* Empower *I know my level of English has changed.* "

Nikita, *Empower* Student, ITMO University, Saint Petersburg, Russia

2 Corpus-informed

Insights
Corpora can provide valuable information about the language items learners are able to learn successfully at each CEFR level.

Content
Two powerful resources – Cambridge Corpus and English Profile – informed the development of the *Empower* course syllabus and the writing of the materials.

Results
Learners are presented with the target language they are able to incorporate and use at the right point in their learning journey. They are not overwhelmed with unrealistic learning expectations.

Rich in practice

1 Language in use

Insights	**Content**	**Results**
It is essential that learners are offered frequent and manageable opportunities to practise the language they have been focusing on.	Throughout the *Empower* Student's Book, learners are offered a wide variety of practice activities, plenty of controlled practice and frequent opportunities for communicative spoken practice.	Meaningful practice makes new language more memorable and leads to more efficient progress in language acquisition.

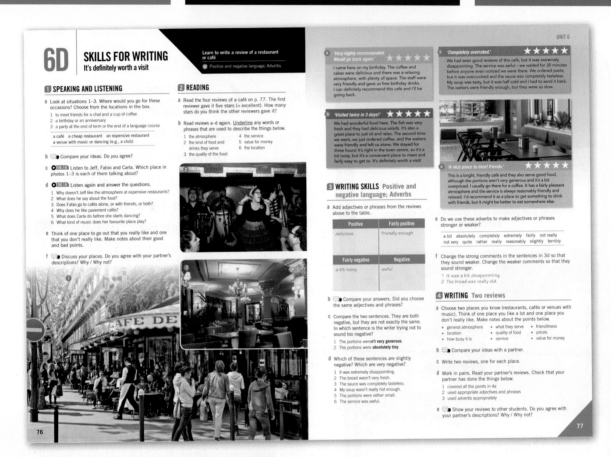

2 Beyond the classroom

> *There are plenty of opportunities for personalisation.*
>
> **Elena Pro, Teacher, EOI de San Fernando de Henares, Spain**

Insights
Progress with language learning often requires work outside the classroom, and different teaching models require different approaches.

Content
Empower is available with a print workbook, online practice, documentary-style videos that expose learners to real-world English, plus additional resources with extra ideas and fun activities.

Results
This choice of additional resources helps teachers to find the most effective ways to motivate their students both inside and outside the classroom.

Unit overview

Unit Opener

Getting started page – Clear learning objectives to give an immediate sense of purpose.

⬇

Lessons A and B

Grammar and Vocabulary – Input and practice of core grammar and vocabulary, plus a mix of skills.

— **Digital Workbook (online, mobile):** Grammar and Vocabulary

⬇

Lesson C

Everyday English – Functional language in common, everyday situations.

— **Digital Workbook (online, mobile):** Listening and Speaking

⬇

Unit Progress Test

⬇

Lesson D

Integrated Skills – Practice of all four skills, with a special emphasis on writing.

— **Digital Workbook (online, mobile):** Reading and Writing

⬇

Review

Extra practice of grammar, vocabulary and pronunciation. Also a 'Review your progress' section for students to reflect on the unit.

⬇

Mid- / End-of-course test

⬇

Additional practice

Further practice is available for outside the class with these components.

Digital Workbook (online, mobile)

Workbook (print)

Components

Resources – Available on cambridgeone.org

- Audio
- Video
- Unit Progress Tests (print)
- Unit Progress Tests (online)

- Mid- and end-of-course assessment (print)
- Mid- and end-of-course assessment (online)

- Digital Workbook (online)
- Photocopiable Grammar, Vocabulary and Pronunciation worksheets

CONTENTS

Lesson and objective	Grammar	Vocabulary	Pronunciation	Everyday English
Unit 6 Different cultures				
Getting started Talk about different cultures				
6A Talk about advice and rules	Modals of obligation	Compound nouns	Word stress: compound nouns	
6B Describe food	Comparatives and superlatives	Describing food	Sound and spelling: /ʃ/ and /tʃ/	
6C Ask for and give recommendations			Sounding interested	Asking for and giving recommendations
6D Write a review of a restaurant or café				
Review and extension More practice		WORDPOWER *go*		
Unit 7 House and home				
Getting started Talk about ideal houses				
7A Describe a building	Modals of deduction	Buildings	Modal verbs: final /t/ and /d/ sounds	
7B Describe a town or city	Quantifiers	Verbs and prepositions	Sentence stress: verbs and prepositions	
7C Make offers and requests and ask for permission			Sounding polite	Making offers and requests and asking for permission
7D Write a note with useful information				
Review and extension More practice		WORDPOWER *over*		
Unit 8 Information				
Getting started Talk about an interesting news story				
8A Talk about podcasts	Reported speech	Sharing information	Sound and spelling: /g/ and /k/	
8B Talk about what other people say	Verb patterns	Reporting verbs		
8C Generalise and be vague			Sound and spelling: /h/ and /w/	Generalising and being vague
8D Write an email summary of a news story				
Review and extension More practice		WORDPOWER *in / on* + noun		
Unit 9 Entertainment				
Getting started Talk about street entertainers				
9A Talk about films and TV	The passive	*-ed / -ing* adjectives	Sound and spelling: final *-ed* in adjectives	
9B Give extra information	Defining and non-defining relative clauses	Music; Word-building (nouns)	Relative clauses: pausing; Word stress	
9C Recommend and respond to recommendations			Showing contrast	Recommending and responding to recommendations
9D Write an article				
Review and extension More practice		WORDPOWER *see, look at, watch, hear, listen to*		
Unit 10 Opportunities				
Getting started Talk about different kinds of opportunities				
10A Talk about new things it would be good to do	Second conditional	Sport; Adjectives and prepositions	Sentence stress: *would*	
10B Talk about imagined past events	Third conditional	Expressions with *do, make* and *take*	Sentence stress: *would* and *have*	
10C Talk about possible problems and reassure someone			Sounding sure and unsure	Talking about possible problems and reassuring someone
10D Write an email with advice				
Review and extension More practice		WORDPOWER Easily confused words		
Communication Plus p. 127	**Vocabulary Focus p. 133**		**Grammar Focus p. 144**	

This page is intentionally left blank.

UNIT 1

TALK

GETTING STARTED

a 💬 Look at the photo and answer the questions.

1 Where do you think the girls are?

2 What do you think the girl on the left is saying? Why do you think that?

3 How do you think the other girl feels? Why?

b Discuss the questions.

1 Do/Did you talk a lot in class in school or at university?

2 Do you talk a lot when you are with your friends? What about with your family?

3 Do you think you should change anything about the way you talk (e.g., talk more, less, more loudly, more quietly)? Why / Why not?

1A | WHO LIKES MY POSTS?

Learn to talk about friendship and communication

G Subject and object questions
V Friendship and communication

1 SPEAKING AND VOCABULARY
Friendship and communication

a 💬 Discuss the questions.

1 How do you usually meet new people – face-to-face or online? Why?
2 Are your online friendships different from your other friendships? How?
3 What kinds of things do you talk about online? Is this different from most of your face-to-face conversations? Why / Why not?

b Match the words in **bold** in sentences 1–6 with definitions a–f.

1 ☐ Social media is a great way to **get in touch** with old friends you haven't seen in a while.
2 ☐ It's really difficult to **express your feelings** online because you can't look people in the eye.
3 ☐ When her brother, Mike, was in hospital, Susanna **reached out** to all his friends to come and visit him.
4 ☐ It's easier to **interact with** people online because you can think about what you want to say before you write it.
5 ☐ With good friends, you often don't have to **put** how you feel **into words**, because you just understand each other.
6 ☐ It's not a good idea to **give your opinion** in an online discussion because it's written. If you change your mind, you can't get rid of what you wrote.

a to communicate with and react to a person or people
b to say or write what you think or believe about something
c to contact someone by phone, email or text message
d to try to communicate with a person or group of people, usually to help or involve them
e to talk about your emotions
f to explain a feeling using language

c 💬 Do you agree with sentences 1–6? Why / Why not?

d ≫ Now go to Vocabulary Focus 1A on p. 133.

2 READING

a Read the article and find out if it has similar ideas to the ones you talked about in 1a.

BUT ARE THEY REAL FRIENDS?

You've probably heard it before, haven't you? 'Facebook and Instagram friends aren't the same as the real thing.' People from generations that didn't grow up with online friendships criticise younger adults who say they have a lot of online friends. They don't think friendships that are made online are as real or as meaningful as face-to-face ones. But it looks like they may be wrong.

Researchers at the University of California have come to the conclusion that online friendships have the same qualities as those in the real world. In a study, the researchers looked at exchanges between online friends and observed the same kinds of behaviours that exist in face-to-face friendships. Online friends share experiences and interests, express their feelings and reveal things about themselves. Sometimes they offer each other practical help, and they can keep each other company at any time of the day or night.

Another way that face-to-face and online friendships are similar is that they take time to develop. You can't just go online hoping to find a friend – it's not as simple as that. Experts say that you need to build online friendships carefully, and they offer the following advice:

👤 Join a discussion or community that talks about something you're interested in.

👤 Make sure it's an app or website where you can exchange ideas and information – not one where you just follow what other people say.

👤 Write a clear and honest profile of yourself. Make it interesting and use a friendly tone.

👤 Don't expect to find a friend immediately – it can take time.

And when you do find a friend ...

👤 Take things one step at a time, but make sure you stay in touch.

👤 Share things about your life, but not very personal things, and try to build trust.

b Read the article again. Are the sentences true (*T*) or false (*F*)? Correct the false sentences.

1 Some older people don't think online friends are true friends.
2 Researchers say there are many differences between face-to-face and online friendships.
3 Online friends can be available to interact with day and night.
4 You will find online friends very quickly.
5 To help an online friendship develop, share some details about yourself and your life.

Here's a checklist of questions you can ask yourself as you explore the world of online friendships:

1 Is it easy to use the app/website? ☐
2 Is this a community I want to join? ☐
3 Are there people I want to communicate with? ☐
4 Am I interested in replying to posts? ☐
5 Are the posts friendly and honest? ☐
6 Do other people like or reply to my posts? ☐

c 💬 Discuss the questions.

1 Do you think the advice in the article is good? Why / Why not?
2 What problems can happen as a result of online friendships? What are the benefits?
3 Do you think people express their feelings more or less carefully online? Why?
4 Do you think it's easier to find someone you have something in common with in the real world or online? Why?

3 GRAMMAR Subject and object questions

a Look at the questions and answers. The main verb is in **bold**. Underline the correct words in the box.

1 **Q:** What do experts **say** about making friends online?
   A: You need to build friendships carefully.
2 **Q:** Who **thinks** online friendships aren't real?
   A: People from generations that didn't grow up with online friendships.

> a In question 1 the subject is *what / experts / making friends*. Question 1 is a(n) *subject / object* question.
> b In question 2, the subject is *Who / online friendships*. Question 2 is a(n) *subject / object* question.
> c We use auxiliary verbs *do, does, did* in *subject / object* questions.

b Are the questions below subject (*S*) or object (*O*) questions?

1 ☐ Who do I give this to?
2 ☐ What happened to your leg?
3 ☐ Which of these books do you want to borrow?
4 ☐ Who gave you the flowers?
5 ☐ Which car uses less petrol?
6 ☐ What did he say to you?

c ≫ Now go to Grammar Focus 1A on p. 144.

d Make subject (*S*) or object (*O*) questions with the words below. You may need to change the verb or add *do, does* or *did*.

1 Who / call / you / yesterday? (*S*)
   _____

2 Who / you / last / text? (*O*)
   _____

3 What / you and your friends / talk about? (*O*)
   _____

4 What / make / you and your friends / laugh? (*S*)
   _____

5 Which of your friends / you / see / every day? (*O*)
   _____

6 What / post / last / make / you laugh? (*S*)
   _____

e 💬 Ask and answer the questions. Try to ask follow-up questions.

4 LISTENING

a 💬 Discuss the questions.

1 Do you think online friends can become face-to-face friends? How can this happen?
2 What are the advantages and disadvantages of this change in friendship?

b ▶ 01.05 You are going to hear Kris, Alex and Kelly talk about online friendships. Listen and put a name with each photo.

1 _____

2 _____

3 _____

c ▶ 01.05 Listen again and complete the information in the chart.

	Kris	Alex	Kelly
Friend's name			
Common interest			
Met – yes or no?			
What have they done together?			

d Which of the three speakers would you like most as an online friend? Why?

5 SPEAKING

a Tick (✓) the things you have done recently. Make notes about the experience.

☐ met someone new face-to-face
☐ met someone new online
☐ met someone face-to-face who you first met online
☐ met an old friend you hadn't seen in a long time
☐ posted a strong opinion on social media or a discussion board
☐ posted a video story on social media
☐ created a playlist of your favourite music
☐ started a new job/course

b Look at the experiences your partner ticked and write three questions to ask them.

> *met someone new*
> Who was it?
> Where were you?
> What did you talk about?

c Ask your partner about their experiences. Try to ask follow-up questions.

1B I'M USING AN APP FOR LEARNING ENGLISH

Learn to describe experiences in the present

G Present simple and present continuous
V Gradable and extreme adjectives

Dy bannee diu   Guten Tag   **Gouden Dai**   **Salut**

Сәлем!   **Bonjour**   **Halito**   Salute

Hallo   Håfa ådai   **Ç'kemi**   Guuten takh

Héébee   Bon die!   Servas   Tungjatjeta

Ola   Ahoj   **Вітаю**   Góðan dag   Hoi

Salud   Hola / Buenos días   **Bom dia**

1 SPEAKING

a 💬 Discuss the questions.

1 How many languages can you say 'Hello' in?
2 How many languages can you order a meal or have a simple conversation in?
3 What language are you best at (apart from your own)?

b Choose one idea below and continue using *because*. Write your idea.

Learning a new language is like …
* making a new friend
* going on a long journey
* being a child again
* growing plants in a garden
* learning a musical instrument.

Learning a new language is like being a child again because you feel like you are starting from the beginning and everything is new.

c 💬 Read your sentences to each other. Do you agree with each other's ideas?

d 💬 Look at photos a–d and discuss the questions.

1 What are the different ways of learning a language in the photos?
2 What are the advantages and disadvantages of each way of learning a language?
3 Which have you tried? Have you tried any other ways?

LEARN GERMAN

START NOW

2 READING

a Read *Can you really learn a language in 22 hours?* quickly and answer the questions.

1 What is Memrise?
2 Why is Jon Foster using it?
3 How much has he learned?

b Read the article again and choose the correct answers for questions 1–4.

1 The writer wants to learn Lingala because he … .
  a loves new languages
  b wants to talk with the people who speak it
  c wants to try Memrise
2 Ed Cooke wants learners to … .
  a enjoy learning more
  b improve quickly
  c do more vocabulary practice
3 A 'mem' is … .
  a a digital plant that you 'water'
  b a translation of a new word
  c a picture that helps people remember new words

4 Where do the mems come from?
  a Ed Cooke creates them.
  b Users can create mems for themselves and other users.
  c Every user creates mems only for themselves.

c Match the words in **bold** in the article with meanings 1–8 below.

1 getting better
2 changes a word from one language into another
3 what someone wants to do
4 learned something so that you remember it exactly
5 something difficult that tests your ability
6 able to communicate freely and easily
7 to make someone remember something
8 do something again

d 💬 Have you used or would you like to use Memrise? Why / Why not?

Can you really learn a language in 22 hours?

We all know that people learn better if they enjoy learning.

Jon Foster reports on an app that makes learning a new language like playing a game.

I've never been very good at languages.

But next month, I'm travelling to a remote area of Central Africa and my **goal** is to know enough Lingala – one of the local languages – to have a conversation. I wasn't sure how I was going to do this – until I discovered a way to spend just a few minutes, a few times a day, learning all the vocabulary I'm going to need.

To be honest, normally when I get a spare moment at home, I go on Facebook or play games on my phone. But, at the moment, I'm using those short breaks for something more useful. I'm learning a foreign language. And thanks to Memrise, the app I'm using, it feels just like a game.

'People often stop learning things because they feel they're not **making progress** or because it all feels like too much hard work,' says Ed Cooke, one of the people who created Memrise. 'We're trying to create a form of learning experience that is fun and is something you'd want to do instead of watching TV.'

And Memrise is fun. It's a **challenge**. It gives you a few new words to learn and these are 'seeds' that you plant in your 'greenhouse'. (This represents your short-term memory.) When you practise the words, you 'water your plants' and they grow. When the app believes that you have really remembered a word, it moves the word to your 'garden'. You get points as your garden grows, so you can compare yourself to other Memrise users. I want to get a high score and go to the next level. And if I forget to log on, the app sends me emails that **remind** me to water my plants.

The app uses two principles about learning. The first is that people remember things better when they link them to a picture in their mind. Memrise **translates** words into your own language, but it also encourages you to use 'mems' – images that help you remember new words. You can use mems that other users have created or you can create your own. I **memorised** *motele*, the Lingalan word for 'engine', using a mem I created – I imagined an old engine in a motel room.

The second principle is that we need to stop after studying words and then **repeat** them again later, leaving time between study sessions. Memrise helps you with this because it's the kind of app you only use for five or ten minutes a day.

I've learned hundreds of Lingalan words with Memrise. I know this won't make me a **fluent** speaker, but I hope I'll be able to do more than just smile and nod when I meet people in the Congo.

Now, why am I still sitting here writing this? I need to go and water my vocabulary!

3 GRAMMAR Present simple and present continuous

a Match present simple sentences a–c with uses 1–3.

a When I get a spare moment at home, I normally **go** on Facebook or **play** games on my phone.
b I **know** this won't make me a fluent speaker.
c People **learn** better if they enjoy learning.

We can use the present simple:
1 to talk about things that are generally true (sentence _____)
2 to talk about habits and routines (sentence _____)
3 with state verbs – verbs about thoughts (e.g., *understand*), feelings (e.g., *want*) and possession (e.g., *own*) (sentence _____).

b Match present continuous sentences a–c with uses 1–3.

a **I'm learning** a foreign language.
b Now, why **am** I still **sitting** here writing this?
c Young people **are spending** more and more time playing video games.

We can use the present continuous to talk about:
1 actions in progress at the same time as speaking/ writing (sentence _____)
2 actions in progress around (before and after) the time of speaking/writing (sentence _____)
3 changing situations (sentence _____).

c Complete the rule about how we make the present continuous.

subject + *am* / _____ / *is* + verb + _____

d ⟫ Now go to Grammar Focus 1B on p. 144.

e 💬 Make questions with the words below. Then discuss the questions.

1 you / think / you / communicate / well in your own language?
2 How often / you / hear / foreign languages where you live?
3 you / think / you / have / a good memory?
4 What / help / you / learn / English grammar?
5 What / you / think / about / right now?
6 you / prepare / for an exam at the moment?
7 more people / learn / languages in your country than before?

f ⟫ **Communication 1B** 💬 Student A: Look at the picture on p. 127. Student B: Look at the picture on p. 129. Follow the instructions on the page.

4 VOCABULARY Gradable and extreme adjectives

a ▶ 01.08 You will hear four short conversations about learning languages. Which conversation is about someone who … ?

1 is having pronunciation problems.
2 has been practising another language a lot.
3 doesn't have good learning material.
4 is very good at learning languages.

b ▶ 01.08 Listen to the conversations again. What word do you hear?

1 I'm OK, but I'm really *tired / exhausted*.
2 I'm trying to, but this book's absolutely *bad / useless*!
3 That's absolutely *amazing / good*. I can only speak one language.
4 It's very *hard / impossible*. I'll never get it right!

c Underline the word that comes before each adjective. Does it make the meaning weaker or stronger?

d Read about gradable and extreme adjectives. Complete sentences 1–6 with a word to make the meaning stronger.

> • With some adjectives (*good, bad, difficult*), we can use words like *very, really* and *extremely* to make their meaning stronger (e.g., *His pronunciation is really good. The exam was extremely difficult.*).
> • Other adjectives already have a strong or extreme meaning (e.g., *perfect, useless*). We can use words like *really* or *absolutely* before these adjectives to add emphasis (e.g., *Her English is absolutely perfect.*).

1 Online dictionaries are often _____ **useful**.
2 That cake's _____ **enormous**.
3 I think Anna's _____ **confident**.
4 I went for a swim in the river and the water was _____ **freezing**.
5 There are only seven houses in my village – it's _____ **tiny**.
6 She's a(n) _____ **important** figure in world politics.

e ⟫ Now go to Vocabulary Focus 1B on p. 134.

5 SPEAKING

a 💬 Talk about learning a foreign language. Use the questions below.

• What do you want to be able to do with English?
• What level of English do you hope to reach?
• How often do you revise what you have learned?
• How often do you watch or read things in English?
• How often do you communicate with native speakers?
• What are you doing at the moment to learn English?
• Are you having any problems with English at the moment?

b Report back to the class about what you found out.

1C | EVERYDAY ENGLISH
Well, if you ask me …

Learn to give and respond to opinions

- **P** Word groups
- **S** Using *me too* / *me neither*

1 LISTENING

a 💬 Discuss the questions.

1 Do you enjoy meeting new people?
2 Do you usually decide what you think of someone from a first impression? Or do you get to know them first?

b 💬 Look at the photo above. What do you think the customer is buying?

c 🎥 ▶ 01.11 Watch or listen to Part 1 to check.

d 🎥 ▶ 01.11 Watch or listen again and <u>underline</u> the correct answers.

1 Becky is buying flowers because she's *going to someone's house* / *getting married*.
2 She doesn't want roses because *she doesn't like them* / *they're too romantic*.
3 She *likes* / *doesn't like* the tulips.
4 She will *buy flowers in another shop* / *come back later*.

e Look at the photo below right and answer the questions.

1 Where are the people?
2 What are they doing?

f 🎥 ▶ 01.12 Watch or listen to Part 2 to check.

g 🎥 ▶ 01.12 Watch or listen again and answer the questions.

1 What will happen to the bookshop?
2 What problem will this cause for Rachel?
3 What is Mark's advice?
4 What does Rachel say happened at work?

2 USEFUL LANGUAGE
Giving and responding to opinions

a ▶ 01.13 Listen and complete the sentences with one word.

1 Well, in my _____, roses are always a good option.
2 I _____ something like tulips might be better.
3 I _____ it's going to be impossible with another florist's in the same street.
4 Well, if you _____ me, it's not worth worrying about until we know for sure.

b Put the words in the correct order to make more formal phrases for giving an opinion.

1 it / me / seems / that / to
2 as / as / concerned / far / I'm

c Look at five ways of responding to an opinion. Does the speaker agree (*A*) or disagree (*D*)?

1 ☐ I know what you mean, but …
2 ☐ I know exactly what you mean.
3 ☐ I'm not so sure about that.
4 ☐ That's right.
5 ☐ I see where you're coming from, but …

d Tick (✓) the sentences you agree with. Change the other sentences so you agree with them.

1 ☐ English is an easy language to learn.
2 ☐ It's difficult to communicate with older people.
3 ☐ First impressions are important when you meet someone.

e 💬 Give your opinions from 2d and respond.

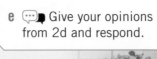

3 PRONUNCIATION Word groups

a ▶ 01.14 Listen to these sentences. Notice where the speaker pauses to make the message clearer.

I'm really worried. Jo phoned today with some bad news.

b ▶ 01.15 Listen to this similar sentence. Does the speaker pause?

I'm really worried I won't make enough money.

c Look at the conversation. Write // where you think the speakers pause.

Rachel Oh, I'm sorry, love. I'm just a bit worried. Jo phoned today and said that the old bookshop is going to be turned into another florist's.

Mark The bookshop on the corner? I didn't know they'd sold it.

Rachel Me neither. But what am I going to do? It's hard enough already to make money, but I think it's going to be impossible with another florist's in the same street.

d ▶ 01.16 Listen and check.

4 CONVERSATION SKILLS
Using *me too / me neither*

a ▶ 01.17 Listen and <u>underline</u> the correct words.

1 **Mark** The bookshop on the corner? I didn't know they'd sold it.
Rachel Me *too / neither*.
2 **Mark** Hey, don't worry about it. Let's just forget about work. Personally, I need a relaxing evening!
Rachel Me *too / neither*.

> 1 We use *Me too* and *Me neither* to say we agree or are in the same situation.
> 2 We use *Me too* after a positive sentence.
> 3 We use *Me neither* after a negative sentence.

b Complete the exchanges with appropriate responses.

1 **A** I need a nice cup of tea.
 B _____ .
2 **A** I don't really like watching football.
 B _____ .
3 **A** I wasn't invited to the wedding.
 B _____ .
4 **A** I'm looking forward to the party.
 B _____ .
5 **A** I don't really eat chocolate.
 B _____ .
6 **A** I hate going out in the rain.
 B _____ .

5 LISTENING

a 💬 Look at the photo. What is happening? What do you think will happen next?

b 🎥 ▶ 01.18 Watch or listen to Part 3 and check your ideas.

c 💬 Discuss the questions.

1 How would you feel in Becky's situation?
2 How would you feel in Rachel's situation?
3 Have you ever made a bad first impression?

6 SPEAKING

a Think of an example of:

• a good way to meet new people
• a good way to make a good first impression
• a good topic of conversation with someone you don't know well
• a good reason to dislike someone you've just met.

b 💬 Discuss your ideas in 6a.

> If you ask me, the best way to make a good impression is to use people's names a lot.

> I'm not so sure about that.

✓ UNIT PROGRESS TEST

➡ **CHECK YOUR PROGRESS**

You can now do the Unit Progress Test.

1D | SKILLS FOR WRITING
Different ways of learning

1 SPEAKING AND LISTENING

a 💬 What do you think are some good ways to learn new vocabulary in English? Talk about the ideas in photos a–e or your own ideas.

b ▶ 01.19 Listen to Maria and Gilberto talking about learning vocabulary. Are you more like Maria or Gilberto?

c ▶ 01.19 Listen again and answer the questions.

1 What system does Maria use for learning vocabulary?
2 What system did Maria's sister use?
3 Does Gilberto think either system will work for him? Why / Why not?

d Read the descriptions of each style. What kinds of learners are Maria and Gilberto?

VISUAL LEARNERS

They prefer to learn by seeing or reading things. They need to see new information written down.

AUDITORY LEARNERS

They prefer to learn by listening to new information. They also like to talk about the new things they've learned.

KINAESTHETIC LEARNERS

They prefer to learn by doing something. They don't like sitting still for very long.

e 💬 Talk about what kind of learner you are and why.

2 READING

a Read *What kind of learner are you?* on p. 17. Answer the questions.

1 Which of Maria's ideas is mentioned?
2 Does the article talk more about understanding new information or remembering it?

b Read the article again. Make notes about the key study techniques for each learning style.

- visual
- auditory
- kinaesthetic

What kind of learner are you?

Different people learn in different ways. In order to find the most useful way to learn new information, it's a good idea to think about the kind of learner you are: visual, auditory or kinaesthetic. Knowing your learning style helps you study more effectively, so you remember what you have learned more easily. Remember, you don't just learn when you study – this advice can also be useful for learning at work or in your free time.

VISUAL LEARNERS

It helps to study in a quiet place so that you can concentrate. To learn new information, try to think of an image in your head, or make a diagram to highlight different points. [1]**This technique helps your memory and it means you can find the information easily when you look at your notes again.**

AUDITORY LEARNERS

Going to a lecture is a good way for you to learn. Read your notes aloud, then cover them and try to say them again from memory. Also, try to use new words when you're talking to people. If you are studying words on a particular topic, you can listen to podcasts that include this vocabulary. [2]**These ideas should help you remember what you need to know.**

KINAESTHETIC LEARNERS

In order to learn new information, you need to be doing something. It helps to study in a place where you can walk around the room, touch things and move as freely as possible. Make sure you take regular breaks and go for a walk. [3]**This will help you to concentrate and remain interested in what you are studying.**

These descriptions are only a guide. Most people have a mixture of learning styles. To study successfully, you need to experiment and find the best method.

3 WRITING SKILLS Introducing a purpose; referring pronouns

a Look at these sentences from the article. Circle the words or phrases in the underlined parts which introduce the purpose in each sentence.

1 In order to find the most useful way to learn new information, it's a good idea to think about the kind of learner you are.
2 Knowing your learning style helps you study more effectively, so you remember what you have learned more easily.
3 To learn new information, try to think of an image in your head.

b Underline other examples of purpose words/phrases in the article.

c Join the sentences using purpose words/phrases. More than one answer is possible.

1 I write the new words in a vocabulary notebook. I remember them.
2 I practise pronunciation. I record myself saying words on my phone.
3 I write grammar rules on a piece of paper. I understand them better.

d Look at sentences 1–3 in **bold** in the article and underline the correct words in the rules.

a *This* and *these* refer to *ideas already mentioned / new ideas*.
b In sentences 1 and 3, *this* refers back to *one word / a complete idea*.
c We sometimes put *a noun / an adjective* after *this* and *these*.

4 WRITING A guide

a Think of a skill you know how to do well. It can be something to do with school, work, sport or a free-time activity. Make notes using these questions.

1 How easy is it to learn this skill?
2 What are the problems people have when learning it?
3 What are good ways to learn this skill?
4 Why are they good ways?

b Write a guide on how to learn this skill. Use words/phrases to introduce purpose and *this* or *these*, if possible, to refer back to ideas.

c 💬 Work in pairs. Read your partner's guide. How easy do you think it would be to learn their skill?

UNIT 1
Review and extension

1 GRAMMAR

a 💬 Complete the questions. Then ask and answer the questions.

1 You live with someone.
Who ___do you live___ with?
2 Something woke you up this morning.
What _____ this morning?
3 You talk to someone every day.
Who _____ every day?
4 You read something yesterday.
What _____ yesterday?
5 Something made you laugh recently.
What _____ recently?
6 Someone speaks to you in English.
Who _____ in English?
7 You know different ways of learning English.
Which different ways of learning English _____?
8 Some ways of learning English work best for you.
Which ways of learning English _____?

b Tick (✓) the four correct sentences. Then correct the mistakes in the other sentences.

1 ☐ John's having a shower.
2 ☐ I think we need a new laptop. Are you agreeing?
3 ☐ I'm hardly ever writing letters.
4 ☐ You look sad, Maria. What do you think about?
5 ☐ Monkeys communicate with sounds.
6 ☐ I don't know at the moment.
7 ☐ Carrie doesn't work this week because she's ill.
8 ☐ I'm getting cold.

2 VOCABULARY

a Complete the sentences with the verbs in the box.

argue   complain   encourage   express
forgive   persuade   refuse   update

1 Are you going to _____ about the terrible food?
2 I'm very sorry. Will you please _____ me?
3 Please _____ me on your progress.
4 I _____ you to try Thai food. It's delicious!
5 He prefers to _____ his feelings in writing.
6 She's trying to _____ me to go on holiday with her.
7 Please don't _____ my request! You have to say yes.
8 I try not to _____ with my boss – even when he's wrong!

b Match the extreme adjectives in the box with gradable adjectives 1–8.

awful   brilliant   enormous   exhausted
filthy   freezing   furious   tiny

1 big   _____
2 dirty   _____
3 small   _____
4 cold   _____
5 tired   _____
6 angry   _____
7 bad   _____
8 good   _____

3 WORDPOWER yourself

a Match sentence beginnings 1–6 with endings a–f.
1 ☐ Why do you keep **talking**
2 ☐ This room needs a lot of work, but you can **do**
3 ☐ Come in! **Make yourself**
4 ☐ Good luck at the interview! Just **be**
5 ☐ Bye! Have a wonderful time! **Look**
6 ☐ Are you OK? Have you

a **after yourself** and have fun – **enjoy yourself**!
b **yourself** and **tell yourself** 'I can do this!'
c **to yourself**? Is it because you're **teaching yourself** German?
d **hurt yourself**?
e **at home** and **help yourself** to food and drink.
f **it yourself** – you don't need to pay someone.

b Underline the correct words in the rule.

We use *yourself* in the phrases in **bold** in 3a because the object of the verb is *the same as / different from* the subject of the verb.

c Underline the correct words.
1 Is it possible to *help / teach* yourself how to swim?
2 You could pay someone to clean the car, or you could *do / do it* yourself.
3 There's a lot of food in the fridge. Please *help / make* yourself.
4 Don't copy other people. *Be by / Be* yourself.
5 Sit down. Make yourself *to / at* home!
6 You should *tell / tell to* yourself 'I'm wonderful!' every day.

d Complete the questions with the correct form of the verbs in the box and *yourself*.

enjoy   hurt   look after   talk to   teach

1 Have you ever _____ how to do something? What was it? Was it easy or difficult to learn?
2 Do you _____? Do you eat well and get enough sleep?
3 Have you ever _____ at home? Did you have to go to hospital?
4 Do you ever _____? What do you say?
5 Are you _____ at the moment? If not, what would make you happy?

e 💬 Discuss the questions in 3d.

⟳ REVIEW YOUR PROGRESS

How well did you do in this unit? Write 3, 2 or 1 for each objective.
3 = very well   2 = well   1 = not so well

I CAN ...	
talk about friendship and communication	☐
describe experiences in the present	☐
give and respond to opinions	☐
write a guide.	☐

UNIT 2

MODERN LIFE

GETTING STARTED

a Look at the photo. Where do you think the person is?

b 💬 Discuss the questions.

1 What else do you think might be in this building? (Think of the furniture, rooms and facilities.)

2 Would you like to work in a place like this? Why / Why not?

3 What would your ideal workplace be like?

2A THEY'VE JUST OFFERED ME THE JOB

1 READING

a 💬 Discuss the questions.

1 Have you ever had a job interview?
2 Was it a good experience? Why / Why not?

b Read *Not the best interview I've ever had!* Who got the job? Who didn't get the job?

c Read the stories again. Match a–d with headings 1–4.

1 ☐ Wrong word!
2 ☐ Better to tell the truth
3 ☐ The interviewer probably felt worse than I did!
4 ☐ An unlucky call

d 💬 Tell your partner which story you liked best. Have you had any embarrassing experiences like the ones in the stories?

> I've received a phone call at a bad moment.

> Really? What happened?

Not the best interview I've ever had!

Most people feel nervous when they go for a job interview, but some interviews are worse than others. Fortunately, they don't all end in disaster!

a "They wanted to test how fast I could type. My fingers were over the keyboard, ready to type. The interviewer said, "Right click to open the file," but all I heard was "Write click," so I typed "click" on a window that was already open. I felt so embarrassed when I realised my mistake, but we both laughed and I got the job. I've worked there for eight months now." **Laura**

b "I've had a lot of good interviews, but this one was a disaster. I had put on my CV that I could speak "some French". I learned some French at school, but I've never really used it and my listening skills are really bad. The three interviewers began the interview by speaking to me in French, and I didn't understand a word. No, I didn't get the job, and yes, I've changed my CV." **Dan**

c "I've never forgotten to turn my phone off in the cinema, but for some reason I forgot when I went for my first job interview. My friend called me to wish me good luck – right in the middle of the interview. Oops! I didn't get the job." **Andy**

d "I had a job interview with two people last week. One of them was leaning back in his chair when suddenly it fell over, and it was soon clear that he couldn't get up again. I didn't know if I should try to help or not, and I was worried I was going to start laughing. Fortunately, the other interviewer asked me to wait outside the room for a minute, and then the interview carried on as if nothing had happened. Guess what? They've just offered me the job!" **Ellie**

2 VOCABULARY Work

a Look at photos a–f below and match them with sentences 1–6.

1 ☐ Hundreds of people **applied for** the job, but only six **candidates** were invited for an interview.
2 ☐ It's hard to balance family life and a **career**.
3 ☐ I'm proud of my practical skills and medical **knowledge**.
4 ☐ There are 200 **employees** in this organisation, but I'm only **in charge of** a small team.
5 ☐ I've got good **marks**, but I haven't got much experience to put on my **CV**.
6 ☐ I've got a lot of **business contacts** who work for **employers** in different countries.

b Match the words in **bold** in 2a with these meanings.

1 a series of jobs you do during your working life
2 people you know who might be useful to you in your work
3 contacted a company to ask for a job
4 people who work for a company
5 the results of your school or university exams
6 the things you know from experience or study
7 people who are trying to get a job
8 responsible for something or someone
9 the people you work for
10 a document that describes your education and the jobs you have had

c 💬 What do managers look for when they employ someone new? Choose the four qualities that you think are most important.

- creative thinking
- good marks
- work experience
- self-confidence
- good problem-solving skills
- a friendly personality
- the ability to work in a team
- a positive attitude at work
- practical skills

3 GRAMMAR Present perfect and past simple

a Look at these sentences from the stories on p. 20. Which verbs in **bold** are in the present perfect and which are in the past simple?

1 I**'ve had** a lot of good interviews, but this one was a disaster.
2 I **had** a job interview with two people last week.
3 They**'ve** just **offered** me the job!

b Complete the sentences using the words in the box.

have/has   irregular   -ed   past participle

a To form the **past simple**, we add _____ to the verb, or we use a(n) _____ past form of the verb.
b We form the **present perfect** with _____ + _____ .

c Complete the rules. Add *present perfect* or *past simple* in the gaps. Match the rules (a–c) with the examples (1–3) in 3a.

a ☐ We use the _____ to talk about events at a particular time in the past.
b ☐ We use the _____ to talk about recent events that have an effect on the present.
c ☐ We use the _____ to talk about experiences at some time in our life.

d ▶ 02.01 **Pronunciation** Listen and choose the sentences you hear. Then practise saying them.

1 a I applied for the job.
  b I've applied for the job.
2 a I had a lot of good interviews.
  b I've had a lot of good interviews.

e ▶ 02.02 Listen and practise saying the sentences.

f ≫ Now go to Grammar Focus 2A on p. 146.

g Complete the sentences with the present perfect or past simple form of the verbs in brackets.

1 I _____ (never / have) a really terrible job interview.
2 Once, I _____ (forget) to turn off my phone when I was at the cinema.
3 Sorry, I can't come with you. My boss _____ (ask) me to work at the weekend.
4 I don't have very much work experience, but I _____ (be) the leader on a project at school.
5 I _____ (get) some useful work experience last year.
6 I _____ (finish) my exams, but I _____ (not / get) the results yet.
7 I _____ (already / work) for more than three organisations.
8 I _____ (know) what career I wanted when I was a child.

h 💬 Which sentences in 3g are true for you? Tell your partner or change them so they are true and give more information.

> Number 1 is true for me. I've only had two or three job interviews, but they've all been OK.

4 LISTENING

a 💬🗨 Think of five reasons why an employer might <u>not</u> offer a candidate a job. Compare your ideas with a partner.

b ▶ 02.06 Listen to the beginning of a radio programme. Answer the questions.

1 Are any of your ideas in 4a mentioned?
2 What quality does Nancy Maynard believe all employers are looking for in a job interview?

c ▶ 02.06 Listen again and complete each sentence with one or two words.

1 People with likeability can _____ with other people.
2 Nancy believes likeability is more important than other abilities in the first _____ of a new job.
3 She advises job hunters to spend time with _____.
4 Nancy encourages people to apply for jobs even if they don't have the right _____.
5 During an interview, it's important to _____ the interviewers by showing that you're friendly, positive and can communicate well.

d ▶ 02.07 Listen to five speakers. Do they agree that being likeable is more important than other skills? Write agree (A) or disagree (D).

Speaker 1 _____   Speaker 3 _____   Speaker 5 _____
Speaker 2 _____   Speaker 4 _____

e ▶ 02.07 Listen again and answer the questions.

1 According to Speaker 1, why don't people know that likeability is important?
2 According to Speaker 2, what's the advantage of developing your 'soft skills'?
3 What does Speaker 3 believe are the most important things in his job?
4 What problem does Speaker 4 have with 'soft skills'?
5 According to Speaker 5, what are the most important things you can offer an organisation?

f 💬🗨 Discuss the questions.

1 Think of different kinds of jobs. When applying for each job, what is more important – likeability or good qualifications? Why?
2 Do you think schools should help students develop 'soft skills'? How could they do this?

5 SPEAKING

a You are going to talk about your experiences. Tick (✓) three things you have done. Then make notes about your experiences.

☐ got qualifications (which?)
☐ learned practical skills (what?)
☐ studied/worked in a foreign country (where?)
☐ chosen a career
☐ worked for no money
☐ visited an interesting office or factory
☐ written a CV
☐ given a talk or presentation
☐ done some online learning
☐ studied or worked as part of a team
☐ been in charge of a project

b 💬🗨 Take turns to talk about your work and training experiences. Ask questions to find out more information.

I've been in charge of a project. It was a small team, and we all worked well together.

Was this at work or at school?

2B | I'VE BEEN PLAYING ON MY PHONE ALL MORNING

1 VOCABULARY Technology

a 💬 Think of things you can do on a smartphone. Compare ideas with other students. Who has the most ideas?

b Match words 1–5 with definitions a–e.

1 ☐ app   3 ☐ icon   5 ☐ username
2 ☐ browser   4 ☐ text message

a a name you need to type (with a password) to start using something
b a written message that you send from one phone to another
c a computer program that you use to read information on the Internet
d a small picture on a computer/phone screen that you click on to open a program or an app
e a small computer program that you can download onto a mobile phone or other device

c Cross out the wrong verb in each group.

1 *turn off / send / delete* an email
2 *download / press / share* a video
3 *install / share / upload* some photos
4 *install / download / press* a new app
5 *turn off / turn on / delete* a phone
6 *upload / press / click on* a button or icon
7 *connect to / send / browse* the Internet
8 *type / change / turn on* a password

d 💬 Think of five things that you've done recently using phrases from 1c. Tell a partner.

> I've just changed my email password.

> Why? Did you forget it?

e 💬 Discuss the questions.

1 What apps have you got on your phone or tablet?
2 Which apps do you like or use the most?
3 Look at the apps on this page. What do you think they do?

23

2 READING

a Read *What's your favourite app?* and answer the questions.

Which app … ?

1 is good for music lovers
2 helps you learn about the stars
3 keeps you interested because you can keep improving
4 helps busy people get organised
5 helps you create and keep photos online
6 helps you make funny photos
7 is useful if you've got too many apps on your phone
8 records your fitness information

b Read the comments again and answer the questions.

1 What do you get from ThingsToDo at the end of each week?
2 How do you find a planet with SkyWatch?
3 What changes can you make to photos with Imagegram?
4 Why does Enzo play Balloon Pop every day?
5 What information does ActivityTracker give you when you run?
6 What information can TuneSpotter tell you about a song?
7 How can StopApp make your phone work better?
8 What kinds of photos does Luke think are funniest on Crazy Faces?

c 💬 Discuss the questions.

1 Do you use any apps like the ones in the article? Which ones? How useful are they?
2 Would you like to use any of the apps in the article? Which ones? Why?

3 GRAMMAR Present perfect and present perfect continuous

a Read the extracts from *What's your favourite app?* and answer the questions.

I**'ve** always **been** keen on photography. I**'ve been taking** photos since I was 12, when I got my first camera.	StopApp is a really useful app and I**'ve been recommending** it to all my friends.	I**'ve had** it for a week, and I**'ve been using** it a lot.

1 Which verbs in **bold** are … ?
   a the present perfect
   b the present perfect continuous
2 Complete this rule.
   To form the present perfect continuous tense, use *have / has* + _____ + _____ .

b Answer these questions about the extracts in 3a.

1 Which verbs are about activities (things you do) and which are about states (the way things are)?
2 Which sentences show how long something has continued up until now?
3 Which verbs are about a repeated activity that started recently?

What's your favourite app?

I've just installed the ThingsToDo app. It's so easy to use – which is really important when you've got a lot of things to do and not much time! You just create a list and then add items to it. Once a week it sends you a list of everything you've done. I've been so busy lately and this app has really helped me! I've only been using it for three weeks and I've already done 30 things on my list. **Juan**

My favourite game at the moment is Balloon Pop. You select groups of coloured balloons and pop them. I've been playing it on the bus every day because I always want to get to the next level – it's very addictive! **Enzo**

ActivityTracker is a great app for running. You just press the start button when you begin your workout and the app records your speed, distance and heart rate. After the workout, you can then upload your information to social networking websites and compare with your friends. I've never found an app as good as this before. **Fay**

Have you heard about SkyWatch? It's great. You just point your phone at the night sky and it tells you the names of the stars. You can also type in the name of a planet and the program tells you where to look for it. **Katya**

I've always been keen on photography. I've been taking photos since I was twelve, when I got my first camera. So Imagegram is a great app for me. You can use different effects to make photos look different, like old-fashioned photos or with brighter colours. Then you can store them online and share them with your friends. **Paul**

c ≫ Now go to Grammar Focus 2B on p. 146.

d Complete the sentences with the present perfect or present perfect continuous form of the verbs in brackets.

1 I _____ this phone for three years. (own)
2 I _____ for my own name online. (never / search)
3 I _____ TV all day. (watch)
4 I _____ for a new tablet, but I haven't got enough money yet. (save up)
5 I _____ the same phone for a few years now, but I don't want to buy a new one. (have)

e ▶ 02.09 **Pronunciation** Listen to sentences 1–3. Is the stress on the main verb (*M*) or the auxiliary verb (*A*)?

1 This app has really helped me.
2 I've been using it more and more.
3 I've been playing it on the bus.

f ▶ 02.09 Listen again and repeat the sentences.

g 💬 Are the sentences in 3d true for you? Change the false sentences so that they are true for you. Tell your partner about your sentences.

4 SPEAKING

a You are going to find out which of your classmates use the most technology. Think of six questions to ask about what people have used recently. Use the topics below or your own ideas.

apps / mobile phones   video games
the Internet   social networking sites

How often have you been on Instagram in the last two days?
What apps have you been using recently?

b 💬 Use your questionnaire to interview different people in the class. Who has used the most and least technology recently? Now think about your own technology use. Could you be addicted to technology?

I've just downloaded TuneSpotter. If you hear a song you like but you don't know what it is, you can use this app. It identifies the name of the song and the singer. And if you like it, you can buy the song really easily. I've had it for a week, and I've been using it a lot.
Mehmet

StopApp is a really useful app and I've been recommending it to all my friends. If too many apps are open on your phone, your phone can be really slow. This app turns them off, which can make your phone faster. **Ana**

I've been using Crazy Faces a lot recently. It's very silly, but it's fun. You just take photos of your friends and then you can change their faces. You can make them look older or younger, taller or shorter, and you can add beards, moustaches and glasses. I've seen a lot of photos where people have put baby faces on adult bodies and they make me laugh every time!
Luke

EVERYDAY ENGLISH
Could you take it back to the shop?

1 LISTENING

a 💬 Talk about a problem you have had recently. What was the problem? Did you solve it? How?

b 💬 Look at the photos. What has just happened?

c 🎬 ▶ 02.10 Watch or listen to Part 1 to check.

d 💬 What do you think Rachel and Becky will do next?

e 🎬 ▶ 02.11 Watch or listen to Part 2. Do they mention any of your ideas?

f 🎬 ▶ 02.11 Watch or listen again. Are the sentences true (*T*) or false (*F*)?

1 Becky's screen is still working.
2 Rachel thinks removing the SIM card might help.
3 Becky is worried about losing all her phone numbers.
4 Becky bought the phone very recently.
5 Becky has got insurance.
6 Rachel heard on the radio about using rice to dry phones.

2 USEFUL LANGUAGE Making and responding to suggestions

a Choose the correct words.

1 Have you tried *turning* / *turn* it off and on again?
2 What about *taking* / *take* the SIM card out and drying it?
3 Could you *taking* / *take* it back to the shop?
4 Can you *claiming* / *claim* on your insurance?
5 You could *trying* / *try* that.

b 🎬 ▶ 02.11 Watch or listen to Part 2 again and check your answers to 2a.

c Complete the responses with the words from the box.

give   idea   why   worth

1 **A** How about just leaving it until it dries out?
  B I'll _____ it a try. What have I got to lose?
2 **A** Why don't you try drying it with a hair dryer?
  B That's _____ a try, but wouldn't the heat damage the phone?
3 **A** Shall we phone Mark and see if he has any ideas?
  B Yes, _____ not? He might know what to do.
4 **A** Let's go to the phone shop and ask for advice.
  B That's a great _____. They should be able to help.

d What solutions can you think of for these problems? Make notes.

1 You missed your bus home and the next one is in an hour. It's raining.
2 You don't have any ideas about what to buy your friend for their birthday.
3 You've spilt coffee on your shirt and you have an important meeting in 20 minutes.
4 The battery in your phone is low and you need to make an important call in an hour.

e 💬 Take turns to ask for advice and make suggestions.

3 LISTENING

a 💬 Look at the photo. Who do you think Becky is talking to?

b 🎥 ▶ 02.12 Watch or listen to Part 3. Does the phone work now? Why / Why not?

4 CONVERSATION SKILLS
Sounding sympathetic or pleased

a ▶ 02.13 Listen and complete the conversations.

1 **Rachel** How's the phone?
Becky Not good. The screen's frozen.
Rachel _____! Have you tried turning it off and on again?

2 **Becky** I hope I haven't lost all my contacts. I haven't saved them anywhere else.
Rachel Oh no, _____.

3 **Becky** My phone's working. That rice trick worked.
Rachel That's _____! I'm really _____ to hear that.

b Look at the completed conversations in 4a. Which phrases sound sympathetic? Which phrases sound pleased?

c 💬 Take turns to say sentences 1–6 below. Respond, sounding sympathetic or pleased. Then ask for more details.

1 I've lost my phone.

2 I've found a new place to live.

3 My car has broken down.

4 I was woken up very early this morning.

5 My sister is coming to visit.

6 I've been offered a great new job.

5 PRONUNCIATION Sentence stress

a ▶ 02.14 Listen to these sentences. <u>Underline</u> the stressed syllables.

1 Have you tried turning it off and on again?
2 What about taking the SIM card out and drying it?
3 Could you take it back to the shop?
4 Can you claim on your insurance?

b We usually put stress on the words which are important for our message. Which syllables do you think are stressed in these sentences?

1 I can't find my phone!
2 My computer's broken. I've lost all my work!
3 I have a very annoying colleague at work – he complains about everything.
4 I'm really worried. I have a big exam tomorrow.
5 My car has been making a strange noise recently. I hope there isn't a problem.

c ▶ 02.15 Listen and check. Then practise saying the sentences.

6 SPEAKING

a Think of a problem you have or might have (e.g., with a colleague, your studies, a car, your computer). Make notes about the problem.

b 💬 Take turns to explain your problem and make suggestions.

✓ UNIT PROGRESS TEST

→ CHECK YOUR PROGRESS

You can now do the Unit Progress Test.

2D SKILLS FOR WRITING
I'm going to look for a new job

1 SPEAKING AND LISTENING

a What changes would you like to make to your life? Make notes about one of the topics below.

> your job   the flat/house you live in
> the town/city you live in   your free-time activities
> your studies   your friends

b 💬 Talk about the changes you would like to make to your life. Give reasons.

c ▶ 02.16 Listen to two friends, Tania and Lin, talking on the phone. What two changes is Tania thinking about?

d ▶ 02.16 Tania writes an email to an IT company in Singapore called PaySNG. Listen to the conversation again and complete the application email.

✉ 📝 ☆ 🏳   ⊗

Application

Dear Sir/Madam,

I'm writing to enquire about the possibility of working for your company. I'm an application software developer. I've been ¹_____ for my current company for just over ²_____ _____ now, but I'd like a change. I'm good at ³_____ thinking and I have excellent ⁴_____ - _____ skills. In addition, I also have a positive ⁵_____ towards my work and my colleagues.

I don't speak Mandarin, but I'm very interested in ⁶_____ _____ and would love the opportunity to live and work in Singapore. I'd be interested in any information you can send me.

Please find my CV attached.

Yours faithfully,

Tania Sampson

---

e 💬 Ask and answer the questions.

1 How common is it for people from your country to work abroad?
2 What are the main reasons they go?
- better work opportunities
- more money
- a cultural experience
- language learning
- other reasons

2 READING

a Read Tania's email to Lin about Singapore and answer the questions.

1 Has Tania got good or bad news?
2 When does she hope to see Lin?

b Read the email again and answer the questions.

1 What did Tania do the day after the interview?
2 What kind of apps will she create in her new job?
3 Will she only work on the company's current products?
4 Does the company pay well?
5 Besides seeing Lin, what would Tania like to do in Singapore?

✉ 📝 ☆ 🏳   ⊗

Singapore!!!

Hi Lin,

I'm sorry I haven't been in touch for the past few days, but it's been a very busy time.

On Monday, I had a job interview with PaySNG, the IT company in Singapore that I emailed. Then the next day, I had to do a practical test. ¹**You won't believe this, but** they've just rung to offer me a job!

The work sounds really interesting – they want me to work on developing apps that can be used for making mobile payments. ²**And what's really exciting is that** they also want me to think of ideas for new products. The job offer is very generous. Apart from giving me a good salary, they're also going to pay me a bonus if I do well. And they'll pay for my flight and help me with accommodation when I arrive.

³**But the best thing is that** I'm going to live in Singapore! Besides seeing you, I'm also looking forward to learning Mandarin. Everyone at PaySNG speaks English, of course, but I'd like to be able to talk to some of the local staff in their preferred language, if that's Mandarin. I've always wanted to learn a second language well, and I'm sure I'll be able to do it when I'm living there.

We'll have to meet when I get there, so you can show me around Singapore. I haven't booked my flight yet, but I'll let you know when I'm arriving. I can't wait to see you.

Tania

---

3 WRITING SKILLS Adding new information

a Look at **bold** phrases 1–3 in the second email. Why does Tania use them? Choose the correct reason.

1 to summarise her news
2 to introduce new information
3 to show she is very busy

b Rewrite phrases 1–3 in the second email using the words in brackets.

1 _____
  (will never)
2 _____
  (brilliant)
3 _____
  (most amazing)

c Put the words in the correct order and add the necessary punctuation to make sentences.

1 but I've / believe this / bought a house / you'll never
  _____

2 is / more amazing / what's even / the location
  _____

3 it wasn't / thing is that / too expensive / but the best
  _____

d Read sentences a–c and underline the correct words in the rules below.

a I have excellent problem-solving skills. **In addition**, I also have a positive attitude towards my work.
b **Apart from** giving me a good salary, they're also going to pay me a bonus if I do well.
c **Besides** seeing you, I'm also looking forward to learning Mandarin.

> - We can use phrases like *in addition (to)*, *apart from* and *besides* when we want to [1]*emphasise / add* information.
> - We use them at the [2]*beginning / end* of a sentence.
> - We use *in addition (to)* in more formal writing.
> - After *apart from* and *besides*, we use an [3]*infinitive form / -ing form* or a noun.
> - In the other part of the sentence, we can use [4]*and / also* to emphasise that we are adding information.

e Read the sentences. Which words/phrases in **bold** mean *as well as* and which mean *except for*?

1 They're going to pay all my expenses **apart from** meals.
2 **Apart from** my travel expenses, they're also going to pay for my meals.
3 **Besides** seeing you, I'm also looking forward to learning Mandarin.
4 I've done everything I can to prepare, **besides** learning Mandarin.

f Rewrite these sentences using the words in brackets. Write two sentences if necessary. There may be more than one possible answer.

1 I have a degree in software development and I have a diploma in interactive media design. (in addition)
2 They'll pay for a hotel when I arrive and they'll pay the first month's rent on a flat. (apart from)
3 They're going to give me a return airfare now, and they're going to pay for another return airfare in the middle of my contract. (besides)

4 WRITING An informal email

a Imagine you have some exciting news. Choose one of the topics below or your own idea. Make notes about extra things you can say about this news.

1 You've won a trip to a tropical island. (How did you win it? When are you going? What have you been doing to prepare?)
2 You've just got a new job. (What's the job? Why did you apply?)

b 💬 Compare your ideas with a partner.

c Write an email to a friend explaining your good news. Use phrases to introduce new information, if possible, and try to use the present perfect and present perfect continuous.

d Work in pairs. Read your partner's email. Is their news similar to yours? Do they use phrases to add information correctly?

UNIT 2
Review and extension

1 GRAMMAR

a 💬🗨 <u>Underline</u> the best answers. Then ask and answer the questions.

1 What job *did you want / have you wanted* to do when you were a child?
2 How long *have you used / have you been using* this book?
3 How many emails *have you written / have you been writing* today?
4 Have you ever *lost / been losing* your phone?
5 How long *have you known / have you been knowing* your colleagues or classmates?
6 *Have you taken / Have you been taking* your driving test yet?

b Complete the text using the present perfect, present perfect continuous or past simple.

¹_____ (you / ever / imagine) what it's like to be a successful game designer? That's my goal.
I ²_____ (always / love) playing games. In fact, I ³_____ (play) video games since I was just three!
I ⁴_____ (leave) school at 18 and studied computer animation at university. Then I ⁵_____ (work) for a software company. I ⁶_____ (develop) some useful skills there, but it wasn't the right job for me.
Then, six months ago, I got an internship at a gaming company. It doesn't pay very much, but I ⁷_____ (already / gain) a lot of experience.
I ⁸_____ (work) on an idea for a game in my free time for the last six months. When it's ready, I'll present it to my company. I know I'll be a success.

2 VOCABULARY

a Complete the words.

1 We have 72 e _ p _ _ _ _ _ _ s at this company. Some of them have worked here for a long time.
2 We have two c _ _ d _ _ _ _ _ _ s for the job. We need to choose one.
3 Schools should teach p _ _ c _ _ _ _ _ l skills, like cooking and driving.
4 He's got great p _ _ b _ _ _ m-s _ _ _ v _ _ g skills.
5 My uncle had a long c _ _ e _ r in the army.

b Match the words in the box with definitions 1–5.

app	browser	icon	text message	username

1 a software program that allows users to find and read information on the web _____
2 a word that you use along with a secret password to log in to a website _____
3 a computer program designed for one purpose _____
4 a small symbol on a computer screen that you point to and click on with a mouse _____
5 something you write and send from one mobile phone to another _____

3 WORDPOWER *look*

a Match questions 1–8 with answers a–h.

1 ☐ What do employers usually **look for**?
2 ☐ Did you see John's office?
3 ☐ What does 'disconnect' mean?
4 ☐ What are you **looking at**?
5 ☐ How do you feel about your trip to Moscow?
6 ☐ What do you think of my new smartwatch?
7 ☐ **Look out**! Didn't you see that bicycle?
8 ☐ Are you coming to the meeting tomorrow?

a It **looks** good. Can I try it?
b I don't know. **Look** it **up** online.
c No, I have to **look after** some customers.
d I'm really **looking forward to** it.
e Someone who is reliable and hard-working.
f No! It came out of nowhere!
g No, we didn't **look around** the building.
h It's an advert for a sales job.

b Match the phrases in the box with definitions 1–8.

look + adjective   look after someone/something
look at someone/something   look around (somewhere)
look for something/someone   look forward to something
look out   look (something) up

1 try to find _____
2 feel excited about a future event _____
3 check a meaning or other fact in a book or online _____
4 explore _____
5 seem _____
6 be careful _____
7 watch _____
8 be responsible for _____

c Complete the sentences with the correct form of *look* and a particle (*after*, *up*, etc.), if necessary. Sometime more than one answer is possible.

1 Do you like _____ trees, flowers and other plants?
2 Have you ever _____ a factory?
3 Do you know anyone who's _____ a job at the moment?
4 Where do you usually _____ new English words?
5 Do you often _____ your sister's children?
6 What are you _____ to doing this year?
7 Does the weather _____ good today?
8 In what situation would you shout '_____!' to someone?

d 💬🗨 Discuss the questions in 3c.

♻ REVIEW YOUR PROGRESS

How well did you do in this unit? Write 3, 2 or 1 for each objective.
3 = very well   2 = well   1 = not so well

I CAN ...	
talk about experiences of work and training	☐
talk about technology	☐
make and respond to suggestions	☐
write an email giving news.	☐

CAN DO OBJECTIVES

- Talk about a friendship
- Talk about families
- Tell a story
- Write about someone's life

UNIT **3**

RELATIONSHIPS

GETTING STARTED

a 💬 Look at the photo and discuss the questions.

1 Where are the two women? What do you think they have been doing?

2 Do you think they have known each other a long time? Why / Why not?

3 What is their relationship like? Think of three words to describe it.

b Complete the sentences.

1 My oldest friend is …

2 My closest friend is …

3 When I'm old, I'll still be friends with …

c 💬 Talk about the people in your answers in b.

3A SHE HAD MOVED THERE 20 YEARS EARLIER

1 SPEAKING AND VOCABULARY Relationships

a 💬 Write down the names of three people you know well and show them to your partner. Ask and answer the questions about each person.

1 How long have you known this person?
2 When did you meet?
3 How often do you see each other?
4 What do you do together?

b Match the words in **bold** in sentences 1–7 with the definitions a–g. Sometimes there is more than one possible answer.

1 ☐ My sister and I **have a lot in common**, but we don't like the same music.
2 ☐ I **get on well with** most of my family, but I don't like my aunt very much.
3 ☐ I **have a good relationship with** my cousin. We're more like friends.
4 ☐ I think you really **get to know** people well when you go on holiday with them.
5 ☐ Most of my friends **come from the same background** as I do. We all grew up in the same neighbourhood and went to the same school.
6 ☐ I'm not very good at **keeping in touch** with friends when they move far away.
7 ☐ My longest **friendship** is with someone I met when I was eight years old.

a to find out what someone is really like
b to see or contact someone often
c to be interested in the same things
d to have someone as a friend
e to like someone and enjoy being with them
f to grow up in the same kind of family and/or social group
g to find it easy to be with someone

c Use the correct form of the words and phrases in **bold** in 1b to complete the sentences. Sometimes there is more than one possible answer.

1 I _____ with my brother, but not as well with my sister.
2 My _____ with Jackie goes back to when we were at primary school.
3 My mother and I both love sport, so we _____ and have plenty to talk about.
4 I still _____ with friends from school on social media.
5 When I went to university, I _____ a lot of new people.
6 My friend Melissa and I don't _____ – she comes from a rich part of the city and I come from a poor one.
7 I _____ most of my colleagues, but not such a good one with my boss.

d 💬 Which sentences from 1b are true for you? Change the others so they are true. Tell your partner.

2 PRONUNCIATION Linking sounds

In a sentence, when one word ends in a consonant sound and the next word starts with a vowel sound, we often link these words. We say them without any pause between the words.

a ▶03.01 Listen to the sentences. Can you hear the linking between the words in **bold**?

1 We don't have **much in** common.
2 I **get on** with **most of** my family.
3 I'm not very **good at keeping in** touch.

b Underline the words you think will be linked in this way (consonant sound + vowel sound).

1 I fell in love with my husband the moment I saw him.
2 Kate lives in the USA, but we keep in touch online.
3 My friends and I have a very silly sense of humour.
4 I don't think a shared background is important.
5 My relatives are all very close.

c ▶03.02 Listen and check. Then practise saying the sentences.

3 READING

a Look at the headline and the photos in the article on p. 33. Answer the questions.

1 What do you think is the relationship between these two people?
2 How do you think they met?
3 How do you think they became friends?
4 Where might they be in these photos?

b Read the article and check your answers.

c Read the article again and answer the questions.

1 Why did Spencer stop playing the game with Rosalind? Why did he start again?
2 Who is Amy Butler? Why is she important in this story?
3 How long did Spencer and Rosalind meet for in Florida? Was their meeting a success? Why / Why not?
4 What kind of reaction was there on social media when Spencer posted his photos? How did Rosalind feel about this?
5 Choose all the words below that describe Rosalind's attitude towards life.

calm	open-minded	prejudiced
old-fashioned	positive	

60 years and 1,000 miles

How a word game brought two unlikely people together

What do a young rapper, a retired woman and an online word-game app have in common? Not much, you might think. In fact, they are at the heart of an incredible true story of friendship.

Spencer Sleyon, a New York rapper in his early twenties, and Rosalind Guttman, an elderly woman living a thousand miles away in Florida, are two people who would seem to have very little in common. And yet the pair became good friends. How did their unlikely relationship begin?

The answer is that they got to know each other online, but not through social media, as you might expect. Their friendship began completely by chance when they both started playing a popular word-game app on their mobile phones.

The two played each other almost every day and soon they also began chatting on the app. Rosalind talked about her life in Florida and Spencer spoke of his plans to move to New York and follow a music career. They soon discovered that they were not only perfect gaming partners, but they also got on really well, even though they came from such different backgrounds.

After some time, though, Spencer decided to delete the app. He was looking for a job in New York and his life was getting too busy. He just didn't have time to play any more. But before he stopped, he asked Rosalind if she had any advice for him. 'Shoot for the stars,' she told him. 'Whatever you want out of life, just go grab it!'

After he had been in New York for a few months, Spencer found he did actually have a little free time. He decided to reinstall the app and he and Rosalind started playing again. Then one day Amy Butler, the mother of one of Spencer's friends, overheard a conversation Spencer and his friends were having. He was telling them about his friendship with an 81-year-old woman who lived in a retirement village in Florida. Amy thought it would be a great idea to arrange a meeting between the two. Soon, she and Spencer were flying down to Florida to meet Rosalind. The meeting was a great success. Spencer and Rosalind found that they got on just as well face-to-face as they did online.

They only spent one day together – they had lunch in a restaurant and Rosalind showed Spencer around her neighbourhood. But when Spencer posted photos of their meeting on social media, they quickly went viral and received more than a million likes. Several newspapers even reported the story of how the pair had become friends. Rosalind said she had enjoyed the meeting, but she wasn't sure why it had become such a big story. She felt that it was quite natural that they should have a good relationship and there wasn't anything unusual about it.

And what happened next? Well, Spencer and Rosalind are still playing the word game online, but now they have a new way to keep in touch – they've become friends on Facebook.

d 💬 Discuss the questions.

1 Why do you think this story went viral? Were the reasons ... ?
   a mainly positive   c both positive and negative
   b mainly negative
2 Do you know of any unlikely friendships or relationships?
   Think about people you know or famous people. Why are
   these relationships 'unlikely'?

4 GRAMMAR Narrative tenses

a Underline the correct words in the summary.

Spencer and Rosalind ¹*first got* / *were first getting* to
know each other through playing an online word game.
Rosalind was living in a retirement community in Florida.
She ²*moved* / *had moved* there 20 years earlier, when
she retired. Spencer was living in Massachusetts, but he
³*looked* / *was looking* for a job in New York because he
wanted a career in music. Later, after he moved to New
York, Amy Butler overheard Spencer talking with his friends.
They ⁴*told* / *were telling* each other who their best friends
were, and that's how she heard about Rosalind. Amy
⁵*decided* / *had decided* to go with Spencer to visit Rosalind
in Florida. Spencer's pictures of the meeting ⁶*went* / *had
gone* viral, and many newspapers reported the story of how
they had met and ⁷*were becoming* / *had become* friends.

b Look at the example sentences from the summary.
Which examples show ... ?

1 an event that took place before another event in the story
2 an activity over a period of time that gives background to
  the story
3 events in the story

a *Rosalind* **was living** *in a retirement community in Florida.*
b *Later, after he* **moved** *to New York, Amy Butler* **overheard**
   Spencer talking with his friends.
c *Many newspapers reported the story of how they* **had met** ...

c Match the verbs in 4b to the tenses 1–4. One tense
is not used.

1 past simple   3 present perfect
2 past continuous   4 past perfect

d Find five more examples of the past continuous and
three more examples of the past perfect in the article.

e Complete the story with the correct form of the verbs
in brackets. Use narrative tenses (past simple, past
continuous, past perfect).

I ¹_____ (meet) my friend Amy in 2015.
She ²_____ (work) in a café at the time
and I ³_____ (go) there often. She
⁴_____ (not be) very happy because she
⁵_____ (just / finish) a degree in art history
and she couldn't find an interesting job. One day she
⁶_____ (notice) that I ⁷_____ (read)
a book about Leonardo da Vinci, and we
⁸_____ (start) talking about art. We realised
we had a lot in common, including a love of Italian
art. A few months later, Amy ⁹_____ (hear)
about an art history course in Italy, and we
¹⁰_____ (decide) to take it together.
We both still live in Rome, and we love it here.

f ≫ Now go to Grammar Focus 3A on p. 148.

5 SPEAKING

a Think about yourself and a close friend, or two people
you know who are close friends. Prepare to tell the
story of how the friendship started. Make notes about
these topics:

• life before you/they first met
• what happened when you/they met
• what happened next
• things you/they have in common.

b 💬 Take turns telling your stories.

> I got to know my best friend at
> secondary school. We had been
> at the same primary school, but
> we were in different classes.

1 READING

a 💬 Discuss the questions.

1 Look at the photos of the twins. Which twins are identical (they look exactly the same)?
2 If you are a twin, what is it like? If you are not a twin, what do you think it would be like?

b 💬 Do the quiz. Answer the quiz questions with your partner. Then check your answers at the bottom of p. 37.

QUIZ: TWIN FACTS

Do you think the following facts about twins are true or false? Not sure? Have a guess!

1 There are about three chances out of 100 of twins being born – they make up 3% of the general population. **T / F**

2 Identical twins have exactly the same DNA. **T / F**

3 Mothers of twins are likely to be a bit taller than other women. **T / F**

4 Most twins would prefer to be an only child. **T / F**

5 When twins are very young, about 40% develop a language of their own. **T / F**

6 Many twins believe they can read each other's thoughts. **T / F**

7 Identical twins have the same fingerprints. **T / F**

8 Cândido Godói in Brazil is the twin capital of the world – between 1959 and 2008, 8% of the births there were twins. **T / F**

9 Many twins are left-handed. **T / F**

10 Film stars Rami Malek, Scarlett Johansson and Vin Diesel each have a twin. **T / F**

Rami Malek

Scarlett Johansson

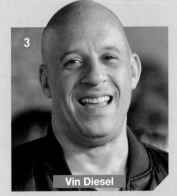
Vin Diesel

c Read *Twin tales* and answer the questions.

1 How do Martina and Bianca feel about being twins?
2 Do they feel the same as each other?

d Read the article again and answer the questions.

1 What does Martina think was typical from their childhood?
2 How does Martina think she is different from Bianca?
3 How does Martina say they were different as teenagers?
4 What is Bianca's view of their childhood?
5 How does Bianca think she is different from Martina?
6 What is the 'crazy thing' that Bianca mentions?
7 What is the life of the twins like now?

e 💬📢 If you've got a brother or sister, compare your relationship to Martina and Bianca's. If you haven't got a brother or sister, would you like to have one? Why / Why not?

2 VOCABULARY Multi-word verbs

a Look at the nine multi-word verbs in **bold** in the article. Match them to the definitions a–i.

a to be similar to an older member of the family
b to meet (when you have planned it before)
c to have a friendly relationship with someone
d to gradually have a less close relationship
e to incorrectly think one person/thing is another person/thing
f to remove or make shorter, using a knife or scissors
g to spend time with a person or people you like
h to gradually become an adult
i to look after a child until they are an adult

b Complete rules 1–3 with the verbs in **bold**.

• I mainly **take after** my dad.
• We started to **grow apart**.
• We'd both **cut** all our hair **off**.
• We'd both **cut off** all our hair.
• We'd both **cut** it **off**.

1 Some multi-word verbs have no object (e.g., _____).
2 Some multi-word verbs are separable (e.g., _____). This means that the object can go either between the verb and the particle or after the particle. (When the object is a pronoun (e.g., *you*, *him*, *it*), it must go between the verb and the particle.)
3 Some verbs are not separable (e.g., _____). When we use a pronoun with these, it goes after the particle.

c ▶️ 03.06 **Pronunciation** Listen to these sentences. Which word in **bold** is stressed?

1 Bianca is the sister I **grew up** with.
2 We didn't **get on with** each other very well.
3 We had both **cut** all our hair **off**.

We usually stress the particle in multi-word verbs, not the main verb. If the multi-word verb has two particles, we stress the first one. If the multi-word verb is separated by an object (e.g., *all our hair*), then we often stress the object.

TWIN TALES

Statistics tell us that one in every 30 people is a twin. If you're one of the other 29, you've probably always wondered what that's like. Are twins closer than other brothers and sisters? Do they know each other's thoughts? Is it fun being an identical twin, or is it annoying when people mix you up? We asked twin sisters Martina and Bianca for the inside story.

MARTINA

When people ask me what it's like being a twin, I don't really know how to answer because I've never *not* been a twin! So, Bianca is the sister I [1]**grew up** with, and that's probably no different from having an ordinary sister. We're identical twins, so when we were growing up, people used to [2]**mix us up** all the time – even our parents! These days we look a little bit different and we don't wear matching clothes.

We also have different personalities. I [3]**take after** my dad a lot more – we're both good at drawing and love art and films. Bianca is more into science, and she's much better at sport than I am. There's one quality we have that probably has to do with being twins. I usually know what Bianca is thinking or feeling, and it's the same for her. I suppose you could say it's a kind of telepathy.

When we were teenagers, we didn't [4]**get on with** each other very well and we both wanted to discover our own identities, but now that we're older, we [5]**hang out** together all the time. We talk on the phone two or three times a day and see each other once or twice a week.

BIANCA

Martina and I had a great childhood – it was so much fun. We did all the things identical twins do at some stage, like exchange classes at school and pretend to be each other. But from the beginning, we had quite different personalities. Martina has always been a bit kinder and more caring than I am, but she's often very forgetful! I'm usually a little more organised and maybe a bit more confident. Our parents understood this from the beginning and [6]**brought** us **up** to be different people. Sometimes twins are treated like they're one person, but that was never the case with us.

Sometimes we do some crazy things that people think are typical of twins. We went to different colleges in different cities. Then, when we came home for the summer, we had both [7]**cut** all our hair **off** so it was really short. But we hadn't told each other we were going to do that. Although we're very different people, we know each other well and Martina is my best friend. We usually [8]**get together** once or twice a week. I don't think we'll ever [9]**grow apart**.

3 LISTENING

a 💬📢 Discuss the questions.

1 Think of a family event from your childhood that you remember well. What happened?
2 Do family members sometimes have different memories of past events? What are some examples from your family or the family of someone you know?

b ▶ 03.07 Listen to Martina and Bianca talk about their childhood. Tick (✓) the topics where they remember the same information.

1 ☐ wearing the same clothes in school
2 ☐ talking together as children
3 ☐ wearing different clothes at secondary school
4 ☐ not liking questions from other people
5 ☐ their parents bringing them up well

c ▶ 03.07 Listen again for more information about the topics in 3b and make notes. Then compare with a partner.

4 GRAMMAR *used to, usually*

a ▶ 03.08 Underline the correct words in the sentences. Sometimes both words are correct. Then listen and check which form is used in the recording.

1 We *wore* / *used to wear* different clothes.
2 That's when you *started* / *used to start* wearing black.
3 I *hated* / *used to hate* being asked the same question all the time.
4 I *usually* / *used to* know what you think about things.
5 I *usually felt* / *used to feel* that people wanted us to compete all the time.

> All answers are true except for 2, 4 and 7.

b Complete the rules with the words in the box.

> *always*   the past simple   *usually*   *used to*

1 We can use _____ to talk about events that happened only once in the past.
2 We can use _____ + infinitive (without *to*) to talk about past habits and states.
3 We can use _____ and _____ with the present simple and past simple to talk about present and past habits.

c ≫ Now go to Grammar Focus 3B on p. 148.

d Complete the sentences so they are true for you.

1 The whole family usually _____ once a year.
2 My mum/dad/parents used to _____ when I was a child.
3 My mum/dad/parents didn't use to _____ when I was a child.
4 My grandmother/grandfather/uncle/aunt used to _____.
5 My brother/sister usually _____.
6 Families in my country usually _____.
7 Families in my country used to _____.

e 💬📢 Talk about your sentences from 4d.

> The whole family usually gets together once a year.

> Really? How big is your family?

> There are about 20 of us.

5 SPEAKING

a You are going to talk about a tradition in your family. Make notes using these questions to help you.

- What's the tradition?
- How often does it happen?
- When/Where does it happen?
- Which family members are involved?
- How did the tradition start?
- Was there anything you used to do that you don't do now?
- Do you like the tradition?
- Do you think the tradition will continue in the future?

b 💬📢 Tell each other about your family traditions. Are your traditions similar?

> We always go out for dinner on my birthday. We used to go for pizza, but now I usually choose a Japanese restaurant – I love sushi!

3C EVERYDAY ENGLISH
You won't believe what I did!

1 LISTENING

a 💬 Discuss the questions.

1 When was the last time you bought a present for a friend or relative? What was it? Did they like it?

2 Do you do a lot of shopping online? Do you buy different things online and in 'real' shops? Which do you prefer?

b 💬 Look at the photo below and the words in the box. What story do you think Mark is telling Tom?

> a desk   Mark's dad   online shopping
> very small   for children

c 📹 ▶ 03.10 Watch or listen to Part 1 and check your ideas. What mistake did Mark make?

2 CONVERSATION SKILLS
Reacting to what people say

a 📹 ▶ 03.10 Watch or listen to Part 1 again. Match Mark's comments 1–4 with Tom's replies a–d.

1 ☐ You won't believe what I did.   a Great!
2 ☐ It was a fantastic price, too.   b What?
3 ☐ So I ordered it.   c Sounds good.
4 ☐ It turned out I'd ordered a desk for a child.   d No way!

b Match responses a–d in 2a with the descriptions below.

1 responding positively ___ , ___
2 showing surprise ___
3 asking for more information ___

c Underline two other ways to show surprise in the exchange below.

A I've just bought my sister's birthday present. She loves running, so I got her a sports watch.

B Wow! That's a coincidence. I ordered one for myself yesterday.

A Really? What make did you get?

d Complete the sentences so they are true for you.

1 I like / don't like …   3 I really want to …
2 Last week, I …   4 I haven't been to …

e 💬 Take turns to say your sentences and then react to what your partner says. Use the phrases in 2a and 2c.

> I don't like chocolate cake.

> Really? I thought everyone liked chocolate cake.

3 LISTENING

a 💬 What do you think Mark did when he discovered his mistake?

b 📹 ▶ 03.11 Watch or listen to Part 2. What did Mark do next? Did he get a desk for his dad in the end?

c 📹 ▶ 03.11 Watch or listen again. Are the sentences true (*T*) or false (*F*)? Correct the false sentences.

1 The company Mark bought the desk from didn't offer a refund.
2 Looking on a freecycling website for a new desk was Rachel's idea.
3 Freecycling is where people can give away unwanted things.
4 Tom already knew about freecycling.
5 Mark is waiting for the desk to be delivered.

d 💬 Have you ever had any problems with online shopping? What happened?

4 USEFUL LANGUAGE
Telling a story

a ▶ 03.12 Complete each sentence with one or two words. Then listen and check.

1 **You won't** _believe_ **what** I did.
2 **The _____ thing is**, it was really, really small.
3 **It _____** I'd ordered a desk for a child.
4 But _____, I still had to find a desk.
5 **In the _____**, Rachel suggested I try one of those freecycling websites.
6 I found the perfect desk straight away, and **the _____ thing is** it's free.

b Add the phrases in 4a to the list below.

* starting a story:
  You'll never guess what (happened to me last week).

  _____

* adding new information:

  _____

  _____

* finishing a story (or part of a story):

  _____

  _____

c 💬▤ Tell each other stories using the notes below and the phrases in 4b.

1 • went to the shops
  • saw an old friend I hadn't seen for years
  • had lunch
  • she knew my wife/husband from work
2 • went shopping
  • wanted new clothes for wedding
  • found perfect dress/suit
  • got 25% discount

5 PRONUNCIATION
Stress in word groups

a ▶ 03.13 Listen to these sentences from the conversation. Notice how the speaker pauses between word groups. Use // to mark where the speaker pauses.

1 The funny thing is, it was really, really small.
2 In the end, Rachel suggested I try one of those freecycling websites.
3 Well, I phoned the company to explain and luckily they agreed to give me a refund.

Notice how, in each word group, one syllable is stressed more than all the others in the group. This is the main stress.

b ▶ 03.13 Listen again. Underline the syllable in each group which is stressed more strongly than the others.

c ▶ 03.13 Listen again and repeat the sentences.

6 SPEAKING

a Think of an interesting thing that happened to you (or someone you know) recently. Choose from the topics below or your own ideas:

* making a stupid mistake
* meeting a new person
* going on an interesting trip

Make notes about what happened. Think about which phrases from 4a you can include when you tell your story.

b 💬▤ Tell each other your stories. Make sure you react to what your partner is saying.

✓ UNIT PROGRESS TEST

→ CHECK YOUR PROGRESS

You can now do the Unit Progress Test.

3D SKILLS FOR WRITING
He wanted to see the world

1 SPEAKING AND LISTENING

a 💬 Discuss the questions.

1 How much do you know about past generations of your family? Are there any interesting stories in your family history?

2 Do you know more about your mother's or your father's side of the family? Why?

b ▶03.14 Listen to Bryan talking to his cousin, Susie, about their family. Which relatives are they talking about?

c Look at the photos. How do you think Bryan and Susie's relatives met?

d Make notes about someone in your family who interests you. Why do they interest you?

e 💬 Tell a partner about the person in your family.

2 READING

a Read Bryan's email to Susie. Why did their great-grandparents decide to live in Australia?

Our great-grandparents

Hi Susie,

I've done some investigating about our great-grandparents, Mary and Joe, and how they ended up living in Australia. I told you that Joe worked as a chef on cruise ships from 1937 until 1939, when World War II started. And you know that while he was working on one of the ships, he met Mary. She was the ship's nurse.

Well, apparently, that ship's destination was Melbourne. When the ship arrived, they spent a couple of days there. That's when Joe proposed to Mary and she said yes. During their stay in Melbourne, they decided that they really liked the city and that they would start a new life in Australia.

However, World War II started and Joe had to go back to England and join the British army. Meanwhile, Mary stayed in Australia because it was much safer. They were separated for several years and missed each other very much. Mary was quite lonely at first, but after a couple of months, she got a job in a hospital and made friends there – she was always very friendly and good at talking to people.

In 1946, Joe returned to Australia and they got married. Five years later, our grandmother was born. After she grew up and got married, she had two daughters – our mothers!

Our great-grandparents lived in the same house in Melbourne for 30 years. I found it over the summer when I was on holiday. Would you like me to take you to see the house one day?

Bryan

b Read the email again and put pictures a–e in the order they are described.

1 ☐ 2 ☐ 3 ☐ 4 ☐ 5 ☐

3 WRITING SKILLS Describing time

a Look at the words in **bold** in the examples. Do they all describe a *point* in time or a *period* of time?

1 Joe worked as a chef on cruise ships **from** 1937 **until** 1939.
2 **While** he was working on one of the ships, he met Mary.
3 **During** their stay in Melbourne, they decided that they really liked the city.
4 They were separated **for** several years.
5 **Meanwhile**, Mary stayed in Australia.
6 I found their house **over** the summer.

b Underline the correct words to complete the rules.

1 We can use *while / during* before a noun or noun phrase.
2 We can use *while / during* before a verb phrase.
3 We *can / can't* use 'during' before lengths of time (e.g., six months).
4 *Meanwhile / Over* means 'at the same time' and is usually at the beginning of a sentence.
5 *Meanwhile / Over* can mean the same as 'during'.

c Underline the correct words.

1 I lived alone *from / until* 2012 *from / until* I got married.
2 I worked as a chef *while / during* the 1990s.
3 I usually go abroad *over / from* the winter months.
4 I lived in Singapore *while / meanwhile* I was working for the government.
5 I had a job in Ankara *from / for* about two years.
6 *Meanwhile / While*, my sister was living in Pattaya.

d Complete the sentences from another life story.

1 He was a soldier in the army _____ five years.
2 He went to India twice _____ he was working on the ship.
3 He was in Italy _____ 1943 until 1945.
4 She was in Rome for about six months. _____, her husband stayed in Milan.
5 From 1950 _____ two years later, he worked as a chef in an Italian restaurant.

e Make notes about some important events in your life (e.g., your job, your studies, your activities).

Over the summer, I worked at a swimming pool.
I started work four years ago. Meanwhile, I was studying for a degree.

f 💬📢 Take turns to read your events to your partner. Ask questions to find out more.

4 WRITING

a You are going to write a biography of someone you know or know about. Choose a person and make notes about the topics below.

1 why this person is important to you
2 what you remember most about this person
3 what the key events in this person's life are

b Write the biography. Use words and phrases to describe time (*from, while*, etc.).

c 💬📢 Work in pairs. Read your partner's biography. Do they use time words correctly? Ask a question about the person they described.

UNIT 3
Review and extension

1 GRAMMAR

a Complete the sentences with the past simple, the past continuous or the past perfect form of the verbs.

1 When I _____ (get) home, everyone _____ (wait) for me. My family and friends _____ (plan) a surprise party for my birthday!
2 When I _____ (wake up) this morning, I _____ (be) shocked. The wind _____ (blow) a tree down and it _____ (block) the front door.
3 As soon as the doctor _____ (show) me the X-ray, I _____ (know) I _____ (break) my leg.
4 As I _____ (sit) on the grass, I _____ (realise) that I _____ (wear) socks that _____ (not match). I _____ (feel) very silly.

b Underline the correct words.

1 We *occasionally / used to* had a big family party.
2 My parents *used to give / gave* me a bike on my eighth birthday.
3 Did you *used / use* to be shy when you were a child?
4 Terry and his twin brother *always wear / used to wear* the same clothes. They wear matching outfits to work and at home.
5 My sister and I *always used to walk / walked always* home from school together when we were young.
6 My aunt doesn't *used to / usually* celebrate her birthday, but I always phone her.
7 I didn't *use to / hardly ever* like George, but now we're best friends.
8 My grandfather says, 'Young people *used to be / always were* more polite than they are now.'

2 VOCABULARY

a Complete the sentences with the correct word.

1 Do you have a lot in _____ with your brother?
2 We became friends at university and our _____ lasted for 50 years.
3 Will you keep in _____ after you move to Lima?
4 He comes from the same _____ as I do. Our childhoods were very similar.
5 I get _____ well with most people I meet.

b Complete the sentences with a multi-word verb that has a similar meaning to the words in brackets.

| bring | cut | grew | grow | hang |
| apart | off | out | up | up |

1 It's a book about how to <u>bring up</u> children. (raise)
2 When did he _____ all his hair _____? (remove)
3 Where did you _____ _____? (live when you were a child)
4 We used to be good friends, but we _____ _____ when she changed schools. (become less close)
5 I often _____ _____ with Martin and his cousin. (spend time relaxing)

3 WORDPOWER *have*

a Complete the conversations with sentences a–g.

a Yes, we did, but we **had an accident** in the car we hired.
b Yes, I did. Well, I **had a go**. I wasn't very good!
c Shall we **have lunch** at a restaurant today?
d Neil **has three brothers**, doesn't he?
e I **have no idea**. What Spanish restaurant?
f Does he **have brown eyes and a beard**?
g You should **have some lessons**.

A ^{1}_____
B Yes, but I only know the oldest one, Carl. I sometimes **have a bite to eat** with him after work.
A ^{2}_____
B Yes, he does.

A How was your holiday? Did you **have fun**?
B ^{3}_____

A ^{4}_____
B Yes, I'd like that. Where's that new Spanish restaurant?
A ^{5}_____
B It's a new place. Let's go into town and **have a look**.

A How was the wedding? Did you dance?
B ^{6}_____
A ^{7}_____
B Yes, maybe I will.

b Add the phrases with *have* in **bold** in 3a to the table.

eating/drinking	possession	experience	other phrases
		have fun	

c Complete the sentences with the correct form of *have* or *have a/an*.

1 When was the last time you _____ special meal?
2 Are any of your friends or family _____ language lessons at the moment?
3 Do you usually _____ breakfast with your family or on your own?
4 Have you ever _____ accident in a car or on a bike?
5 Did you _____ good time last weekend? Why / Why not?

d 💬 Ask and answer the questions.

⟳ REVIEW YOUR PROGRESS

How well did you do in this unit? Write 3, 2 or 1 for each objective.
3 = very well   2 = well   1 = not so well

I CAN ...	
talk about a friendship	☐
talk about families	☐
tell a story	☐
write about someone's life.	☐

 CAN DO OBJECTIVES

■ Describe people and their abilities
■ Describe feelings
■ Offer and ask for help
■ Write an informal online advert

UNIT 4

PERSONALITY

GETTING STARTED

a 💬 Look at the photo and discuss the questions.

1 What three words would you use to describe the child on the right?
2 What three words would you use to describe the other child?

b 💬 Discuss the questions.

1 Who in your family is most similar to you in personality? What is that person like?
2 Which of your friends is most different from you in personality? What is that person like?

4A | I COULD SING VERY WELL WHEN I WAS YOUNGER

Learn to describe people and their abilities

- **G** Modals and phrases of ability
- **V** Ability

1 READING AND VOCABULARY
Ability

a Write down three things you were good at as a child. Think about sport, school subjects, art and music or other skills.

b 💬 Talk about what you were good at.

> I was good at drawing people's faces. I won a prize in a drawing competition when I was ten.

c Read *When will I be famous?* What problems did Christian Bale have? How does he feel about his success now?

d Read the article again and <u>underline</u> the correct words.

e Complete the table with the words you chose in the text.

adjective	noun / noun phrase	verb
successful	ability	

f Complete each sentence with the preposition *about*, *at*, *to* or *towards*. Sometimes more than one answer is possible.

1 She is **good** _____ making friends.
2 I'm not very **talented** _____ art.
3 It's important to have **a positive attitude** _____ your work.
4 She has the **ability** _____ pass exams without even trying.
5 He is **confident** _____ his ability to pass the exam.

g Complete the sentences so they are true for you.

1 It's important to have a positive attitude and not give up because …
2 I'm talented at …
3 I'm not very good at …
4 If you want to be successful in life, you need to …
5 One of my biggest achievements was …

h 💬 Talk about your sentences in 1g.

When will I be famous?

Who remembers Mara Wilson and Jake Lloyd? Both were big stars as children in films like *Matilda* (Wilson) and *Star Wars: The Phantom Menace* (Lloyd) but neither had successful film careers in later life. Read about one child star who did make it …

The Dark Knight, *The Big Short*, *Vice* – ¹*successful / confident* films starring Christian Bale. He's now thought of as one of the world's biggest stars, but his was a career that almost ended before it began. The story of how this ²*talented / positive* performer went from promising child actor to Hollywood leading man is itself like something from a film.

Bale had an unusual childhood – his father was an entrepreneur* and his mother was a circus performer, so they moved around a lot. As a young boy, Christian was good at ballet and playing the guitar, but it was his sister's interest in theatre that first gave him the idea of trying acting. From early on, it was clear he had real ³*achievement / ability*. Although he was a(n) ⁴*intelligent / successful* child, school work didn't interest him nearly as much as performing.

Christian's first acting role was in a TV advert, when he was just eight years old. Further roles in TV dramas followed, before his big break in 1987, playing the lead in Steven Spielberg's *Empire of the Sun*. Despite his early ⁵*achievement / ability*, he didn't always enjoy the film star attention he received. He almost decided to ⁶*give up / achieve* acting, until a director offered him a role in a film version of Shakespeare's *Henry V*. This experience gave him a more ⁷*positive attitude / positive success* towards his profession.

Bale left school when he was 16 years old and he was ⁸*determined / confident* to become a successful actor. In the 1990s, he played a wide range of characters from romantic hero to rock star. Then, in 2005, he starred in Christopher Nolan's film *Batman Begins*. The rest, as they say, is history. Nowadays, Bale is famous as one of Hollywood's best 'method' actors, meaning he often changes his appearance or body shape for a film. He also manages to change his personality and 'become' the person he is playing.

Despite all his success, he's still not ⁹*confident / talented* that he will continue to get roles and worries about where the next job will come from.

*****entrepreneur** (n) someone who starts their own business

2 LISTENING

a ▶️ 04.01 Listen to a radio programme about age, talent and success. Complete the table.

Name	What do they have a talent for?	Did they show this talent at a young age?	At what age did they first become famous or successful?
Tsung Tsung			
Lionel Messi	playing football		
Vivienne Westwood			
Andrea Bocelli	singing		

b ▶️ 04.01 Listen again. Are the sentences true (*T*) or false (*F*)?

1 Tsung Tsung first became famous when he appeared on a TV programme.
2 As a boy, Messi could play football better than the older boys.
3 A recent study showed that most talented children do much better than other adults when they grow up.
4 Vivienne Westwood was a teacher before she became a successful designer.
5 Bocelli's solo classical album became an international success when he was in his forties.
6 Ed believes that talented people don't usually make mistakes.

c 💬🔊 Do you agree with these statements?

1 Talented children don't succeed as adults because they don't develop good social skills.
2 It's better to be successful when you are young – you can enjoy it more.
3 If you want success in a creative job, hard work is more important than talent.

Vivienne Westwood

Lionel Messi

Andrea Bocelli

3 GRAMMAR Modals and phrases of ability

a Underline the words and phrases used to talk about ability in these sentences.

1 Tsung Tsung <u>could</u> play the piano when he was three.
2 He said his dream was to be able to play like Mozart.
3 He was so good that he was able to join the Barcelona junior team when he was 11.
4 Less than 5% managed to become very successful adults.
5 He's been able to sing well since he was a child.
6 Say to yourself: 'I can do it!'
7 They'll be able to do it when they're a bit older.

b Look at the sentences in 3a. Complete rules 1–5 with the words in the box.

> be able to   can   will be able to
> could   manage to   was/were able to

> 1 We use _____ and *be able to* to talk about ability in the present.
> 2 In the past, we usually use _____ to talk about general ability and _____ to talk about a single time.
> 3 There is no present perfect or infinitive form of *can*, so we use forms of _____ instead.
> 4 We can't say 'will can', so we say _____ instead.
> 5 The verb _____ means to succeed in doing something difficult.

c ▶ 04.02 Pronunciation Listen to this sentence from 3a. Which is stressed more: *could* or *play*?

Tsung Tsung could play the piano when he was three.

d ▶ 04.03 Now listen to this sentence. Which word is stressed the most?

Say to yourself: 'I can do it!'

e Underline the correct words in the rules below.

> 1 We *usually / don't usually* stress words and phrases that talk about ability, unless we are emphasising something.
> 2 We *usually / don't usually* stress the main verb we are focusing on (e.g., *play the piano*).

f Complete the sentences with forms of *can, could, be able to* and *manage to*. More than one answer may be possible.

1 I took my exam today and I _____ finish all the questions before the end.
2 After trying for 20 minutes, we _____ open the door.
3 I've _____ ski since I was five years old.
4 Lisa _____ already read simple books when she was three years old.
5 I live near the sea, but I _____ swim.
6 My Spanish is getting better. I'll _____ speak to my Spanish friends on the phone soon.

g ≫ Now go to Grammar Focus 4A on p. 150.

h Make notes about these topics.

1 three things you could do when you were a child that you can't do now
2 two things you managed to do after a lot of hard work
3 one thing you want to be able to do better in the future
4 two things you didn't manage to do last week because you had no time

i 💬 Talk about the topics in 3h. Ask each other questions to find out more information.

4 SPEAKING

a Think about ways in which you have succeeded (e.g., learned a new skill, passed an exam, solved a problem). Tick (✓) the things that helped you to be successful.

☐ a positive attitude
☐ patience
☐ working long hours
☐ knowing the right people
☐ good luck
☐ good health
☐ talent
☐ support from friends and family
☐ self-confidence
☐ intelligence

b 💬 Which of the things from 4a helped you to be successful? Which do you think are the most important?

> My parents helped me a lot when I was at university. You definitely can't succeed without the support of your family.

4B | ARE YOU AN INTROVERT?

1 SPEAKING AND READING

a 💬 Discuss the questions.

1 Do you prefer spending time alone or with other people?
2 Do you think you are an extrovert (confident and sociable) or an introvert (quiet and happy to be alone)?

b Complete the quiz and compare your answers with your partner. Then go to p. 128 to see your results. Do you agree with them?

QUIZ

Are you an INTROVERT?

Read each statement and tick **Yes** or **No**.

1 I can be alone for a long time without feeling lonely.
Yes ◯ No ◯

2 In class, I prefer listening to talking in groups.
Yes ◯ No ◯

3 I express myself better in writing than speaking.
Yes ◯ No ◯

4 I don't always answer my phone when it rings.
Yes ◯ No ◯

5 I prefer working on my own or in a small group of people.
Yes ◯ No ◯

6 I don't like other people seeing my work before I've finished it.
Yes ◯ No ◯

7 People often describe me as quiet.
Yes ◯ No ◯

Number of *Yes* answers = ☐

2 LISTENING

a 💬 Discuss the questions.

1 Do you think you can tell whether a person is an extrovert or an introvert from their appearance? Think about the following topics.

body language	clothes	hairstyle	make-up

2 Look at these people. Which person seems outgoing and sociable and which person seems serious and reserved? Why?

Kate

Alex

b ▶ 04.05 Listen to the two people. What number do you think they are on the scale on p. 128?

c ▶ 04.05 Listen again. What do Kate and Alex say about the topics below?

Kate:
1 parties
2 being alone
3 other people's opinions of her
4 speaking in public

Alex:
1 parties
2 being alone
3 making people laugh
4 chatting with people

3 VOCABULARY Personality adjectives

a Match words 1–8 with definitions a–h.

1 [e] sociable   a likes talking a lot
2 [ ] outgoing   b not confident with other people
3 [ ] talkative   c full of energy
4 [ ] shy   d quiet and doesn't laugh a lot
5 [ ] reserved   e likes being with other people
6 [ ] lively   f feels emotions deeply and
7 [ ] serious   often easily upset
8 [ ] sensitive   g doesn't show what they're
               feeling or thinking
          h friendly and interested in
               meeting new people

b 💬 Which adjectives would you use to describe Kate and Alex? Why?

c Read about these people. Which adjectives would best describe them? Sometimes more than one answer is possible.

1 Lisa loves romantic poetry. It often makes her cry. _____
2 Louis doesn't say much when he's with people he doesn't know. _____
3 Stefan always has something to say. _____
4 Jon loves parties and meeting new people. _____
5 Anna doesn't talk to many people, but you can have an interesting discussion with her. _____

d 💬 Which adjectives in 3a best describe you? Explain your choices.

4 READING

a Look at the four photos of famous people. Then answer the questions.

1 What do you know about these people?
2 Do you think they were/are introverts or extroverts? Why?

b Read *Why the world needs introverts* quickly to check your ideas.

c Read the article again and answer the questions.

1 What is the attitude that Susan Cain calls the 'Extrovert Ideal'?
2 How do people organise classrooms and offices to make them better for extroverts?
3 How are extroverts useful to introverts?

d 💬 Discuss the questions.

1 Do people in your culture think that being quiet is a good thing? Why / Why not?
2 Are schools and offices in your country designed for extroverts? How?

Why the world needs *introverts*

It's good to be sociable! It's good to be confident! It's good to be loud! In her book *Quiet*, Susan Cain points out how deeply this belief is held by society. Very often the qualities of extroverts – being active and lively, making quick decisions and working well in a team or group, for example – are valued more than the shy, serious and sensitive qualities of introverts.

Susan Cain calls this attitude the 'Extrovert Ideal'. In her book, she looks at the way society places such value on the Extrovert Ideal that many modern schools and workplaces are built around it. Desks in classrooms are pushed together so students can work in groups more easily. In Europe and the USA, employees are frequently put in shared offices so they can work in teams. Students and employees are also expected to be confident and talkative.

Why are the needs of introverts ignored in this way when introverts have so much to offer? Introverts need

Mahatma Gandhi was an introvert, as were Vincent van Gogh and Albert Einstein.

less excitement around them than extroverts, it's true, but that doesn't make them less exciting people. Many of the world's greatest ideas, art and inventions have been produced by introverts. The Indian leader Mahatma Gandhi was an introvert, as were the artist Vincent van Gogh and the physicist Albert Einstein.

Then there was Rosa Parks, who helped start the US civil rights movement in 1955 by bravely and quietly saying no when a white passenger wanted to sit in her seat on a bus.

Famous introverts in modern times include Angelina Jolie and Lorde. Jolie, a hugely successful actor, supports charities that help people in war zones. She describes herself as an introvert, saying she loves to spend time alone or with small groups of people because it helps her develop as a person.

And despite seeming incredibly comfortable on stage, pop singer Lorde also sees herself as an introvert and says she is 'really a shy, library person'.

But let's not forget that we need extroverts, too – because introverts can come up with great ideas but they may need help in communicating those ideas to the world. Songwriters need singers. Designers need salespeople. In other words, extroverts and introverts need each other.

Mahatma Gandhi

5 GRAMMAR Articles

a Read Laura's post. Which personality adjectives in 3a do you think best describe ... ?

  a Laura   b her husband

Laura

> I have always been ¹an introvert. At ²school, I was really shy, and I have always preferred to spend hours alone with ³a good book or to go for a long walk. I hate ⁴clubs and groups. For example, I went to ⁵a birthday party last week and I felt really nervous. But I tried to look happy at ⁶the party because I didn't want people to think I was strange.
> My husband is totally different. He's ⁷the friendliest person in ⁸the world. He loves going out and being with people. Every so often he says to me, 'You really don't like ⁹people, do you?'

b Match the examples in Laura's post (1–9) with the descriptions (a–h). Sometimes more than one answer is possible.

a, an

a one of several people or things (*I bought **a** new car.*)

  _____

b when we mention a person or thing for the first time (*They have **a** boy and **a** girl.*) _____

c one of a particular type or group (*He's still **a** child.*)

the

d when it is clear which one we are talking about (*I'm going to **the** supermarket.*) _____

e when there is only one of something (***The** sun was shining.*) _____

f when we mention a person or thing again, especially to make it clear which one we mean (*They have a boy and a girl. ... **The** boy is 10 ... .*) _____

no article

g to talk about people or things in general (*I never play **video games**.*) _____

h in some fixed phrases about places (*Are they at **home**?*) _____

c ›› Now go to Grammar Focus 4B on p. 150.

d Write a short paragraph about one of the topics below. Try to use articles correctly.

- someone you know who is an extrovert/introvert
- an interesting book you would recommend
- a famous person you admire

e Read and check your partner's paragraph. Are there any mistakes with articles?

6 SPEAKING

a Choose one of the topics below. Make brief notes about the person. Include some of the adjectives from 3a.

- someone you know who is an extrovert/introvert
- a famous person you admire
- a person in your family you admire

b 💬 Work in groups. Tell other students in your group about the person you chose and answer any questions.

c 💬 Tell the class about one of the people you talked about in your group.

Rosa Parks

Angelina Jolie

Lorde

4C EVERYDAY ENGLISH
Do you need a hand?

Learn to offer and ask for help
- (S) Question tags
- (P) Intonation in question tags

1 LISTENING

a 💬 Discuss the questions.

1 Do you think that you're a helpful person? Why / Why not?
2 Do you know anyone who's very helpful? Have they helped you?

b 💬 Look at the photo. What do you think Tom is offering to do to help?

c 🎥 ▶ 04.07 Watch or listen to Part 1 and check your answers to 1b.

d 🎥 ▶ 04.07 Watch or listen to Part 1 again. Underline the correct answers.

1 Becky is showing Rachel photos of her *holiday* / *house*.
2 Rachel asks Becky to take photos for *her website* / *fun*.
3 Mark is going to *buy* / *pick up* the desk on Saturday.
4 Becky suggests that *Mark goes alone* / *Tom helps Mark*.

e What favour do you think Tom might ask Rachel?

2 CONVERSATION SKILLS
Question tags

a ▶ 04.08 Listen to the questions below and look at the question tags in **bold**. Match the question tags with uses a or b.

1 ☐ That's the hotel you stayed in, **isn't it**?
2 ☐ You know I'm making a new website, **don't you**?

a a statement checking something you already think is true
b a real question

b Match 1–4 with a–d to complete the rules.

1 ☐ We usually use a positive question tag
2 ☐ We usually use a negative question tag
3 ☐ If there is an auxiliary verb (*do/have/be*), and *be* is not the main verb,
4 ☐ If there is no auxiliary verb, and the main verb isn't *be*,

a after a positive sentence.
b after a negative sentence.
c use *do/don't* in the question tag.
d use the auxiliary verb in the question tag.

c Complete the question tags.

1 You don't drink coffee, _____?
2 It's cold in here, _____?
3 You've eaten, _____?
4 It was you I saw, _____?
5 Steve's gone to France, _____?
6 You didn't come to class yesterday, _____?

3 PRONUNCIATION
Intonation in question tags

a ▶ 04.09 Listen to this sentence. Here, the speaker thinks she knows the answer. Does the intonation go up or down on the question tag?

> That's the hotel you stayed in, isn't it?

b ▶ 04.10 Now listen to the same sentence with a different intonation on the question tag. This time, the speaker isn't sure about the answer. It is a real question. Does the intonation go up or down on the question tag?

> That's the hotel you stayed in, isn't it?

4 LISTENING

a ■ ▶ 04.11 Watch or listen to Part 2 and <u>underline</u> the correct words.

1 Tom wants Rachel to help him to *ask Becky to marry him / buy a ring*.
2 Rachel *agrees / refuses* to help Tom.

b 💬 Look at the photo. What do you think is happening?

c ■ ▶ 04.12 Watch or listen to Part 3 and check your ideas.

d 💬 Which of these things have you done to help a friend? Were you happy to do it? What happened?

- move furniture / help them move house
- use your creative skills (e.g., taking photos)
- talk through a problem they have
- buy a present
- give them a lift in your car

5 USEFUL LANGUAGE
Offering and asking for help

a ▶ 04.13 Complete each sentence with one word. Listen and check.

1 **Do you think you** _____ take them?
2 **Do you** _____ **a hand?**
3 **Could I** _____ **you a favour** in return?
4 So **what do you** _____?
5 **I** _____ **if you could** come with me to buy the ring.

b Add the phrases in **bold** in 5a to the table.

Offers to help	Asking for help

c Add these questions to the table in 5b.

1 Can you do something for me?
2 Can you give me a hand (with something)?
3 Is there something I can do?
4 How can I help you?

d Complete the conversations with the phrases in 5b. There may be more than one answer.

1 **A** I'm having a fridge delivered this evening.
   B _____?
   A No, it's fine, thanks.

2 **A** _____ with this report?
   B Of course, what do you need?
   A _____ check it and see if it makes sense?

3 **A** _____?
   B Depends what it is.
   A _____ look after my plants while I'm away.

6 SPEAKING

a ≫ **Communication 4C** 💬 Student A: Go to 6b below. Student B: Go to p. 128.

b You are going to have two conversations offering and asking for help. Read the information and think about what you are going to say.

> **Student A**
> 1 You need some help to buy a new computer. You think Student B knows about computers. You would like Student B to come shopping with you.
> 2 You have a big car. Student B would like your help with moving some furniture. You are free at the weekend, but you aren't free on Friday.

c 💬 Have conversations using the language in 5b.

✓ UNIT PROGRESS TEST

→ CHECK YOUR PROGRESS

You can now do the Unit Progress Test.

4D | SKILLS FOR WRITING
No experience needed

1 SPEAKING AND LISTENING

a 💬 Discuss the questions.

1 Which of these things do you usually prefer to do on the Internet?
- buy or sell things
- book trips or holidays
- meet other people or join groups
- find work

2 What do you think are the advantages and disadvantages of using the Internet for these things?

b ▶ 04.14 Listen to three people talking about websites they have used. What is the purpose of each website?

c ▶ 04.14 Listen again. What do the speakers in brackets say about each topic?

1 how she travelled in India (Sheena)
2 her personality (Sheena)
3 earning money (Alya)
4 teaching children (Alya)
5 his skills (Brad)
6 being serious (Brad)

d 💬 Would you use websites like these? Why / Why not?

2 READING

a Read adverts a–c quickly. Which of these topics does each advert mention?

dates or times   money   travelling   types of people   work

b Read the adverts again and answer the questions.

Advert a
1 Where is the trip?
2 How many people are they looking for?
3 What kind of person are they looking for?

Advert b
1 What are the main responsibilities of the job?
2 When does the work start?
3 What kind of person are they looking for?

Advert c
1 What does the job involve?
2 What experience is needed?
3 How long is it for?

---

a
TRAVELGROUPS
🏠 Home   👤 Profile   ▪ Account

North India and the Himalayas – come and join us in October!
Hi there,
We're planning a trip to North India and the Himalayas this October and we're looking for people to join us.

We'll be doing some climbing (not too much!) and also travelling around North India. We're meeting up in Delhi in mid-October and spending about four weeks on the road.

We're looking for one or two people, male or female, under 30, reasonably fit, and able to live cheaply. Climbing experience preferred (and experience in India would be good, too). Ideally you should be sociable and not too serious.

If this sounds like the trip for you, send a reply plus a photo and we'll get back to you!
Cristina, Matt and Rob

● ● ● ● ▶

b
VC
Volunteer Community Project
home   about us   community projects   accommodation   applications

Volunteer needed

Duties include teaching English, art, maths, etc., as well as leading educational play groups. Support will be given by local teachers or project staff. Occasionally, volunteers will be asked to help with domestic duties such as preparing meals and keeping the classrooms and gardens clean to help create a happy and healthy atmosphere for the children.

Volunteers should be available to start work next month. No qualifications required, but candidates should have a positive and outgoing personality and be good with young children.

Please send a CV and a short personal profile.

3 WRITING SKILLS The language of adverts

a Read about the language used in the adverts. Which adverts do sentences 1–6 describe? Write *a*, *b* or *c*.

1 Sentences start with *we* or *you*. _a, c_
2 Sentences start with impersonal nouns like *jobs* or *duties*. _____
3 Sentences use formal words like *candidates* or *volunteers*. _____
4 Passive verb forms are often used. _____
5 The advert uses conversational expressions (e.g., *Hi there, get back to, fixing things*). _____
6 Some sentences and phrases end in exclamation marks. _____

b Which features in 3a make the adverts seem …?

a more personal and friendly
b more impersonal and official

c Look at advert a. What is the purpose of each section? Match sections 1–4 with these descriptions.

a ☐ tells the reader what to do next
b ☐ gives details of the situation (work, travel, plans, etc.)
c ☐ shows briefly what the advert is about
d ☐ says what kind of person they're looking for

d In adverts and messages, we often use fixed 'reduced' expressions. Find expressions in the adverts that mean the following:

1 You don't need any experience.
2 We'd prefer a person with climbing experience.
3 We need a volunteer.
4 We don't require you to have any qualifications.

e Look at some more examples of reduced expressions in writing. How can you express the same ideas in full sentences?

1 Assistance urgently needed.
2 Driving licence required.
3 Male or female under 40 preferred.
4 Accommodation included.

4 WRITING An informal online advert

a Write an advert. Choose one of these situations.

- You're travelling somewhere and you want more people to join you to make a group.
- You're organising charity work and you want some volunteers to help you.
- You want to employ someone to work for you for a couple of weeks.

Follow this plan.

1 Create a heading to draw attention to the advert.
2 Describe the situation (the job, your plans, etc.).
3 Say what kind of person you're looking for.
4 Ask for a reply.

b Read and check your advert.

1 Do you think it's too formal, not formal enough or about right?
2 Have you used any reduced expressions?

c Read another student's advert and write a reply.

1 Say you're interested.
2 Give details about yourself.
3 Ask any further questions.

c SHORTWORK

Home   Profile   Account

Wanted – help with garden and house

We're a big family (three small children) and we need help with work on our garden and house for two weeks.

Jobs that need doing include general work in the garden, painting in the house and fixing minor electrical problems.

No experience needed, but you should be good at fixing things and willing to work hard. Payment to be arranged.

Reply to: Mel and Nick

UNIT 4
Review and extension

1 GRAMMAR

a Tick (✓) the correct sentences. Sometimes both are correct.

1. ☐ a I can kick a ball, but I can't play football!
   ☐ b I manage to kick a ball, but not manage to play football!
2. ☐ a Were you able to answer all the questions?
   ☐ b Did you manage to answer all the questions?
3. ☐ a Unfortunately, I couldn't relax.
   ☐ b Unfortunately, I wasn't able to relax.
4. ☐ a You need to can swim.
   ☐ b You need to be able to swim.

b Underline the correct words. (Ø means 'no article'.)

The COLOURFUL WORLD of AELITA ANDRE

Aelita Andre is [1]*a / Ø* young artist from Melbourne, Australia. She loves [2]*the / Ø* colours and her paintings are bright and wild. She sometimes adds [3]*the / Ø* small toys to her pictures, such as plastic dinosaurs and butterflies.

[4]*A / The* young painter has already earned a lot of money, and [5]*Ø / the* people have described her as 'the youngest professional artist in [6]*Ø / the* world'. When Aelita was five, her work was on display in [7]*the / an* art gallery in New York.

Aelita's mother says, 'You know how [8]*Ø / the* young children paint for a few minutes and then lose interest? When Aelita was two, she often painted for an hour without stopping.'

c 💬🔊 Complete the questions with *a*, *an*, *the* or *Ø*. Then ask and answer the questions.

1. Do you like spending time in ___ countryside?
2. How many times ___ year do you go to ___ cinema?
3. Can you remember ___ first time you went to school?
4. Have you ever called ___ police?
5. Did you go anywhere interesting ___ last week? If so, where?
6. Can you play ___ piano or any other musical instrument?
7. Would you like to be ___ artist? Why / Why not?

2 VOCABULARY

a 💬🔊 Underline the correct words. Which sentences are true for you?

1. People think I'm *talented / confident*, but in fact I'm very shy.
2. I'd like to be a *determined / successful* businessperson.
3. I've already *succeeded / achieved* a lot of my goals.
4. I'm very *patient / bright* with young children.
5. I'm very *talkative / sensitive*, so people often tell me to be quiet.

b Complete the sentences with *ability*, *attitude*, *confident* or *good* and a preposition.

1. I'm not very _____ languages. I only speak English.
2. How _____ are you _____ passing your driving test?
3. I used to have a positive _____ my job, but now I don't care much.
4. You need the _____ solve problems to be a good project manager.

3 WORDPOWER *so* and *such*

a Match statements and questions 1–6 with responses a–

1. ☐ How many people were in the group?
2. ☐ Julie works **so** hard!
3. ☐ How many pages have you written?
4. ☐ Simon's a bit of an introvert, isn't he?
5. ☐ You're getting married. That's **such** good news!
6. ☐ We're going to need a lot of stuff!

a. Yes, paper, glue, paint, scissors **and so on**.
b. About 20 **or so**, I think. I didn't speak to all of them.
c. Absolutely! **So** he wouldn't like to give the presentation.
d. Yes, I'm **so** happy!
e. Ten **so far**, but I haven't finished yet.
f. I know. And she's **such** a nice person, too.

b Find examples of rules 1–3 in 3a.

1. We use *so* + clause to describe a result. ___
2. We use *so* before an adjective or adverb to add emphasis. ___, ___
3. We use *such* before an adjective + noun to add emphasis. ___, ___

c Match the words in the box with the meanings.

and so on   or so   so far

1. up to now _____
2. there are more things on the list _____
3. more or less _____

d Complete the sentences with one, two or three words. One of the words must be *so* or *such*.

1. Emma speaks _____ quickly!
2. We need to leave in 10 minutes _____.
3. It was too difficult, _____ I asked for help.
4. She's _____ interesting person.
5. I've been trying to find a present for my brother, but I haven't had much success _____.
6. I don't like _____ hot weather.
7. We need simple food for the picnic, like bread, cheese, crisps, fruit _____.
8. It was _____ big achievement for me.

e 💬🔊 Think of famous people who match the descriptions below.

1. … is such an amazing singer.
2. … is so funny.
3. … is so rich.
4. … does such good things for other people.

🔄 REVIEW YOUR PROGRESS

How well did you do in this unit? Write 3, 2 or 1 for each objective.
3 = very well   2 = well   1 = not so well

I CAN ...	
describe people and their abilities	☐
describe feelings	☐
offer and ask for help	☐
write an informal online advert.	☐

UNIT **5**

THE NATURAL WORLD

GETTING STARTED

a 💬 Imagine you are the person in the photo. How do you feel? What would you do next?

b 💬 How much do you know about this animal?

  1 Where does it live?   3 Is it dangerous?
  2 What does it eat?   4 Is it endangered?

c 💬 Is protecting the environment and endangered animals important to you? If so, what kinds of things are you doing about it? What other things could you do?

1 VOCABULARY Environmental issues

a Match the words in **bold** in sentences 1–8 with the descriptions in a–h below.

1 Is air **pollution** a problem where you live? If yes, how can we **prevent** it?
2 What **wildlife** or natural environments are **endangered** in your country?
3 Are there any **conservation projects** to help **protect** animals and plants in your local area?
4 How important is it to **save** our natural environments?
5 Have new roads and buildings **damaged** the environment near you?
6 Do most people in your country care about **climate change**?
7 What can ordinary people do to help **the environment**?
8 Should people always buy **environmentally friendly** products and **recycle** their glass and plastic?

a a noun that means the air, land and water where people, animals and plants live
b four verbs that are used to talk about solutions
c a verb that means 'destroy' or 'spoil'
d a noun and a noun phrase that are environmental problems
e a noun phrase that can be a solution to environmental problems
f a noun that means 'animals that are not pets or farm animals'
g an adjective that describes animals and plants that may disappear
h a phrase that means 'not bad for the environment'

b ▶ 05.01 **Pronunciation** How is the <u>underlined</u> letter *a* pronounced in each word below? Complete the table. Listen and check.

<u>a</u>nim<u>a</u>ls ch<u>a</u>nge clim<u>a</u>te conserv<u>a</u>tion d<u>a</u>maged
end<u>a</u>ngered gl<u>a</u>ss n<u>a</u>tural p<u>a</u>per pl<u>a</u>nts

/eɪ/	/ɑː/	/æ/	/ə/
			animals

c ▶ 05.01 Listen again and repeat the words.

d 💬 Choose two questions from 1a that interest you. Discuss your answers to the questions.

e ≫ Now go to Vocabulary Focus 5A on p. 135.

2 READING

a Read about the Whitley Fund for Nature below and answer the questions.

1 Who do they give money to?
2 How much money do they give?
3 What can winners do with the money?

THE WHITLEY FUND FOR NATURE

WFN

The **WFN** is a UK-based charity that aims to help the environment in different parts of the world. They give money to people who are trying to save their local environment from danger. They believe that the best projects:

🦋 are practical

🦋 are based on good science

🦋 help local people but also depend on local people's help.

Every year, they give awards of up to £45,000 to help people run projects that will bring long-term positive change to the environment. With the help of the Whitley Award money, these people will be able to increase the size of their projects and become better known, both in their own country and abroad.

b You are going to read about three people who have won a Whitley Award to help their local environments. Look at the photos on p. 57. What do you think their projects are?

c Work in groups of three. Each group member should read one part of the article (a, b or c) on p. 57 and answer the questions below.

1 Where does the person work?
2 How did they first get interested in conservation?
3 What wildlife are they trying to protect?
4 Do they work with local people? What do they do?
5 What do they hope will happen in the future?

d 💬 Work in your group. Use your answers from 2c to discuss these questions.

1 What do the people and their projects have in common?
2 Do you think one project is more important than the others? Why / Why not?
3 Which project would you like to visit or help? Why?

a Ekwoge Enang Abwe

The Ebo Forest in Cameroon covers almost 2,000 km^2 and is home to a unique mix of 11 primates, including gorillas and the Nigeria–Cameroon chimpanzee, the most endangered of the chimpanzees. These amazing chimps use tools to fish and open fruit. In addition, the spectacular Goliath frog, the largest frog in the world, lives here.

The Cameroon government is considering turning the Ebo Forest into a national park, with a focus on conservation research and tourism, but there are still threats from local people and large companies who want to use the land for farming.

Ekwoge Enang Abwe grew up in a village in Cameroon, so his love for chimpanzees began at an early age. He has played an important role in the area for over a decade and, since 2010, he has been managing the Ebo Forest Research Project.

As well as encouraging local communities to be proud of the forest's unique biodiversity, this project has been doing biological research in the forest. The project has regular contact with communities through environmental and conservation education. They hope they will be able to create a safe future for the Ebo Forest.

Alexander Blanco b

The harpy eagle is one of the world's largest eagles – its wings stretch six feet (1.83 metres) from end to end! These eagles live in forests all the way from Mexico to northern Argentina. Unfortunately, environmental problems like logging, deforestation and poaching have endangered the species. Since 1996, veterinary surgeon Alexander Blanco has been working to save these important birds in Brazil and Ecuador, as well as in his home country of Venezuela. 'After my first experience of tagging an eagle chick nearly 20 years ago, I decided that this was what I wanted to do,' he explained. Now he leads a national programme to protect the species. His vision is to develop protection strategies so that local people can help to save the harpy eagles and the land around them. By working with communities, he hopes to reduce deforestation and protect a greater number of places where the birds nest.

c Çağan Şekercioğlu

Turkey has a huge variety of natural environments, from Mediterranean forests to coastal mountains. But many of these areas are threatened by the construction of new dams and roads. Çağan Şekercioğlu has been working hard to protect some of these areas. He is the first conservationist to win two Whitley Gold Awards.

In 2008, he won his first award for his work to protect the natural environment around Lake Kuyucuk, home to over 40,000 birds of 227 species. This work included researching the local wildlife, creating environmental education programmes for schools and promoting nature tourism to support the local economy.

He won the award again in 2013 after he persuaded the government to create Turkey's first Wildlife Corridor. Approximately 4.5 million trees will be planted to connect the Sarıkamış-Allahuekber Mountains National Park to the forests along the Black Sea coast and the Caucasus Mountains in neighbouring Georgia. This will allow large animals such as the wolf, brown bear and Caucasian lynx to move freely and safely.

Çağan's interest in conservation began when he was a teenager in Istanbul and a local wetland area, where he had played as a small child, was destroyed. This early experience inspired his life's work of protecting Turkey's wildlife habitats. For his next mission, he hopes to stop the construction of a dam that could destroy one of the world's most important wetlands.

a ▶05.03 Masha is going to Costa Rica to work on an environmental project. Listen to her talking about it. How much does she know about the project?

b ▶05.03 Listen again. Are these sentences true (T) or false (F)?

1 The government in Costa Rica wants to save the rainforests.
2 Masha will find out more about her project soon.
3 She knows exactly who she's going to work with.
4 She promises to send Phil regular emails.

4 GRAMMAR Future forms

a Match the future verb forms in 1–4 with uses a–d.

1 ☐ It takes quite a long time for forests to recover. **They'll probably grow** back, but not immediately.
2 ☐ Tomorrow **I'm meeting** someone who worked on the project.
3 ☐ **I'm going to make** the most of my time in Costa Rica and learn some Spanish, too.
4 ☐ **I'll write** regular updates on the blog and you can follow that.

a to talk about an intention or plan
b to make a prediction about the future
c to make an offer, promise or quick decision to do something in the future
d to talk about something you have arranged to do in the future

b Look at the future forms in **bold** below. How sure do they sound: very or a bit? What words change the meaning?

1 **They'll probably grow** back, but not immediately.
2 But **I'll definitely be able to** save some turtles!
3 **Perhaps I'll work** with local people as well.
4 **I'm sure you'll have** a great time.

c Underline the best phrases in Masha's blog.

MY BLOG
Home   About me   Follow

Welcome to the first entry in my blog! Amazing news! ¹I'm going / I'll go to Costa Rica tomorrow for six weeks! ²I'll work / I'm going to work on a turtle conservation project on the west coast.
³It will definitely be / It's definitely being hard work – but so interesting! ⁴I'm going to work / I'm working with turtles every day – counting them and collecting their eggs.
⁵I'm probably going have / I'm probably going to have some Spanish lessons while I'm there. Perhaps ⁶I'll be / I'm being fluent in a few weeks!
⁷I'll leave / I'm leaving tomorrow and I'll be back at the beginning of March.
⁸I'll write / I'm writing again soon with more details. Probably not tomorrow because ⁹I'll be / I'm being tired after the flight. But definitely as soon as I can.

d ⟫ Now go to Grammar Focus 5A on p. 152.

e Work in pairs. Write six imaginary predictions about your partner's future. Use the ideas in the box, and try to use different future forms from 4a and 4b.

be famous   get a new job   get your hair cut
learn another language   live in a different country
travel around the world

I think you'll …   I think you're going to …
You're probably going to …   I'm sure you'll …
You probably won't …

f 💬 Discuss your predictions.

> I'm sure you'll get a good job after you graduate.

> I hope so!

5 SPEAKING

a Read predictions 1–6. Do you agree with them? If not, change them so you do.

In the future …
1 people will stop killing endangered animals and cutting down trees.
2 we will lose some animal or plant species forever.
3 people will discover new wildlife species.
4 pollution will continue to get worse in big cities.
5 more areas of my country will become national parks.
6 people will behave in a more environmentally friendly way (recycle more, use public transport more, etc.).

b 💬 Discuss your ideas. Do you generally agree with each other? Are you optimistic or pessimistic about the future?

> In general, our group is quite hopeful about pollution. It will take time, but we think it will get better. We think that people will recycle more in the future.

5B IF NATURE CAN DO IT, WE CAN COPY IT

1 LISTENING

a 💬 Look at photos a and b and discuss the questions.

1 What do you think each photo shows?
2 What is the material in photo b used for?
3 What is the connection between the things in the two photos?

b Read the TV guide and check your ideas.

SPOTLIGHT ON ...

IF NATURE CAN DO IT, WE CAN COPY IT

In this series, Professor Leslie Cook takes a closer look at common objects that were invented by humans but inspired by nature.

Episode 1: Professor Cook explores Velcro, a material we use every day on our shoes, clothes and bags. It was inspired by the 'hook and loop' system that some plants use to move their seeds. In 1948, Swiss engineer George de Mestral was walking with his dog in the country when he noticed that little seeds from a plant were sticking to his dog's fur. He studied the plants more closely and saw how the hooks on the plant attached themselves to the loops and curls of an animal's fur. This gave him the idea for making Velcro.

WATCH NOW ⊙   SAVE FOR LATER 🔖

c 💬 Match the things from the natural world (1–3) with the related objects (a–c).

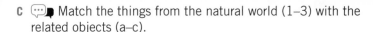

dragon lizard

spider

seashell

robot

safety helmet

water collection device

d ⊙ 05.07 Listen to part of the TV programme and check your answers.

e ⊙ 05.07 Listen again and complete the summary with one word in each gap.

- One reptile, the thorny dragon lizard, can pull up water through pipes in its [1]_____. It has inspired a device that can [2]_____ water. This will help people who live in very [3]_____ environments.
- Most spiders can move [4]_____ and make themselves very small. This has inspired the invention of a [5]_____ robot, which will help people who are trapped in [6]_____ spaces.
- Seashells are very [7]_____ and light. This has inspired the production of material for safety [8]_____ such as gloves and helmets.

f Which of the inventions do you think is the most useful? Why?

g 💬 Compare your ideas in 1f. Do you agree about the most useful invention?

2 GRAMMAR Zero and first conditionals

a Look at the conditional sentences from the TV programme and choose a or b to complete the rules.

1 Zero conditional, e.g., *If the lizard puts a foot somewhere wet, its skin pulls the water up and over its body.*
This is about something that … .
a may happen in the future   b is generally true

2 First conditional, e.g., *If we're successful, the device will provide water for people who live in very dry environments.*
This is about something that … .
a may happen in the future   b is generally true

b Put words from the box in the gaps.

present simple   verb   will

zero conditional
if + subject + present simple, subject + ¹_____

first conditional
if + subject + present simple, subject + ²_____ +
³_____

c Complete the text below with the correct form of the verbs in the box.

attach   fall off   make   save   succeed   try

BIOFOULING —
Do sharks have the answer?

If tiny plants and animals ¹_____ themselves to the surface of a ship, they ²_____ the ship slower. They call this 'biofouling' and it costs ship owners a lot of time and money to fix. Yet if the same plants and animals ³_____ to attach themselves to a shark's skin, they ⁴_____. This is because shark skin is made of a lot of tiny scales that look like tiny teeth. Scientists are working on a new kind of paint for ships based on this clever natural design. If they ⁵_____, ship owners around the world ⁶_____ millions of pounds each year.

d >> Now go to Grammar Focus 5B on p. 152.

e 💬 Complete the sentences so they are true for you. Work in pairs and compare your sentences.

1 If I get a cold, I usually …
2 If I need to study for an exam, I …
3 If I go to a party where I don't know anyone, I …
4 If it rains today, I …
5 If I'm not too busy this weekend, I …
6 If I get up early tomorrow, I …

3 READING AND VOCABULARY
The natural world

a Look at the photos on p. 61. Which animals or plants can you see? Read *Animals have adapted to survive everywhere* quickly and check your answers.

b Look at the words in the box. Which can you see in the photos?

branch   feathers   fur   leaf   paws
petals   scales   skin   tail   web

c Read the article on p. 61 again and complete the sentences with the words in 3b.

d ▶ 05.10 **Pronunciation** Words with several consonants together can sometimes be difficult to pronounce correctly. Listen and practise saying these words, paying attention to the underlined parts.

a<u>dapt</u>   ba<u>ckgr</u>ound   <u>br</u>anch   de<u>str</u>uction
mu<u>shr</u>oom   <u>scr</u>eam   <u>spl</u>ash   <u>spr</u>eading   <u>thr</u>eatened

e 💬 Which animal or plant on p. 61 do you think is the most amazing? Do you know any other animals that can do amazing things?

f 💬 Describe the animals and plants in the box using the words in 3b. Do not say what you are describing. Try to guess your partner's word.

chicken   goldfish   monkey   orangutan   palm tree
parrot   pine tree   rose   shark   snake   spider

> It's tall and has short branches. It has little leaves. It doesn't lose its leaves in the winter.

> A pine tree?

g >> Now go to Vocabulary Focus 5B on p. 136.

ANIMALS HAVE ADAPTED TO
SURVIVE
EVERYWHERE

The natural world is full of animals that have adapted in amazing ways to gain an advantage in the race for survival. Polar bears are a great example. They have layers of fat under their ^{1}_____ , which means they can swim in freezing water. Not only that, but it's very difficult for other animals to see them in the snow. Because they have completely white ^{2}_____ , they can easily run up to other animals and attack with their huge ^{3}_____ .

Another amazing animal is the ptarmigan. This Arctic bird is also white, which helps it hide in the snow. However, when the snow melts, the bird's ^{4}_____ change colour. From its head to its ^{5}_____ , it turns grey to match the rocky environment.

Plants have adapted, too. This bee orchid looks exactly like it has a real bee resting on its ^{6}_____ . This 'bee' is actually part of the flower, and it's nature's way of attracting real bees to the orchid.

Many fish can change the colour of their ^{7}_____ instantly to match their background.

At first, you might think that this is a ^{8}_____ . But it's really an Indian leaf butterfly, sitting on the ^{9}_____ of a tree. Because it doesn't look like a butterfly, it can hide from other animals that would like to eat it.

This Amazon jungle spider also has an inventive way of protecting itself. It creates a ^{10}_____ that looks like a much larger spider, possibly to frighten other animals.

4 SPEAKING

a You are going to recommend the best place to experience the natural beauty of your country. Make notes on the topics below.

- beautiful places
- what you can see there (rivers, forests, beaches, etc.)
- animals or plants you can see
- what you can do
- the best time of year to go

b 💬 Practise talking about the places on your list. Try to use conditional sentences.

> If you go to the beach near here, you will be able to see dolphins.

> If you like forests, you can go to …

c 💬 Work with another pair. Take turns to describe your places.

1 LISTENING

a 💬 Discuss the questions.

1 What hobbies and interests do you have?
2 Could any of your hobbies become a job? Would you like to do those jobs?

b 💬 You are going to watch Rachel and Becky talking about Rachel's job. Discuss the questions.

1 Why do you think Rachel became a florist?
2 What might the advantages of the job be?

c 🎬 ▶ 05.13 Watch or listen to Part 1. Do Rachel and Becky mention your ideas?

d 🎬 ▶ 05.13 Watch or listen to Part 1 again. Complete each sentence with one or two words.

1 Tina spent the morning _____.
2 Tina _____ to be in the photos.
3 Becky thinks that being a florist is good because you can be your own _____.
4 Becky doesn't like dealing with other people's _____.
5 Rachel suggests that Becky could be a _____.

2 USEFUL LANGUAGE
Giving reasons, results and examples

a Complete the sentences with the words/phrases in the box.

for instance   such as   like   because of

1 That's _____ Tina. She spent the morning cleaning up!
2 Oh, lots of things. _____, all I seem to do is deal with other people's problems, _____ issues with their pay or holidays.
3 **Becky** I wish I had a job where I could travel the world, spread my wings, be free!
   Rachel _____?

b ▶ 05.14 Listen and check your answers.

c Add the words/phrases in the box to the table.

as a result   because   because of   due to   for example
for instance   like   since   so   such as

Giving reasons	Giving results	Giving examples

d Read this conversation and <u>underline</u> the correct words/phrases.

A So, do you still want to be a vet?
B Oh, yes. That's my dream. I've always wanted to work with animals, [1]*for example / due to*, in a zoo or something like that.
A A zoo! Wow, that would be good.
B Well, I need to do lots of things first, [2]*since / like* finding the best university to go to.
A I see. And is it easy to become a vet?
B Not really. It takes years at university [3]*because of / so* all the things you have to study. But that's OK. I really want to do it, [4]*so / for example* I'm sure I won't find it too difficult.
A Well, if there's anything I can do to help, [5]*so / such as* looking at university websites, let me know!

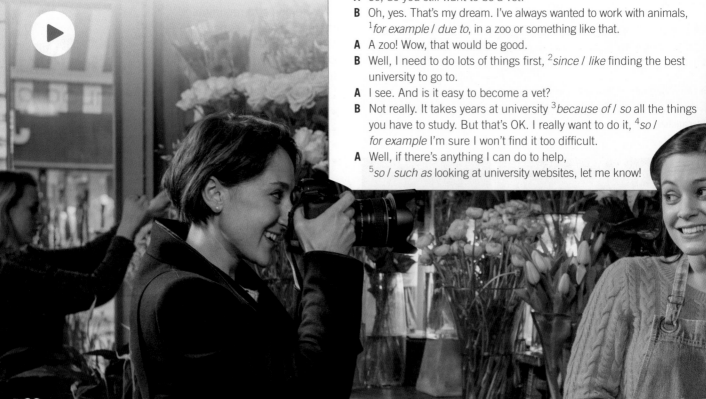

3 LISTENING

a 💬🎤 Look at photos a–c above. Which one do you think would be best for Rachel's website? Why?

b 🎥 ▶ 05.15 Watch or listen to Part 2. Which photo does Rachel suggest using first? Does Becky agree?

c Answer the questions.
1 What is Rachel looking at on the computer?
2 Do they choose a photo for Rachel's website in the end?

d 💬🎤 Do you think that Becky should give up her job and become a photographer?

4 CONVERSATION SKILLS
Giving yourself time to think

a ▶ 05.16 Listen and complete the extract.

Becky Rachel, we can't see you in that one.
Rachel OK, _____ . I think this one.

b Complete the exchanges with the words in the box.

Just   Let   sure   That's   Well

1 **A** When did you meet Frankie?
   B _____ me see, I think it was in 2004.
2 **A** This thermometer says it's 21°C in here.
   B I'm not _____. I think that's wrong.
3 **A** How old were you when you decided to work with animals?
   B _____ a good question … I was about 15, I think.
4 **A** What time does the restaurant open?
   B _____ a second, I'm not sure. I'll check on their website.
5 **A** Why did you decide to resign?
   B _____, I was bored in my job.

c 💬🎤 Ask and answer the questions. Give yourself time to think using phrases from 4b.
1 What's your dream job?
2 What's your favourite natural place? (e.g., the beach, mountains, forest)

> Let me see … I think my dream job involves working with animals …

5 PRONUNCIATION
Voiced and unvoiced consonants

a ▶ 05.17 Listen to these words from the conversation which begin with the sounds /p/ and /b/.

pay	people	Becky	being

b Repeat the words in 5a. Touch your throat when you try to say them. Then complete the rules with /b/ and /p/.

1 When you say _____, there is a sound in the throat.
2 When you say _____, there is no sound in the throat.

c ▶ 05.18 Listen and <u>underline</u> the words you hear.
1 pay / bay
2 pie / buy
3 pair / bear
4 rope / robe
5 pride / bride

d ▶ 05.19 Listen and repeat the words in 5c. Which sounds are voiced in the throat? Which sounds are not voiced?

6 SPEAKING

≫ Communication 5C 💬🎤 Student A: Read the information below. Student B: Go to p. 128.

Student A
1 You don't like your job and you want to quit. Think about the answers to these questions.
   • Why don't you like it?
   • What are you going to do next? Why?

2 Student B will tell you they are going to move to another part of the country. Ask them about their decision, including why they have decided to do this.

✅ UNIT PROGRESS TEST

→ **CHECK YOUR PROGRESS**

You can now do the Unit Progress Test.

1 SPEAKING AND LISTENING

a 💬🔊 How much do you know about whales?

b 💬🔊 Look at *The Whale File* on the right. Which sentence is NOT true? Check your answer on p. 127.

c ▶05.20 Liz Kerr is an environmental journalist who is helping whales that have come ashore. Listen to her audio diary and answer the questions.

1 How many whales is Liz taking care of?
2 Is she working alone or in a group?
3 What happened at the end?

d ▶05.20 Listen again and complete the suggestions for saving whales that have come ashore. Write one word in each gap.

1 Don't try and do things on your own – talk to the Marine _____ Service.
2 Put on a wetsuit – it can get quite _____.
3 Cover the whale with _____ towels.
4 Pour buckets of water over the whale to keep her _____.
5 Make sure you don't _____ the whale's blowhole.
6 Make a _____ in the sand around the whale to fill with water.
7 When the tide comes in, _____ the whale out to sea again.

The Whale File

TRUE or FALSE?

1 Whales aren't fish, so they need to come to the surface to breathe.

2 All whales have teeth.

3 Female whales are bigger than male ones.

4 Whales never sleep because they need to breathe.

5 Whales breathe every 15 minutes.

6 Whales can communicate by singing to each other.

7 Whales sometimes swim onto the shore and can't get back out to sea.

2 READING

a Read Tomas's essay about water pollution below. In his opinion, who should do something about this kind of pollution?

b Read the essay again. Are the sentences true (*T*) or false (*F*)?

1 Tomas suggests that we probably don't complain when people throw rubbish in water.
2 He suggests there's more rubbish in lakes than on beaches.
3 Eating plastic can make animals and birds ill.
4 Forgotten bits of fishing net can kill fish.
5 Tomas thinks water pollution is worse than air pollution.

c 💬 What do you think should be done about water pollution?

Keeping our water clean

1 If you walk down the street and see someone throw a plastic bottle on the ground, you'll probably get annoyed. You might even say something to that person. But do we react in the same way when we see people throwing rubbish into the sea? We all know how rubbish damages the environment on land, but we often forget the effect that it can have on environments like the sea, lakes and rivers, too.

2 First of all, water pollution looks terrible. Beautiful beaches can become covered in rubbish when whatever we have thrown into the water comes ashore. Even rivers and lakes have some plastic bags and bottles floating in them.

3 Secondly, rubbish can hurt animals and birds that live in or by the water. If they see a plastic bottle, they may think it is food. However, when they try and eat the bottle, it can get caught in their mouth or stomach and stop them from eating anything else. Plastic bottles can also stop dolphins from breathing. Sometimes, fishing boats leave bits of fishing net behind in the water. Fish can get caught in this and die.

4 Finally, people forget that plastic contains chemicals that stay in the water. This is very bad for both fish and plants. If you eat fish containing these chemicals, then you can also get ill.

5 In conclusion, I would say that we need to worry about water pollution as much as we care about land or air pollution. We should all protect the seas, lakes and rivers, and remember to take our rubbish away with us.

3 WRITING SKILLS Organising an essay; Signposting language

a How is the essay organised? Tick (✓) 1 or 2.

1 ☐ introduction ➜ a discussion of different points connected to the topic ➜ conclusion
2 ☐ introduction ➜ points in favour of the topic ➜ points against the topic ➜ conclusion

b Look at the sentence below and answer the questions.

First of all, water pollution looks terrible.

1 Which paragraph of the essay does the sentence come from?
2 Does the signposting phrase in **bold** refer to something that has already been mentioned or introduce a new topic?
3 What other signposting phrases in the essay are similar to this one?

c Read the essay again and answer the questions.

1 In the first paragraph, does *you* refer to 'people in general' or 'the reader'?
2 In the first paragraph, what does *we* refer to?
3 Why does Tomas use these two pronouns?
4 In paragraph 5, what phrase does Tomas use to introduce his opinion?

4 WRITING

a Plan an essay on an environmental issue. Choose one of the topics below or your own idea. Make notes about your topic. Try to think of at least three main points with examples.

air pollution   cutting down forests
climate change   illegal hunting of animals

b 💬 Compare your ideas with a partner.

c Write the essay. Use one of the structures in 3a. Use signposting expressions to organise your ideas. Make sure you communicate directly with the reader in the introduction and conclusion.

d 💬 Read each other's essays. Do you agree with the other students' opinions?

UNIT 5
Review and extension

1 GRAMMAR

a <u>Underline</u> the correct words.

1 The flowers close when you *will touch* / *touch* them.
2 They've decided they aren't *building* / *going to build* a road through the forest.
3 *Shall* / *Am* I pick the apples, or do you want to do it?
4 Unless the government does more to stop illegal hunting, tigers *are dying out* / *will die out*.
5 If you find a plant that you haven't seen before, *don't* / *you won't* touch it, please.
6 Don't eat wild mushrooms *unless* / *if* you know they're safe.

b Complete the sentences with the correct future form of the verbs in brackets. Sometimes there is more than one possible answer.

1 This weekend, I _____ (not / do) anything special – just staying at home.
2 _____ (you / continue) learning English when you _____ (finish) this course?
3 It's very cold. I think it _____ (snow) this evening.
4 If the sky _____ (be) red in the morning, it _____ (rain) later in the day.

2 VOCABULARY

a <u>Underline</u> the correct words.

1 The children jumped across the *stream* / *river* / *lake*.
2 A *valley* / *rainforest* / *national park* is a tropical, wet place with a lot of trees.
3 The sun was shining, but it was completely dark inside the *bay* / *coast* / *cave*.
4 We could see the monkey hanging from the *leaf* / *skin* / *branch* of a tree.
5 The fish's *scales* / *feathers* / *wings* were blue, white and black.
6 Dogs and bears have *webs* / *shells* / *paws*.

b Complete the words.

1 The w _ _ d _ _ _ e in the national park is amazing – from butterflies to parrots to elephants.
2 The blue whale and the mountain gorilla are both e _ _ _ _ g _ _ _ d s _ _ _ _ _ s.
3 Most countries r _ c _ _ _ e paper, glass and cardboard.
4 The cl _ _ _ a _ e is changing; some places are getting hotter and some are getting colder.
5 Building new roads d _ m _ _ _ es the environment.
6 They want to c _ t d _ _ _ n the trees so they can use the land for farming.

3 WORDPOWER *problem*

a Match pictures a–f with sentences 1–6.

1 ☐ His shoelaces are untied, but he **isn't aware of** the problem.
2 ☐ Juan's car won't start, but he**'s fixing** the problem.
3 ☐ They**'re facing** a lot of problems. Their bills are huge this month.
4 ☐ Bad weather has **caused** a lot of problems for traffic.
5 ☐ Lena is upset, but her parents are trying to **solve** the problem.
6 ☐ The fire quickly got out of control, but they**'re tackling** the problem.

b Replace the words in **bold** with the correct forms of the verbs in the box. Sometimes there is more than one possible answer.

be aware of	cause	face	fix	solve	tackle

1 Most people in my country **know about** the problem of rising sea levels. _____
2 My country is **dealing with** the problem of pollution in big cities. _____
3 I'm good at **finding an answer to** problems with computers. _____
4 I express my opinions strongly and that sometimes **creates** problems. _____
5 Damage to the environment is a problem that everyone should **try to stop**. _____
6 Engineers will soon **end** the problem of people not having enough clean drinking water. _____

c 💬 Do you agree with the sentences in 3b?

♻ REVIEW YOUR PROGRESS

How well did you do in this unit? Write 3, 2 or 1 for each objective.
3 = very well   2 = well   1 = not so well

I CAN ...	
talk about the future	☐
talk about *if* and *when*	☐
give reasons, results and examples	☐
write a discussion essay.	☐

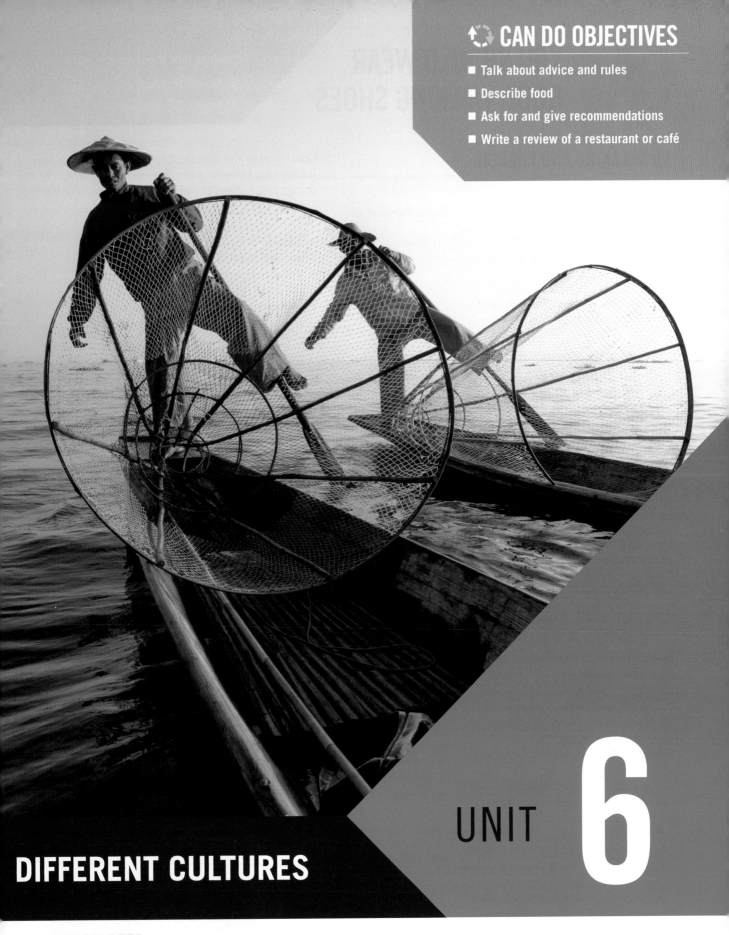

↻ **CAN DO OBJECTIVES**

- Talk about advice and rules
- Describe food
- Ask for and give recommendations
- Write a review of a restaurant or café

UNIT **6**

DIFFERENT CULTURES

GETTING STARTED

a 💬 Look at the photo. Ask and answer the questions.

1 In which part of the world do you think the photo was taken?
2 What job are the men doing?
3 How is this similar to or different from the same job in your culture?
4 Are there any jobs in your country that still use traditional methods? Give details.

b 💬 Have you met people from different cultures? If you have, what did you have in common? How were you different? If you haven't, what do you think they would find interesting or surprising about your country's culture?

6A YOU SHOULD WEAR GOOD WALKING SHOES

1 SPEAKING AND READING

a 💬 Discuss the questions.

1 What do you think the phrase 'culture shock' means? What difficulties might culture shock cause?

2 Think of a country you would like to visit. How do you think it is different from your own country? Think about the words in the box.

> cities and streets   customs   food
> getting around   people

b Quickly read the article about CultureMee, an app for tourists travelling to other countries. Which of the things below does the app provide?

1 'insider tips' about the culture
2 information about main tourist sites
3 a history of the country
4 detailed descriptions of famous buildings
5 lists of recommended hotels and restaurants
6 tips about how to behave in the country
7 information about local attitudes and customs

CULTURE SHOCK? THERE'S AN APP TO DEAL WITH THAT

Many travel apps and guidebooks can help you to book a cheap homestay or an expensive hotel with a swimming pool, and they can tell you where to go windsurfing or what restaurants serve the best seafood. But what if you want information on how to greet people politely in Tokyo, how much to tip a taxi driver in Madrid or where to meet local people in Rio de Janeiro? Well, a new app for your smartphone can now do all that for you.

The app is called CultureMee, and it not only gives straightforward travel advice, but it also provides **insights** into the culture of the country you're visiting. It was set up by an Irish couple, John and Dee Lee, and has quickly grown in popularity. Thousands of people are already using the app, which now covers locations all over the world. It has also won several international awards.

The idea for the app came to them while they were on holiday in East Africa a few years ago. They had guidebooks that told them about places to visit, but they found it difficult to find out about what kind of plug they needed for their hair dryer or exactly what vaccinations they needed.

They realised that it would be very useful to have an app that could give people this kind of basic travel advice. They also wanted to help people understand the culture of any country they might visit, so this became an **integral** part of the app's content.

The couple decided not to take the conventional **approach to** culture, which is already a feature of standard guidebooks, but rather to focus on the everyday lives of people in the country. There are plenty of apps available that can help you book holidays and places to stay, and that give you information about tourist sights and museums. However, John and Dee felt that most travel apps didn't focus on ordinary people, so they decided to put this **at the heart of** what CultureMee does.

CultureMee offers a wide range of cultural content, including background information about the country and its history, details on contemporary culture and advice on dealing with culture shock. Users can access videos, produced by the couple themselves, that **supplement** the core content of the app. Many of these give tips on how to engage with local people and how to behave in an appropriate way. They are based on interviews with people who have visited the country, and who can talk **with authority** about it from a visitor's point of view. There are also interviews with local people who provide insights into how they view their own culture.

So, imagine that someone from the UK wants to travel to Thailand. They can select the appropriate culture video and hear a Thai person talking about Thai culture. They can also watch a video of a non-Thai person talking about how to get on with Thai people and understand their culture.

An essential aim of John and Dee's project is to create an online community of people who are interested in travel and culture. As the app becomes more popular, they hope this community will continue to augment* it with their own stories and viewpoints.

*augment (v) to increase the size or value of something by adding to it

A screenshot from CultureMee

John and Dee Lee, founders of Cultur

68

c Read the article again. Decide if the sentences are true (*T*) or false (*F*). Find phrases in the text that tell you the answer.

1 The new app only gives cultural advice, not practical travel advice.
2 CultureMee has already been successful.
3 John and Dee's guidebook on East Africa didn't tell them everything they needed to know.
4 John and Dee decided to interview ordinary people who know about a country.
5 All the interviews are with people who come from the country they talk about.
6 They would like people who use the app to contribute to it and improve it.

d What do the words in **bold** mean in the context of the article? Choose a or b.

1 **insights**
   a knowledge of something
   b suggested places to visit
2 **integral**
   a additional, extra
   b central, essential
3 **approach to**
   a information about
   b way of looking at
4 **at the heart of**
   a feeling strongly about something
   b central to something
5 **supplement**
   a add to something
   b use instead of something
6 **with authority**
   a knowledgeable about something
   b having permission to talk about something

2 VOCABULARY Compound nouns

a Read the information below about compound nouns, then <u>underline</u> the compound nouns in the title and introduction to the article on p. 68.

Compound nouns combine two words. We write some compound nouns as one word (e.g., *lunchtime*) and others as two words (e.g., *living room*). They are usually formed by:
• noun + noun (e.g., *newspaper*)
• verb + *-ing* + noun (e.g., *washing machine*)
• noun + verb + *-ing* (e.g., *ice skating*)

b ▶ 06.01 **Pronunciation** Listen to the compound nouns from the article. Which part is stressed – the first or the second word? Practise saying the words.

c Complete the compound nouns with the words in the box.

baseball book insect pack screen shop tour walking

1 _____ guide
2 sun_____
3 souvenir _____
4 _____ cap
5 back_____
6 guide_____
7 _____ shoes
8 _____ repellent

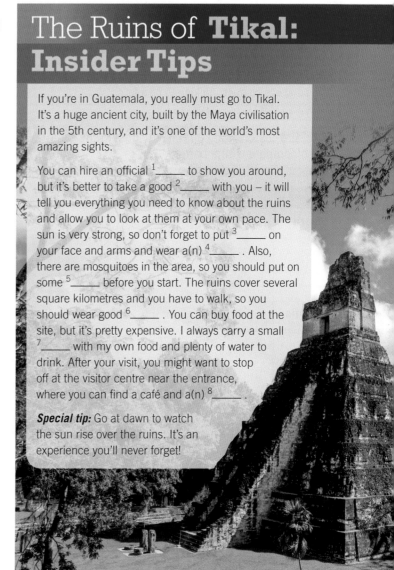

The Ruins of Tikal: Insider Tips

If you're in Guatemala, you really must go to Tikal. It's a huge ancient city, built by the Maya civilisation in the 5th century, and it's one of the world's most amazing sights.

You can hire an official [1]_____ to show you around, but it's better to take a good [2]_____ with you – it will tell you everything you need to know about the ruins and allow you to look at them at your own pace. The sun is very strong, so don't forget to put [3]_____ on your face and arms and wear a(n) [4]_____ . Also, there are mosquitoes in the area, so you should put on some [5]_____ before you start. The ruins cover several square kilometres and you have to walk, so you should wear good [6]_____ . You can buy food at the site, but it's pretty expensive. I always carry a small [7]_____ with my own food and plenty of water to drink. After your visit, you might want to stop off at the visitor centre near the entrance, where you can find a café and a(n) [8]_____ .

Special tip: Go at dawn to watch the sun rise over the ruins. It's an experience you'll never forget!

d Read the travel tips for Tikal in Guatemala. Complete the text with compound nouns from 2c.

e ≫ **Communication 6A** 💬 Student A: Go to p. 130. Student B: Go to p. 132.

3 LISTENING

a 💬 Look at the photos and the information about Kim, Will and Tasia. What cultural differences do you think they noticed when they lived overseas? Compare your ideas with other students.

Kim from England went to live in Brazil.

Will from the USA worked for a company in Nigeria.

Tasia from Greece went to live in the UK.

b ▶ 06.02 Listen to Kim, Will and Tasia. Which of these topics do they talk about? One topic is not mentioned.

being on time   children   getting up early   going to bed   making eye contact   talking to people

c ▶ 06.02 Listen again and make notes in the table. Then compare with a partner.

Country	Cultural difference	Example(s)	Comments they make about it
Brazil			
Nigeria			
UK			

d 💬 Think about the three cultural differences in the table. Have you ever been in similar situations? What happened?

4 GRAMMAR Modals of obligation

a Complete these sentences from the interviews with the words in the box. You will use some of the words more than once.

can   can't   have to   don't have to   must   mustn't   should   shouldn't

Kim
1 If a meeting starts at 10 o'clock, you _____ be there at 10:00. You _____ come maybe fifteen or twenty minutes later, and that's fine.
2 They expect me to show up on time. They always say, 'You _____ be late. You _____ come on time.'

Will
3 If you're talking to someone you don't know well, you _____ look right at them.
4 In the USA, you _____ definitely look the other person in the eye when you talk.

Tasia
5 At a certain time, maybe 7:00 or 8:00, all the children _____ go to bed.
6 In Greece, children _____ usually stay up as long as they want … They _____ go to bed at a fixed time.
7 I just think children _____ join in the life of the family and it's a pity if they _____ be part of it.

b ▶ 06.03 Listen and check your answers.

c ≫ Now go to Grammar Focus 6A on p. 154.

d Complete these rules about transport in your country. Use the modals in the box.

can   can't   have to   don't have to   must   mustn't   need to   don't need to   should   shouldn't

Buses
1 You _____ buy a ticket in advance.
2 You _____ buy a ticket on the bus.

Walking and cycling
3 You _____ use a pedestrian crossing when you want to cross the street.
4 You _____ wear a bike helmet.
5 You _____ ride a bike on the pavement.
You _____ use cycle lanes.

Cars
6 Passengers _____ wear a seat belt.
7 You _____ drive with your lights on during the day.

Taxis
8 You _____ stop taxis in the street.
9 You _____ book taxis in advance.
10 You _____ give taxi drivers a tip.

e A foreign visitor is coming to live in your country for six months. Prepare to give them some advice. Use the ideas in the box and your own ideas to make a list of rules and tips.

clothes   eating and drinking   going out at night   language   parks and public spaces   public transport   roads, pavements and cycle lanes   talking to people who are older than you

You shouldn't eat or drink when walking in the street. You should always give your seat to an older passenger on the bus.

f 💬 Take turns to read your rules and tips aloud. Discuss the questions.

1 Which rules and tips are about safety?
2 Which are about being polite to people?
3 Which rules and tips are the most important?

5 SPEAKING

a Work with a partner. Think about a foreign culture you both know something about. How is it different from your culture? Think about these topics and make brief notes.

children   greetings   how people dress   meals   men and women   older people   time

b 💬 Work in groups. Tell your group about the differences in the culture you chose. Ask the other students questions about the culture they chose. Do you agree with them?

6B IT'S TASTIER THAN I EXPECTED

Learn to describe food

- **G** Comparatives and superlatives
- **V** Describing food

1 VOCABULARY Describing food

a 💬 Look at photos a–e and discuss the questions.
1. Which food would you most like to eat?
2. What country do you think each dish comes from?
3. What ingredients does each dish contain?
4. Which of the dishes could a vegetarian eat?

b Match descriptions 1–5 with photos a–e.

1. tasty Moroccan meatballs cooked in a tomato sauce, served with couscous and fresh herbs
2. creamy Mexican avocado and tomato dip with crunchy tortilla chips
3. white fish cooked in a spicy Thai sauce with hot green chillies
4. Japanese noodles with vegetables in a light soup served with an egg
5. a slice of rich Austrian chocolate cake with a bitter orange filling

c Underline all the adjectives in 1b. Which could you use to describe … ?
a a salad   b a bowl of soup   c a curry

d ≫ Now go to Vocabulary Focus 6B on p. 137.

e ▶ 06.08 **Pronunciation** Listen and repeat these words. Pay attention to the pronunciation of the letters *sh* and *ch*.

/ʃ/	/tʃ/
fresh	chocolate
mash	chop
ship	rich
shape	crunchy

f 💬 A visitor has come to your town. You're going to give advice about where to eat and what typical dishes to try.

Student A: Give the visitor advice.
Student B: You are the visitor. Listen and ask further questions.

g 💬 Now change roles and have a second conversation.

2 LISTENING

a 💬 Look at the photo on the right and discuss the questions.
1. Do you have vending machines in your country? What do they sell?
2. How often do you use them? What do you usually buy?

b ▶ 06.09 Listen to part of a radio show about vending machines in Japan.
1. What types of food and drink are mentioned?
2. What are the advantages for customers of vending machines over buying things from a shop?
3. What does the reporter think of the hot meal?

c 💬 Would you buy hot food from a vending machine? Why / Why not?

3 GRAMMAR Comparatives and superlatives

a ►06.10 Complete the sentences with the words in the box. Then listen and check your answers.

a bit longer than   as good as   by far the highest
much better than   much cheaper   the best

1 Japan has _____ number of vending machines per person in the world.
2 It's _____ for sellers to run a vending machine than it is to run a shop.
3 But is curry and rice from a machine _____ curry and rice from a restaurant?
4 It's taking _____ I imagined.
5 It's actually _____ I expected.
6 I think it might be _____ vending machine meal I've ever eaten.

b Circle the adjectives in the sentences in 3a. Then answer the questions.

1 Which expression(s) talk(s) about something that is number one in a category?
2 Which expression(s) talk(s) about a difference?
3 Which expression(s) talk(s) about two things that are similar?
4 These words change the meaning: *by far, much, a bit.* Which mean a big difference? Which mean a small difference?

c ⟫ Now go to Grammar Focus 6B on p. 154.

d Use the ideas below to write sentences with comparatives, superlatives and (*not*) *as ... as.*

cheap   fun   good for you   healthy
interesting   nice   spicy   sweet   tasty

• street food / food in expensive restaurants / home-made food
• Japanese food / Mexican food / Indian food
• vegetarian food / meat dishes / fish dishes
• food from my country / food from other countries

Japanese food isn't as spicy as Mexican food.

e 💬 Read your sentences aloud. Do you agree or disagree with each other?

Hungry ADVENTURES

'Have you eaten?' 13th May

Singaporeans are my kind of people – they're passionate about food and eating!

People here eat often – they have five or six meals a day. Instead of 'Hello' or 'How are you?' they ask, 'Have you eaten?' And it's hard to believe just how many different kinds of dishes you can get in this tiny country – Chinese, Indian, Arabic, European and many, many more.

The best meal of the day today was lunch. The main course was *muri ghonto* or fish head curry – far more delicious than it sounds! It's a southern Indian dish. You can have it with rice, but we had it the way the Chinese do, with a soft bread roll.

Dessert was *cendol* – coconut milk, ice and green noodles. It's a typical Southeast Asian dish. It wasn't as sweet as I expected, but the noodles were lovely – a bit like jelly.

There are places to eat here to suit everyone – from food stalls in shopping centres to more upmarket (and more expensive!) restaurants. My plan is to try as many as I can in the short time I'm here.

4 READING

a 💬 Look at the photo on the left. Which country do you think it is?

b Read the blog *Hungry Adventures.* Check your answer to 4a.

c Read the blog again. Find the descriptions of the dishes and match them with the food photos a–d.

1 ☐ chicken *satay*   3 ☐ *cendol*
2 ☐ *muri ghonto*   4 ☐ *thosai*

d 💬 Discuss the questions.

1 Did the blog writer enjoy the dishes in 4c?
2 Which of the dishes would you like to try?

Travelling and eating around the world

Hawker centres – street food, but not on the streets

14th May

Singapore is famous for its street food, but it's been illegal to sell cooked food in the streets for many years. So, if you're looking for Singapore's famous street food, hawker centres are the places to go. These are indoor food courts with stalls that sell freshly cooked food. You choose your hawker stall according to what kind of cuisine you want – Thai, Malay, Chinese, Indian, Japanese or Korean.

I went to the Golden Mile Food Centre – it was amazing to see so many different food stalls under one roof. *Sup tulang*, a Malay–Indian dish of beef bones in a red spicy sauce, looked very tasty. But in the end I wanted something lighter, so I chose *ayam buah keluak*, a Paranakan (Chinese–Malay) dish. It's chicken with Indonesian black nuts, served with steamed rice. A good choice – one of the most unusual dishes I've ever tasted.

Little India, big appetite

15th May

This part of Singapore was full of the sights and smells of India. I ate *thosai* – crispy Indian pancakes made from rice and lentils. They were served with rich and spicy dips and vegetable curry. The meal was light and fresh – delicious!

Still full from my Indian lunch, I explored the Arab Quarter. There was plenty of great food available, but sadly I wasn't hungry! I'll have to come back to Singapore. I didn't have a chance to explore Chinatown either.

By the evening I was hungry again, so I tried some of the barbecued food at Lau Pa Sat, an old market. I went for Malaysian chicken *satay*, pieces of chicken on sticks served with spicy peanut sauce. Absolutely delicious!

e Read the blog again and answer the questions.

1 What two habits show that the people in Singapore love food?
2 What did the blog writer eat with her fish head curry?
3 Why can't you buy cooked food on the street in Singapore?
4 Why didn't she have *sup tulang* at the Golden Mile Food Centre?
5 Why didn't she eat anything in the Arab Quarter?
6 Which area of Singapore did she not go to?

f 💬🔊 Imagine you are visiting Singapore. Where will you go? What will you eat?

> I'd really like to go to a big hawker centre, so we can see all the different options.

5 SPEAKING

a You are going to talk about a special meal. Make notes about one of these meals. Use the ideas in the box to help you plan what to say.

- the most special meal you've ever made
- the most delicious meal you've ever eaten
- a meal you'll never forget

where?   when?   who with?   ingredients?
how was the food cooked?   taste, smell, colour?

b 💬🔊 Take turns to describe your meals. Then talk about which of the meals sounds the most delicious.

> The most delicious meal I've ever eaten was in a little restaurant near my grandparents' house. I ate …

6C

EVERYDAY ENGLISH
Do you think I should take her somewhere special?

Learn to ask for and give recommendations

P Sounding interested

S Asking for and giving recommendations

1 LISTENING

a 💬 Discuss the questions.

1 Which of these do you think is the most romantic?
- flowers
- dinner at a restaurant
- a home-made meal
- a handwritten love letter
- an expensive gift (e.g., jewellery)

2 Have you ever bought/done these things for anyone?

b 💬 Look at the photo below. Where are Tom and Rachel? What are they doing? What do you think they are talking about?

c 📹 ▶ 06.12 Watch or listen to Part 1 and check.

d 📹 ▶ 06.12 Watch or listen again. Are the sentences true (*T*) or false (*F*)?

1 Tom isn't going to ask Becky to marry him.
2 Tom is going to take Becky to Paris.
3 Mark asked Rachel to marry him at a special place.
4 Becky and Tom used to work together.

e 💬 Do you agree with Rachel's advice? Where should Tom propose to Becky?

2 USEFUL LANGUAGE
Asking for and giving recommendations

a Look at the phrases in **bold** below. Which ones are asking for recommendations? Which are giving recommendations?

1 **Do you think I should** take her somewhere special?
2 **If I were you, I'd** take her somewhere special.
3 **It's probably worth** asking her where she wants to go.
4 **What would you do** about the ring?
5 **Would you recommend** buying a very expensive ring?
6 **It's much better to** buy something that's her style.
7 **It's not a good idea to** ask her what she likes.

b Complete the conversations with the correct form of the verbs in brackets. Look back at the phrases in 2a to help you.

1
A What do you think I should ¹_____ Dad for his birthday? (get)
B If I were you, I ²_____ him what he wants. (ask)
A But that will ruin the surprise.
B It's much better ³_____ him what he wants though. (get)
A True, I suppose.

2
A Where would you recommend ¹_____ the party? (have)
B It's probably worth ²_____ Laura if she can recommend a restaurant. She knows lots of great places. (ask)
A And what about the cake? What would you ³_____? (do)
B Get it from a bakery. And it's a good idea ⁴_____ them as soon as you can. They get very busy. (contact)

4 PRONUNCIATION
Sounding interested

a ▶ 06.14 Listen to this extract. Is the intonation flat or not? <u>Underline</u> the correct word in the rule.

Rachel I am so excited. I still can't believe you're going to ask Becky to marry you.

Sometimes, intonation is more important than the words we use. If we use *varied* / *flat* intonation, we may sound as if we're bored or don't care about the subject.

b ▶ 06.15 Listen to exchanges 1–3. Which of the B speakers sounds bored?

1 **A** I've got a new job.
  B Wow. That's incredible.
2 **A** I've just bought some new shoes.
  B That's amazing.
3 **A** We lost the game last night.
  B That's terrible.

c Practise saying the exchanges in 4b. Try to sound interested.

3 CONVERSATION SKILLS
Expressing surprise

a Look at the sentences about the next part of the story. Which option do you think is most likely?

1 Rachel advises Tom to buy *a huge diamond* / *something that's Becky's style*.
2 Tom thinks that the rings in the jewellery shop are very *expensive* / *cheap*.
3 Rachel and Tom see Becky and *say hello to her* / *hide in the shop*.

b 🎥 ▶ 06.13 Watch or listen to Part 2 and check your answers to 3a.

c 🎥 ▶ 06.13 Watch or listen to Part 2 again and complete the sentences.

1 **Tom** So, what about the ring? What would you buy? A big diamond, right? So she can show it to her friends?
  Rachel _____? Tom, do you know Becky at all?
2 **Rachel** It's £1,500.
  Tom I _____ _____ _____! That's ridiculous.
3 **Rachel** Tom! It's Becky! Over there.
  Tom _____ _____! What should we do?

d 💬 Take it in turns to say the sentences below and express surprise.

1 I'm getting married.
2 I passed all my exams.
3 That coat costs £300.
4 I lost my phone yesterday.

5 SPEAKING

≫ Communication 6C 💬 Student A: Read the instructions below. Student B: Go to p. 130.

Student A
1 You have been offered an amazing job. The salary is very high and it is a great opportunity. The problem is that you need to move to New York next month! Tell your partner your news and ask for some recommendations about what to do.
2 Listen to your partner's surprising news and give some recommendations.

I've been offered a new job. It's in New York!

No way! That's great.

Do you think I should take it?

✓ UNIT PROGRESS TEST

→ CHECK YOUR PROGRESS

You can now do the Unit Progress Test.

6D SKILLS FOR WRITING
It's definitely worth a visit

Learn to write a review of a restaurant or café

W Positive and negative language; Adverbs

1 SPEAKING AND LISTENING

a Look at situations 1–3. Where would you go for these occasions? Choose from the locations in the box.

1 to meet friends for a chat and a cup of coffee
2 a birthday or an anniversary
3 a party at the end of term or the end of a language course

a café   a cheap restaurant   an expensive restaurant
a venue with music or dancing (e.g., a club)

b 💬 Compare your ideas. Do you agree?

c ▶ 06.16 Listen to Jeff, Fabio and Carla. Which place in photos 1–3 is each of them talking about?

d ▶ 06.16 Listen again and answer the questions.

1 Why doesn't Jeff like the atmosphere at expensive restaurants?
2 What does he say about the food?
3 Does Fabio go to cafés alone, or with friends, or both?
4 Why does he like pavement cafés?
5 What does Carla do before she starts dancing?
6 What kind of music does her favourite place play?

e Think of one place to go out that you really like and one that you don't really like. Make notes about their good and bad points.

f 💬 Discuss your places. Do you agree with your partner's descriptions? Why / Why not?

2 READING

a Read the four reviews of a café on p. 77. The first reviewer gave it five stars (= excellent). How many stars do you think the other reviewers gave it?

b Read reviews a–d again. Underline any words or phrases that are used to describe the things below.

1 the atmosphere
2 the kind of food and drinks they serve
3 the quality of the food
4 the service
5 value for money
6 the location

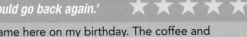

a *'Very highly recommended. Would go back again.'* ★★★★★

I came here on my birthday. The coffee and cakes were delicious and there was a relaxing atmosphere, with plenty of space. The staff were very friendly and gave us free birthday drinks. I can definitely recommend this café and I'll be going back.

b *'Completely overrated.'* ★★★★★

We had seen good reviews of this café, but it was extremely disappointing. The service was awful – we waited for 30 minutes before anyone even noticed we were there. We ordered pasta, but it was overcooked and the sauce was completely tasteless. My soup was tasty, but it was half cold and I had to send it back. The waiters were friendly enough, but they were so slow.

c *'Visited twice in 3 days!'* ★★★★★

We had wonderful food here. The fish was very fresh and they had delicious salads. It's also a great place to just sit and relax. The second time we went, we just ordered coffee, and the waiters were friendly and left us alone. We stayed for three hours! It's right in the town centre, so it's a bit noisy, but it's a convenient place to meet and fairly easy to get to. It's definitely worth a visit!

d *'A nice place to meet friends.'* ★★★★★

This is a bright, friendly café and they also serve good food, although the portions aren't very generous and it's a bit overpriced. I usually go there for a coffee. It has a fairly pleasant atmosphere and the service is always reasonably friendly and relaxed. I'd recommend it as a place to get something to drink with friends, but it might be better to eat somewhere else.

3 WRITING SKILLS Positive and negative language; Adverbs

a Add adjectives or phrases from the reviews above to the table.

Positive	Fairly positive
delicious	friendly enough

Fairly negative	Negative
a bit noisy	awful

b 💬 Compare your answers. Did you choose the same adjectives and phrases?

c Compare the two sentences. They are both negative, but they are not exactly the same. In which sentence is the writer trying not to sound too negative?

1 The portions weren**'t very generous**.
2 The portions were **absolutely tiny**.

d Which of these sentences are slightly negative? Which are very negative?

1 It was extremely disappointing.
2 The bread wasn't very fresh.
3 The sauce was completely tasteless.
4 My soup wasn't really hot enough.
5 The portions were rather small.
6 The service was awful.

e Do we use these adverbs to make adjectives or phrases stronger or weaker?

a bit   absolutely   completely   extremely   fairly   not really
not very   quite   rather   really   reasonably   slightly   terribly

f Change the strong comments in the sentences in 3d so that they sound weaker. Change the weaker comments so that they sound stronger.

1 It was a bit disappointing.
2 The bread was really old.

4 WRITING Two reviews

a Choose two places you know (restaurants, cafés or venues with music). Think of one place you like a lot and one place you don't really like. Make notes about the points below.

- general atmosphere
- location
- how busy it is
- what they serve
- quality of food
- service
- friendliness
- prices
- value for money

b 💬 Compare your ideas with a partner.

c Write two reviews, one for each place.

d Work in pairs. Read your partner's reviews. Check that your partner has done the things below.

1 covered all the points in 4a
2 used appropriate adjectives and phrases
3 used adverbs appropriately

e 💬 Show your reviews to other students. Do you agree with your partner's descriptions? Why / Why not?

UNIT 6
Review and extension

1 GRAMMAR

a Read the text and <u>underline</u> the best words. Sometimes more than one word is possible.

Essaouira, in Morocco, is a wonderful place to visit. You [1]*must / should / can* enjoy walking through the streets, shopping at the market or tasting local food.

It's often windy in Essaouira, so you [2]*don't have to / should / have to* bring warm clothes. The wind means that the beach isn't good for sunbathing, but you [3]*ought to / shouldn't / must* go kite-surfing – it's really exciting!

If you like history, you [4]*don't have to / have to / should* explore the old part of town. There are a lot of market stalls here. If you want to buy something, discuss the price with the stallholder. You certainly [5]*shouldn't / ought to / must* pay the first price you hear!

Many people here speak English, Spanish or French, so you [6]*don't have to / should / mustn't* learn Arabic, although you [7]*should / must / have to* probably learn a few useful phrases. You [8]*can't / don't have to / mustn't* stay in expensive hotels; there are other options, including *riads*, which are hotels that feel like family homes.

b Complete the sentences with the correct form of the words in brackets. Add any extra words you need.

1 A burger in my country is _____ (slightly cheap) a burger here.
2 Indonesia is _____ (a bit hot) Jamaica.
3 On average, trains in Japan are _____ (much fast) trains in India.
4 Thai food is _____ (by far spicy) I've ever eaten.
5 Travelling on this Metro isn't _____ (nearly expensive) travelling on the London Underground.

2 VOCABULARY

a Complete each pair of sentences with compound nouns made from the words in the boxes.

air	crossing	conditioning	pedestrian

1 It's safer to use a _____ . There's so much traffic on this road.
2 **A** It's so hot!   **B** I'll turn the _____ on.

hour	public	rush	transport

3 Let's go at ten o'clock, when _____ is over.
4 Should we drive or use _____?

jam	lights	traffic	traffic

5 Sorry I'm late. I got stuck in a _____ .
6 Wait for the _____ to change from red to green.

cycle	vending	lane	machine

7 That car shouldn't be in the _____!
8 I'd like a cold drink. Is there a _____ near here?

b Complete the sentences with words for describing food.

1 I'm not hungry. Can I have something _____, like a salad?
2 I love _____ foods like chocolate and cake!
3 This hasn't been cooked properly. Look! The vegetables are still _____ .
4 This juice is really _____ . There's too much lemon in it.

3 WORDPOWER *go*

a Match questions 1–6 with responses a–f.

1 ☐ Where does that path **go**?
2 ☐ How did your trip **go**?
3 ☐ This is my new dress. Do these shoes **go** with it?
4 ☐ Where's the milk?
5 ☐ Where's the cake you were making?
6 ☐ Was there food at the party?

a Really well. I met some very nice people.
b No, they're the wrong colour.
c To the beach, I think.
d Yes, but when I got there it had all **gone**.
e It **went** off. I threw it away.
f It **went** wrong. I threw it away.

b Match the phrases with *go* in 3a with these descriptio
We can use:
- *go* to mean *disappear* _d_
- *go* (*with*) to mean *look similar / look good together* ___
- *go* to mean *go towards* ___
- *go wrong* to mean *develop problems / not succeed* ___
- *go* + adverb to describe how things happen (e.g., *go badly*) ___
- *go* + adjective to describe a change (e.g., *go grey*) ___

c Complete each sentence with the correct form of *go* and a word or phrase from the box, if necessary.

around	bad	orange	really well	with my eyes	wrong

1 In the autumn, the leaves _____ .
2 I had a job interview yesterday. It _____ . I got the job!
3 Don't worry if it _____ . Just start again.
4 When I turned to speak to Fred, he had already _____ .
5 The road _____ the lake. It's a nice drive.
6 The shop assistant said the scarf _____ .
7 Milk that is not refrigerated will eventually _____ .

d 💬 Look at what the people are saying. Think of two things that each person might be talking about.

1 It went very well, thanks.

2 It went completely white.

3 It goes very well with cheese.

4 Oh, no! It's gone bad!

5 It goes over the river.

6 It's gone. Good!

◎ REVIEW YOUR PROGRESS

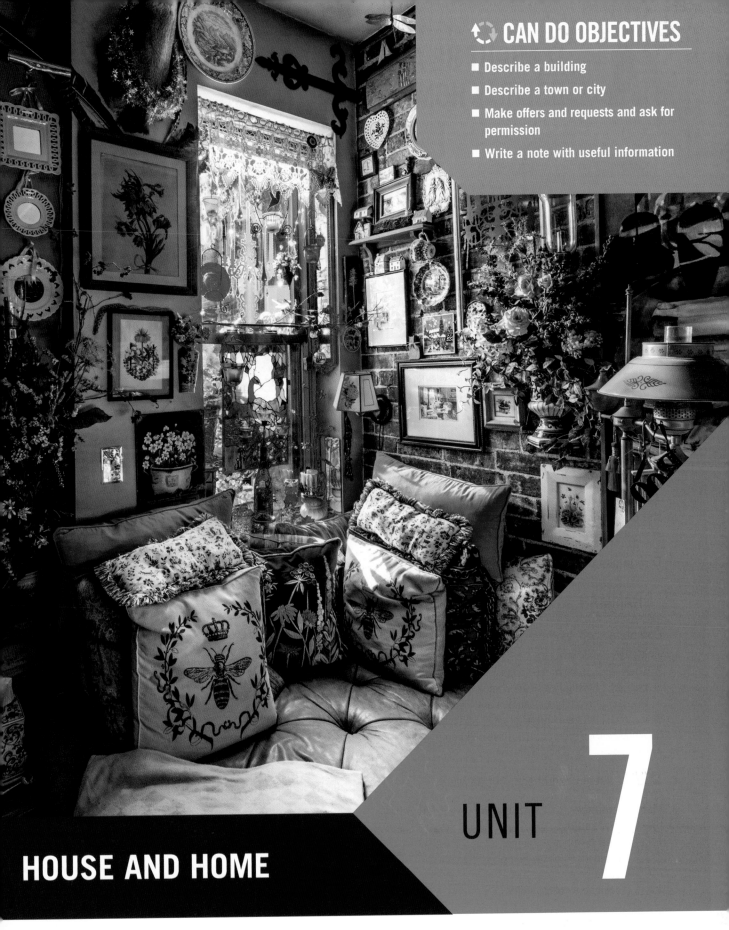

HOUSE AND HOME

UNIT **7**

GETTING STARTED

a 💬 Look at the photo and answer the questions.

1 Which room in the house is this? What items can you see?
2 Would you like to have a room like this in your home? Why / Why not?
3 What is your favourite room in your home? Describe it.

b 💬 Talk about your ideal home.

1 What would it look like?
2 How big would it be?
3 Where would it be?
4 Who would live there with you?

79

7A | IT MIGHT BE A HOLIDAY HOME

1 LISTENING

a 💬🔊 Look at photos a–d and discuss the questions.

1 Where do you think the buildings are? Are they in the city or the country? Which country? Explain your answers.
2 Who do you think lives in each building? A large family? A young married couple? Explain your answers.

b ▶07.01 Listen to four people talking about photos a–d. Which photo is each person talking about?

Speaker 1 ____   Speaker 3 ____
Speaker 2 ____   Speaker 4 ____

c ▶07.01 Listen again. Where do the speakers think the buildings are? Who do they think lives there? Are their answers the same as yours in 1a?

d Do you like these buildings? Why / Why not?

2 GRAMMAR Modals of deduction

a Complete each sentence with one word.

1 It's very small, so it _____ belong to a big family.
2 There _____ be much space in there!
3 It _____ belong to a single person or a couple.
4 It _____ be on the outskirts of any big city.
5 It _____ not be a house.
6 Whoever lives there _____ have children.
7 Or it _____ be a holiday home.

b ▶07.02 Listen and check your answers.

c Match sentences 1–4 with meanings a–c. Two have the same meaning.

1 ☐ It **must** be a holiday home.
2 ☐ It **might** be a holiday home.
3 ☐ It **could** be a holiday home.
4 ☐ It **can't** be a holiday home.

a I think it's a holiday home (but I'm not sure).
b I'm sure it's a holiday home.
c I'm sure it's not a holiday home.

d Look again at the sentences in 2c. What verb form comes after *must*, *might*, *could* and *can't*?

e ≫ Now go to Grammar Focus 7A on p. 156.

f ▶07.04 **Pronunciation** Listen to the sentences in 2c. Underline the correct word in the rule.

> When the final *t* or *d* in a word is followed by a consonant sound, it is often *easier / harder* to hear the *t* or *d* clearly.

g ▶07.05 Listen and tick (✓) the sentences where you hear the final *t* or *d*. Practise saying the sentences.

1 ☐ It can'**t** get much sun.
2 ☐ You coul**d** be right.
3 ☐ She mus**t** earn a lot of money.
4 ☐ It migh**t** be very expensive.
5 ☐ You mus**t** enjoy living here!

h 💬🔊 Discuss the questions.

1 What do you think it might be like to live in the homes in 1a?
2 What would you see from the windows?
3 Would you have a lot of space? Are there a lot of rooms?

3 VOCABULARY Buildings

a Read the email and underline the correct words.

✉ ✎ ☆ 🏳   ⊗

Hi Jamal,

I'm ¹*moving house / moving my house* next Friday, so here's my new address: Flat 4b, 52 Stevens Road, Leighton, NR17 3AQ. I'm ²*renting / buying* the flat for six months and if I like it, I'll stay longer. It's on the fourth ³*level / floor* of a modern ⁴*house / block* of flats, and it's got ⁵*views / sights* of the sea!

It's in a good ⁶*location / located*. The ⁷*neighbour / neighbourhood* is quiet, but there are some nice cafés and shops nearby. You should come and visit. If it's sunny, we can sit on the ⁸*upstairs / balcony* and look at the sea!

I've got to move out ⁹*of / to* this house on Tuesday, but I can't move ¹⁰*of / into* my new place until Friday, so I'll be staying with my parents for a few days next week. Are you going to be in the area?

Hope to see you soon,
Alex

b ≫ Now go to Vocabulary Focus 7A on p. 139.

4 READING

a 💬🔊 Imagine you're going to stay for three nights in a city that you don't know. Discuss the questions.

1 What are the advantages and disadvantages of staying in:
- a hotel?
- a rented flat?
- a spare room in a local person's house?

2 Where would you prefer to stay? Why?

b Read the introduction of *A more personal place to stay* and choose the best summary.

1 How to be less like a tourist on holiday
2 How to find out about a place before you visit
3 How to find out the price of accommodation

c 💬🔊 Would you like to stay in someone else's home? What would be good or bad about it?

d Read *What the guests say …* and answer the questions. Write Letizia (*L*) or Kumi (*K*).

1 ☑L Who stayed in a modern building?
2 ☑K Who felt at home in the neighbourhood?
3 ☑K Who could easily get around the city?
4 ☑K Who cooked their own food?
5 ☐ Who is going to see their host(s) again?

e 💬🔊 Which of the places would you rather stay in?

A MORE *Personal* PLACE TO STAY

Do you want to live like a local when you go on holiday? Popular websites such as Airbnb help travellers find privately owned rooms, flats and houses to rent.

Hosts create profiles of places to rent. Guests can browse the profiles, read reviews written by guests and make reservations online. Prices range from about £35 to £300 per night, depending on the accommodation and the location.

But what's it like to stay at a stranger's house when you're on holiday? And if you're a host, what's it like to open your home to people you don't know? We spoke to some guests and hosts to find out.

👤 WHAT THE GUESTS SAY …

KUMI I've stayed in Berlin a few times, but I've always stayed in a hotel. This experience was completely different. I had the entire top floor of an old house, and the rent included a bicycle, too, which was great for travelling around the city. The hosts (Karl and Alexandra) were very kind, and we had good conversations at every meal. They let me use the kitchen, which was great since the restaurants nearby were very expensive. The shopkeepers in the area knew I was staying at Karl and Alexandra's and they were all very friendly. I felt like a local by the end of the week!

LETIZIA My friends and I stayed in this amazing modern villa in California for ten days. It had eight bedrooms, a pool and the biggest kitchen I've ever seen (in which Jeff, our host, cooked fantastic breakfasts for us!). Jeff was so nice. He gave us a lot of information about the local area and invited us to join him for dinner. We ended up becoming good friends – he's going to stay in my house when he comes to Italy next year.

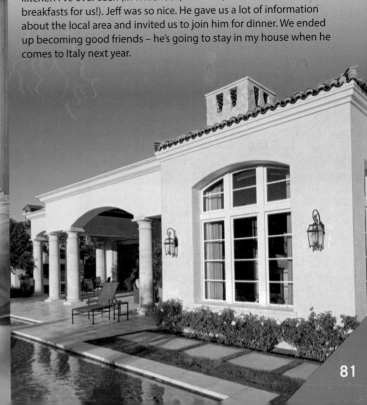

f 💬 What do you think are the advantages and disadvantages of being an Airbnb host?

g Read *What the hosts say …* . Do they mention the advantages and disadvantages you talked about?

🏠 WHAT THE HOSTS SAY …

ROBERTO I've been an Airbnb host for three years. In that time, I've met some wonderful people – musicians, families, athletes, professors, hikers and students – who've needed **accommodation** for different reasons. They've come from different parts of the world, and it's been a **pleasure** to get to know them. The only problem is that you have to do so much laundry and cleaning!

LISA Some people worry about **theft**, but I've had more than 100 guests and no one has ever stolen anything from me. Some guests are nicer than others, of course, but overall they've been charming and friendly. I usually ask people why they're travelling when they make a **reservation**. It's a good way to get to know a bit about them.

CLARA My family has a holiday **cottage** in Scotland. We decided to rent it out when we're not using it. It was easy to set up the profile on the website. You have to trust people to treat your **property** as if it were their own home, but we only accept reservations from guests who have good reviews.

Scotland, UK

h Read the texts above again and match the words in **bold** with the definitions.

1 a building that someone owns
2 place(s) to stay
3 a small house in the country *cottage*
4 an enjoyable experience *pleasure*
5 the crime of stealing something *theft*
6 an arrangement to stay somewhere *reservatio* (e.g., a hotel room)

5 SPEAKING

a 💬 Look at the buildings below and discuss the questions

1 How old is each building?
2 What do you think it's like inside?
3 Would you like to live there?

b 💬 Imagine you are going on holiday with your partner. Discuss which of the houses/flats you would like to stay in. Can you agree on one house/flat to visit?

> I'd like to stay in the flat in photo e. New York must be a really great city to visit.

a Cappadocia, Turkey

b Amsterdam, The Netherlands

c Essex, UK

d Cork, Ireland

f Miami, USA

e New York City, USA

7B THERE ARE PLENTY OF THINGS TO DO

1 LISTENING

a 💬 Where did you grow up – in a big city or a small town? What was good and bad about it?

b Read *Five reasons why small towns are better than cities*. Do you agree with the reasons in the list? Can you add any more reasons?

c 💬 Think of five reasons why cities are better places to live than small towns. Tell a partner.

d ▶ 07.08 Listen to Tim and Kate's conversation. Are Tim's reasons the same as yours in 1c?

e ▶ 07.08 Listen again. Are these statements true (*T*) or false (*F*)?

1 Kate grew up in a small town. T
2 Tim wouldn't want to live in a small town. F
3 Kate thinks small towns are safer. T
4 More people have car accidents in the city than in the country. F
5 People who live in the country have a smaller carbon footprint. F

f 💬 Discuss the questions.

1 Where do you think it's safer to live – in the city or in the country? Think about:
   • driving   • crime   • hospitals   • other ideas
2 Is your (nearest) city designed in a way that's good for the environment? Why / Why not?
3 How could your (nearest) city be better? Think about:
   • public transport   • cycle lanes   • other ideas

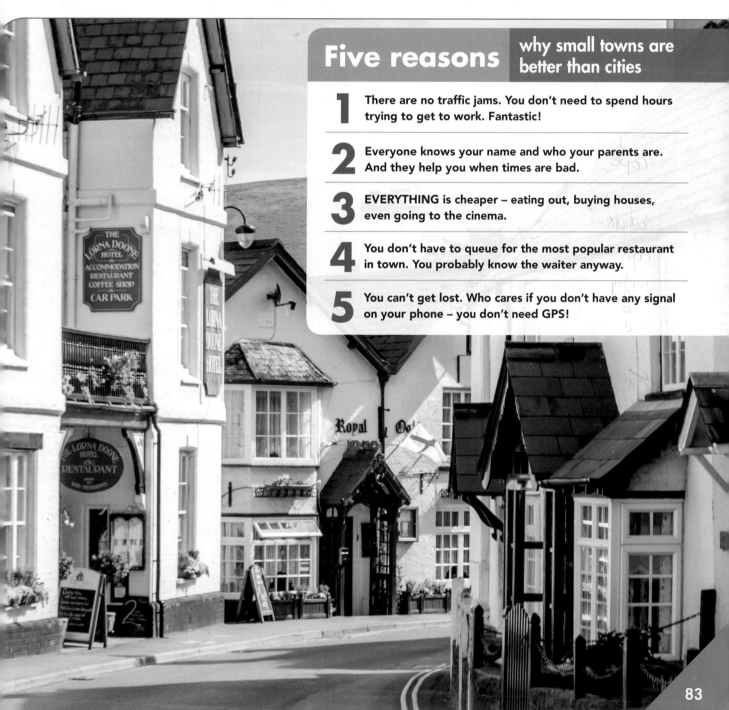

Five reasons why small towns are better than cities

1 There are no traffic jams. You don't need to spend hours trying to get to work. Fantastic!

2 Everyone knows your name and who your parents are. And they help you when times are bad.

3 EVERYTHING is cheaper – eating out, buying houses, even going to the cinema.

4 You don't have to queue for the most popular restaurant in town. You probably know the waiter anyway.

5 You can't get lost. Who cares if you don't have any signal on your phone – you don't need GPS!

2 VOCABULARY Verbs and prepositions

a Complete the sentences with the words in the box.

about (x2)   on   to

1 People care _abt_ you.
2 It's like you belong _to_ one big family.
3 That makes sense if you think _abt_ it.
4 You can't rely _on_ public transport in the countryside like you can in the city.

b ▶07.09 **Pronunciation** Listen and check your answers to 2a. Then complete the rule.

When we use a verb and a preposition, we _usually_ / don't usually stress the verb and _stress_ / _don't stress_ the preposition.

c ▶07.09 Listen again and practise saying the sentences.

d Match the verbs in the box with the prepositions. Use some verbs more than once.

apologise   argue   believe   belong   care
complain   cope   depend   ~~pay~~   ~~rely~~
succeed   ~~think~~   ~~wait~~   worry

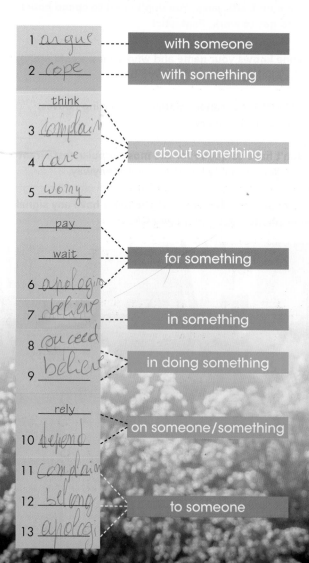

1 _argue_ ---- with someone
2 _cope_ ---- with something
  think
3 _complain_
4 _care_ ---- about something
5 _worry_
  pay
  wait ---- for something
6 _apologi_
7 _believe_ ---- in something
8 _succeed_
9 _believe_ ---- in doing something
  rely
10 _depend_ ---- on someone/something
11 _complain_
12 _belong_ ---- to someone
13 _apolog_

e Complete each sentence with the correct form of a verb + preposition from 2d.

1 Do I like living in the countryside? That _can depend_ the weather – when it's warm and sunny, I love it!
2 My friend has just moved from the countryside to the city and she's finding it hard to _cope with_ all the noise.
3 He moved here to look for work, but he hasn't _succeed in_ finding a job yet, unfortunately.
4 I'd like to _apolo for_ what I said earlier. I didn't mean to be so rude.
5 I _argued with_ the traffic warden about the fine for ten minutes, but in the end I had to pay it.
6 People _complain_ is bus the traffic here, but it isn't bad compared to a big city.
7 **A** Do you _believe in_ bad luck?
  B No, not really. I think people are in control of their own lives.
8 All of the land near the river is private – it _rely on_ the university. You can't walk there. _belong to_

f 💬 Complete the game instructions below with the correct prepositions. Then play the game in teams.

'TWO' Think of two things for each category. You win a point for each answer that no other team has written.

a ways you can pay _for_ things
  1 _cash_   2 _card_

b things hotel guests often complain _about_
  1 _property_   2 _nose_

c ways you can apologise _for_ being late
  1 _bus_   2 _wakker_

d things people often do when they're waiting _for_ a bus or train
  1 _listen to music_   2 _____

e things that a lot of adults worry _about_
  1 _be old_   2 _money_

f things that a lot of children believe _in_
  1 _sinterklaas_   2 _easter_

3 GRAMMAR Quantifiers

a 💬 Discuss the questions.

1 Are there parks and other green spaces where you live?
2 What activities can people do there?
3 How often do you use parks and other green spaces?

b 💬 Look at the photo of the Turia Gardens in Valencia, Spain. What do you think you can do there? Make a list. Then compare lists with a partner.

go jogging
have a picnic

c Read the article and check. Which things on your list are mentioned?

TURIA GARDENS VALENCIA, SPAIN

At one time the River Turia flowed through the beautiful city of Valencia. The trouble was – it often flooded. After a particularly serious flood in 1957, the local government decided to change the course of the river and move it further south. In its place they created nine kilometres of parks and gardens, still crossed by the river's 18 bridges. The Turia Gardens are now home to hundreds of species of plants, a network of paths for cycling and walking and even a 70-metre-long giant lying in the sand, whose body you can climb up and slide down. There are areas to play volleyball and do yoga – or you can just lie about on the grass. The Turia Gardens are a great place for tourists and locals.

What the locals say

I love the Turia Gardens. Calm and beautiful, especially if you go early in the morning when it's quiet.

Pablo

It used to be a lovely quiet place to go. Now it's full of tourists. Don't go at the weekend! But one good thing is that it's quite clean and tidy – they clean up all the rubbish regularly.

Ana

Make sure you allow plenty of time. You need about three hours to see it properly. One thing to remember – there are very few public toilets in the park, so you may need to go to a café.

Rosalia

d Read the article again. Underline the correct words.

1 There are *a lot of* / *too many* different kinds of plants in the Turia Gardens.
2 There are *much* / *plenty of* things to see and do in the park.
3 Pablo goes there early in the morning because there aren't so *many* / *much* people.
4 Ana thinks there are *too many* / *enough* tourists there.
5 There's *very few* / *very little* rubbish in the park.
6 Rosalia thinks there *aren't any* / *aren't enough* public toilets in the park.

e ≫ Now go to Grammar Focus 7B on p. 156.

f Write sentences about each of the places below. Use quantifiers and the words in the box, and your own ideas. Don't include the name of the place.

• a city area that you know
• a country area that you know

| cafés | crime | flowers | noise | people | pollution |
| shops | space | things to do | traffic | views | wildlife |

It's a great place. There isn't much traffic and there's very little pollution.

g 💬 Read your sentences aloud. Can your partner guess where the places are?

A lot of people go there at weekends, but there's enough space for everyone. There aren't many shops or cafés.

Is it the beach?

4 SPEAKING

a You are going to talk about the area where you live. Make notes about these questions:

• Is it a healthy or safe place to live? Why / Why not?
• What do people like about it? (e.g., parks, restaurants)
• What do people complain about? (e.g., the noise, the roads)

b 💬 Take turns to talk about your areas. Would the places you talk about be good to live in for each of the people below? Why / Why not?

• a teenager who likes films and music
• a family with young children
• an elderly couple
• someone who likes sport and outdoor activities

7C EVERYDAY ENGLISH
Is there anything we can do to help?

Learn to make offers and requests and ask for permission

- **P** Sounding polite
- **S** Imagining people's feelings

1 LISTENING

a 💬 Discuss the questions.

1 Do you take presents when you visit someone's house? What might you take?
2 What should you do to be polite when visiting someone's house? (e.g., arrive on time, take your shoes off)

b 💬 Look at the photos on this page. What do you think is happening? How do you think the people feel?

c ▶ 07.14 Watch or listen to Part 1 and check your ideas.

d ▶ 07.14 Watch or listen again. Are the sentences true (*T*) or false (*F*)?

1 Becky hasn't met Tom's parents before. T
2 Michael wants to watch a football match. F
3 Becky got Charlotte's name wrong. T
4 Charlotte is a teacher. F
5 Tom tried to tell his parents that Becky is a vegetarian. F

e Do you think that Becky has been a good guest? Has she made a good first impression?

2 USEFUL LANGUAGE Making offers and requests and asking for permission

a Match questions 1–5 with responses a–e.

1 c **Is there anything we can do to help**?
2 b **Do you think you could** give me a hand?
3 a **Let me** get you something else.
4 e **Is it OK if I** just have some bread and butter?
5 d **I'll** get you a green salad.

a No, it's fine, really.
b Sure.
c Oh no, it's all under control!
d OK, that would be lovely. Thanks.
e No, we can do better than that.

b What phrases in **bold** in 2a do we use to ...

1 offer something politely? 1,3,5   3 ask for permission? 4
2 ask for help politely? 2

c Match requests 1–5 with responses a–e.

1 b Do you mind if I borrow some money?
2 e May I sit here?
3 a Do you think I could have a glass of water?
4 c Can I use your phone for a moment?
5 d Would you mind if I opened the window?

a Yes, of course. Let me get you one.
b Not at all. How much do you want?
c Sure. Here it is.
d Not at all. It's hot in here.
e Of course. There's plenty of space.

UNIT 7

3 LISTENING

a 💬 Look at the photo. What do you think Tom and Michael are talking about?

b 🎥 ▶ 07.15 Watch or listen to Part 2 and check.

c 🎥 ▶ 07.15 Watch or listen again. Are the sentences true (*T*) or false (*F*)?

1 Tom thinks Becky hasn't made a good impression. *T*
2 Michael doesn't like Becky. *F*

4 CONVERSATION SKILLS
Imagining people's feelings

a ▶ 07.16 What word is missing in each sentence? Listen and check.

1 I *imagine* you're excited about the match this afternoon.
2 Tom tells me you're an architect. That *would* be very interesting.

b Read the exchanges and underline the phrases we use to imagine what someone else is feeling.

1 **A** I'm doing three part-time jobs at the moment.
  B You must be very tired!
2 **A** I'm going to meet my boyfriend's parents for the first time.
  B I imagine you're a bit nervous!

c 💬 Look at the sentences below. Respond with *must* and an appropriate adjective.

1 I'm planning a holiday to France.
2 I've just broken my tooth! *gives you have pain*
3 I've lost my smartphone – and I can't remember any of my friends' numbers. *lost, bad*
4 I'm learning Japanese at the moment. *That must be exausti*

I'm planning a holiday to France.

That must be exciting!

d 💬 Tell your partner about some of the things below. Answer with a phrase from 4a or 4b.

- something you're planning on doing soon
- a hobby you have
- a problem you have at school/work

I go to Spanish lessons at 7:30 in the morning before I go to work.

That must be tiring.

Yes, but I really enjoy them.

5 PRONUNCIATION Sounding polite

a ▶ 07.17 Listen to these sentences spoken twice. Which sentence sounds more polite, a or b?

1 Do you think you could give me a hand? a / b
2 It's lovely to meet you at last. a / b

b ▶ 07.18 Listen to three more pairs of sentences. Which sentences sound more polite, a or b?

1 How long are you staying? a / b
2 She seems really great. a / b
3 I'm really happy to hear that. a / b

c 💬 Practise saying the sentences in 5b with polite intonation.

6 SPEAKING

≫ Communication 7C 💬 Student A: Read the instructions below. Student B: Go to p. 132.

Student A

1 You are staying with Student B in their home. During the conversation, ask permission to:
- use the Internet
- have a shower
- wash some clothes

2 Student B is a new colleague in your office. Ask them how it's going and try to sound interested (e.g., *That must be ...*). They will ask you permission to do things. Decide whether or not to give permission.

✓ UNIT PROGRESS TEST

→ CHECK YOUR PROGRESS

You can now do the Unit Progress Test.

87

Learn to write a note with useful information

 Offering choices

1 SPEAKING

a 💬 Talk about a recent holiday.

1 What kinds of activities did you do?
2 Did the people you were with want to do the same things as you or different things?
3 Think of a holiday you would like to go on. What would you do on the holiday?

2 READING AND LISTENING

a 💬 You're going to read about going on holiday in Miami. Before you do, discuss the questions.

1 Where is Miami? Have you ever been there? Do you know anyone who's been there?
2 What is it like, or what do you imagine it's like? Talk about the points below.
   - the weather
   - the people
   - the buildings
   - the atmosphere
   - things to see and do

b 💬 Read about the top five things to do in and around Miami. Which things would you like to do? Why? Are there any things you would *not* want to do? Why not?

c ▶07.19 Sue is talking to a colleague, Jon. Listen to their conversation and answer the questions.

1 How many people are in Sue's family?
2 Where are they staying?
3 Which of the 'top five things' are they going to do?

d ▶07.19 Listen again and make notes in the table.

	Where do they want to go?	Why do they want to go there?
Sue's daughter		
Sue's son		
Sue's husband		
Sue		

e 💬 Do you think Sue is looking forward to the holiday? Why / Why not?

TOP FIVE THINGS TO DO
... in and around Miami, Florida

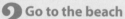

1 Admire the architecture of Miami Beach
Wander the streets of Miami Beach and admire the art deco hotels and houses from the 1930s. The film stars from the 1930s stayed here when they came to Miami. Many of the buildings have been repainted in their original colours.

2 Go to the beach
Miami has endless sandy beaches along the coast. You can find crowds if you want them or you can have a beach to yourself. And the water is always warm.

3 Visit the Everglades
Ninety minutes from Miami are the Everglades, a huge area of natural swamp that is home to alligators, snakes and rare birds. Take a boat through the area and get a close-up view of the wildlife.

4 Spend a day at Disney World
Disney World is not very far from Miami – a great day trip. You can find all the characters from Disney films and have hours of fun with (or without) your kids.

5 Take a trip to Cape Canaveral
North of Miami is Cape Canaveral, where the USA sends some of its rockets into space. You can tour the Kennedy Space Center and see where they built the Apollo rockets that went to the moon.

3 READING

a Read the note below that Sue's cousin, Tess, left in the apartment in Miami. <u>Underline</u> the correct words.

1 The streets are safe *during the day / all the time*.
2 The apartment is *in the centre of / just outside* Miami.
3 The apartment is *right next to / quite far from* the sea.
4 Tess will be away for *a week / more than a week*.

b Which adjectives in the box best describe the tone of the note? Which words or phrases in the note helped you decide?

friendly	formal	funny	practical

c Match the purposes a–f with sections 1–6 of the note.

a ☐ to explain options for buying food
b ☐ to give information about going to places further away
c ☐ to finish the note
d ☐ to greet the reader and say what the note is about
e ☐ to give safety advice about the area around the apartment
f ☐ to give information about things in the apartment

d What general order are the sections in? Choose the correct answer.

1 things they need to know now → things they need to know later
2 things that are very important → things that are less important
3 things that are less important → things that are more important

---

① Welcome to Miami! Hope you have a nice stay in the apartment. Here are a few things you need to know …

② Please make yourselves at home and help yourselves to anything in the kitchen. There's some chicken in the fridge and a lot of fruit and salad, so that should be enough for a couple of meals. I also got a couple of pizzas for the kids – they're in the freezer.

③ After that, you'll need to go shopping. The best place is the Sunshine Center. Go out of the main entrance of the apartment and turn left, and you'll see it about 100 metres down the road. It's got a couple of supermarkets, a big bookshop and a few nice places to eat. Otherwise, there's a good place for burgers a bit further down the road. Apart from that, there are some good restaurants by the sea, but they're a bit further away.

④ By the way, if you do go out in the evening, don't walk around late at night – the streets round here are not very safe at night, although they're OK during the daytime.

⑤ Anyway, the car's in the car park, so you can use that for any trips. If you're going into Miami, another possibility is to take the train, but you'll find the car easier! You'll also need the car to go to the beach. The nearest one is Golden Beach, about a 15-minute drive away. Another option is Ocean Beach, about 30 minutes further north, which is usually much less crowded. Alternatively, you could try Miami Beach, but it can be difficult to park there.

⑥ Enjoy your stay and see you in two weeks!
Love,
Tess

---

4 WRITING SKILLS Offering choices

a What do the words in **bold** below mean?

1 The Sunshine Center has got a few nice places to eat. **Otherwise**, there's a good place for burgers a bit further down the road.
a if you don't like that idea
b however
c finally
2 The nearest one is Golden Beach, about a 15-minute drive away. **Another option is** Ocean Beach, about 30 minutes further north.
a a different direction is
b a different choice is
c a much better beach is

b Read the note again and find three more words or phrases that you could use instead of *Otherwise* or *Another option is … .*

c Use words or phrases from 4a and 4b in the second sentences below.

1 If you drive north, you can visit Disney World. You can also go to the Space Center at Cape Canaveral.
Another option is the Space Center at Cape Canaveral.
2 There are a lot of good restaurants at Miami Beach. Or you can try the restaurants at South Beach.
3 You can get an inter-city bus to go to the West Coast. You can also hire a car for a few days.
4 You can drive through the Everglades to look at the birds and alligators. You can also see them by boat.

5 WRITING A note with useful information

a You are going to write a note for someone who will be staying in your home while you are away. Think about:

- things in the house/flat
- things they can and can't do
- things you want to ask them to do
- food and shopping
- things to do in the area.

b 💬 Compare your ideas with a partner.

c Read another student's note and answer the questions.

1 Did you understand all the information?
2 Did they put the information in a logical order?
3 Did they use words and phrases from 4a or 4b correctly?

UNIT 7
Review and extension

1 GRAMMAR

a <u>Underline</u> the correct answer.

1 There are *a lot* / *too many* / *too much* stairs in this building!
2 There isn't *enough light* / *light enough* / *enough of light*. It's always dark.
3 There's too *many* / *few* / *much* noise outside.
4 It's got *a lot* / *a lot of* / *much* windows.
5 There are very *little* / *much* / *few* buildings in the area.
6 It hasn't got *many* / *much* / *little* floors.

b 💬 Discuss the pictures. Use *must*, *might*, *could* and *can't*.

1 What kind of person are they?
2 How old are they?
3 Where are they?

(a)

(b)

2 VOCABULARY

a Complete the text with the words in the box.

block	floor	location	neighbourhood	views

Holiday home swap

This summer, we exchanged homes with the Acuna family from Lisbon. Our home is in a quiet ¹_____ in the north of England, with beautiful ²_____ of the Pennine hills. The Acunas live on the third ³_____ of a ⁴_____ of flats in the Portuguese capital. The flat is in a lively ⁵_____ and there are a lot of places to visit nearby. Home swapping is a fantastic way to discover new places.

b Complete each sentence with a preposition.

1 Don't worry _____ the neighbours.
2 Who does that house belong _____?
3 You'll have to wait a long time _____ a bus.
4 How do you cope _____ the cold winters here?
5 You can't rely _____ public transport here.
6 We succeeded _____ finding a good hotel.
7 Are you going to complain _____ the noise?

3 WORDPOWER *over*

a Match questions 1–6 with responses a–f.

1 ☐ When did you paint the house?
2 ☐ How many people live in Hong Kong?
3 ☐ How long was the meeting?
4 ☐ Can we start the test?
5 ☐ What's the matter?
6 ☐ Was the hotel room nice?

a Yes, we had a view **over** the lake.
b **Over** the summer.
c Yes, turn your papers **over** and begin.
d **Over** 7 million.
e You're getting mud all **over** the floor!
f It started at 2:00 and it was **over** by 3:15.

b Match the meanings of *over* with sentences a–f in 3a.

1 ☐ finished
2 ☐ across / from one side to the other
3 ☐ more than
4 ☐ during (a period of time)
5 ☐ the other way up
6 ☐ covering

c Complete each sentence with *over* and the words in the box. One sentence only needs *over*.

16   a lifetime   someone   the last few days
the next few days   the world   your city

1 Where can tourists go to get views _____?
2 What businesses from your country are known all _____?
3 How much work have you done _____?
4 What can you do in your country when you are _____? How about 18?
5 What kinds of things do people learn _____?
6 When was the last time you were sad that something was _____?
7 Imagine you spill a drink _____ else in a restaurant. What would you do?
8 What are you going to do _____?

d 💬 Ask and answer the questions in 3c.

⟳ REVIEW YOUR PROGRESS

How well did you do in this unit? Write 3, 2 or 1 for each objective.
3 = very well   2 = well   1 = not so well

I CAN ...	
describe a building	☐
describe a town or city	☐
make offers and requests and ask for permission	☐
write a note with useful information.	☐

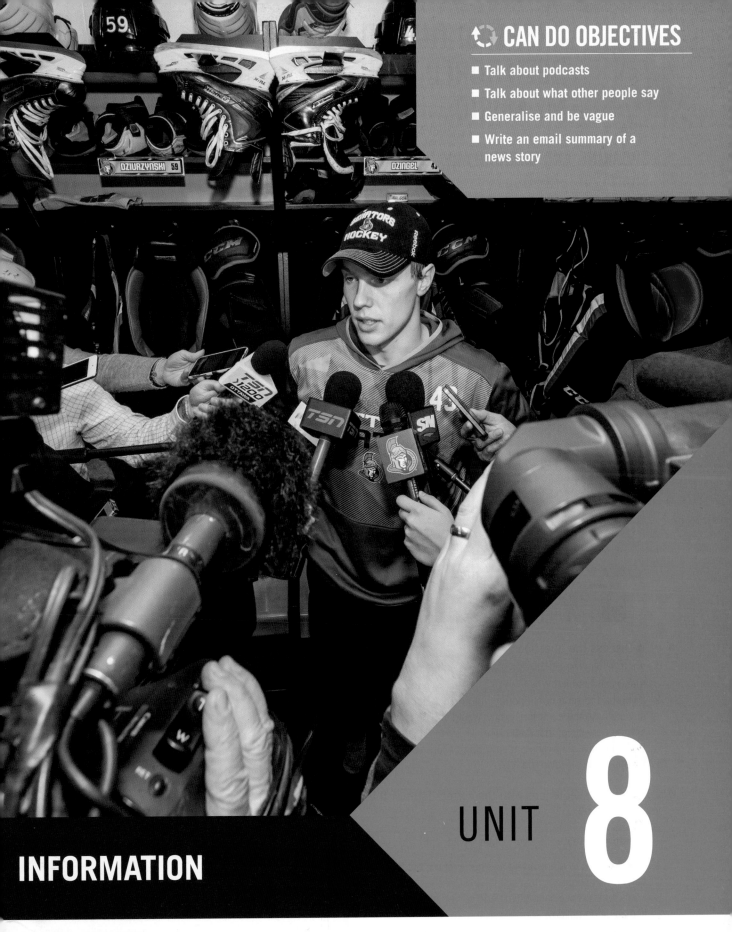

CAN DO OBJECTIVES

- Talk about podcasts
- Talk about what other people say
- Generalise and be vague
- Write an email summary of a news story

UNIT 8

INFORMATION

GETTING STARTED

a 💬🗨 Ask and answer the questions.

1 What is happening in the photo?
2 What do you think happened before the photo was taken?
3 What might happen next?
4 What would be a good caption for this photo if it appeared in a newspaper or online?

b 💬🗨 Talk about an interesting story you heard recently. Where did you hear it (e.g., in the news, on a podcast, on social media)? Ask and answer questions to find out more about each other's stories.

8A | I REPLIED THAT I'D BEEN BORED WITH MY MUSIC

Learn to talk about podcasts

G Reported speech

V Sharing information

1 SPEAKING AND VOCABULARY
Sharing information

a 💬 Discuss the questions.

1 What do you think is the best way to share information with friends and family? Why?
2 If you had to send out important information at university, at work or in the community, how would you do this? What are the benefits of that method?
3 Do you ever want to share ideas and opinions with others? What's the best way to do this?

b Complete the sentences with the correct form of the verbs in the box.

brainstorm create deliver hold post put up send

1 I _send_ a text to Monica and told her to come ten minutes earlier if she could.
2 I only _post_ on social media if I do something interesting, like going on holiday.
3 The best way to advertise the book sale is to _put up_ posters all around the university.
4 She loves local history so much that she has decided to _create_ a podcast series about it.
5 When I was younger, I used to _deliver_ newspapers on my bike.
6 Before we write our essays, we should all _brain_ ideas together as a group.
7 Last week, the city council _held_ a meeting to get feedback on the new cycle lanes.

c 💬 Look at the verb phrases in 1b. Have you done any of these things recently? Tell your partner.

d ≫ Now go to Vocabulary Focus 8A on p. 140.

2 READING

a 💬 Discuss the questions.

1 Do you ever listen to podcasts? How often? Where?
2 Why do you think podcasts have become popular?
3 How easy or difficult do you think it is to make a podcast? Explain your answer.

b 💬 Read the article about making podcasts. In your opinion, does it sound easy or difficult?

Thinking of Making a Podcast?
JUST GIVE IT A TRY!

Not so very long ago, people got their news from the radio, their entertainment from television and their knowledge from books. But, in case you hadn't noticed, times are changing. These days people can get all of that from one source: podcasts.

More than seven million adults in the UK listen to at least one podcast every week. And many of us just can't get enough of them. Podcasts are really popular with young people – 67% of people between the ages of 15 and 35 listen on a weekly basis. They are fun and they are informative, but, most of all, they are portable. Our favourite places to listen are at home, in the car or on public transport. Podcasts are perfect for taking the pain out of long traffic jams or boring trips to work on the bus or train!

Not only are a lot of people listening to podcasts, but a lot of people are now also making them. In some ways, they are very easy to make. Anyone can do it – all you need is a microphone and a computer. However, making a podcast that people really want to listen to is a little more challenging. You need to think about what's going to make people listen – what's going to get their attention? And more importantly, what's going to make them tune in again ... and again ... and again?

The best way to learn to make a podcast is to do it. You'll learn a lot by just giving it a try. Here are some useful tips to guide you in the process:

c Read the article again and make notes on the following topics.

1 podcast listening in the UK _7 Mio_
2 places where people listen _home, car, pt_
3 basic requirements to make a podcast _micro, compu_
4 making sure your content is good _____
5 talking on a podcast _____
6 before uploading _inviting guest_
7 after you've uploaded _edit_
8 building your number of listeners _____

d Find expressions in the article that match these meanings. The first example is done for you:

1 make other people notice you _get their attention_
2 try to do something _give it a try_
3 pleased or satisfied with something _happy with_
4 do what you say you will do _deliver on your prom_
5 learned from doing something _gained from the experi_

3 LISTENING

a 💬 What are the best and worst places to listen to podcasts? Why?

b ▶ 08.01 Listen to Andrea. She is being interviewed on a podcast about podcasts. Answer the questions.

1 How did she start listening to podcasts? _pt => more please_
2 What different types of podcasts does she listen to? _cook_

CONTENT

Before you grab a microphone and start talking, think about what you want to say. Your podcast series should have an overall aim or purpose, and each episode should feel like it's taking your listeners somewhere. It helps to think of your podcast as a kind of journey. You will probably need to plan what you say – not many people are great at improvising.

RECORDING and EDITING

If you record yourself on your podcast, try to sound as natural as possible. Don't use a special voice – just imagine you're talking to your friends. If your podcast isn't trying to be serious, make it sound like you're enjoying yourself. Finding and inviting interesting guests on your podcast can really help. You will probably record more material than you want to upload. This means you should edit it and only use what's relevant and interesting.

UPLOADING

Once you're happy with your episode, all you need to do is upload it. But don't imagine that thousands of people are going to find and listen to what you have to say. Use social media to tell people about your podcast, and be realistic about the number of listeners you can expect to attract when you are starting out. It takes time to build an audience. However, you should always treat your audience with respect and deliver on your promises. If you say you're going to produce one episode a week, make sure you do that. And if you're running late one week, let your listeners know.

Podcasts are fun to do. If yours doesn't end up being a big hit, it doesn't matter. You might lose some of your time, but you will have gained from the experience. So what are you waiting for? Get out there and give it a try!

c ▶ 08.01 Listen again. Are the following sentences true (*T*) or false (*F*)? Correct the false sentences.

1 She first listened to podcasts at home and used her computer. ✓
2 She found it hard not to laugh at the comedy podcast on the train. /
3 Listening to the comedy podcast made the trip to work take longer. /
4 The first podcast she listens to each day is the news.
5 On the train she always listens to a comedy podcast.
6 From podcasts, she has picked up a lot of ideas about baking cakes.
7 She really enjoys true crime podcasts.
8 She's found out useful information for her job from podcasts.

d ▶ 08.02 **Pronunciation** Listen to the words below from the podcast. How are the letters *c*, *g* and *k* in bold pronounced?

pod**c**ast a**g**o **g**uess **c**ommute wor**k**
giving **c**oncentrate ba**k**ing **g**ood or**g**anisation

e Complete the rules with /g/ or /k/.

1 When we say _g_, there is a sound in the throat.
2 When we say _k_, there is no sound in the throat.

f ▶ 08.02 Listen again and repeat the words.

g 💬 If people listen to music or podcasts on public transport, they can't hear what's going on around them. What kinds of problems can this cause?

4 GRAMMAR Reported speech

a Andrea wrote an email to a friend about some of the things she said in the interview. Read the message and <u>underline</u> any reported speech.

Hi Sandy,

The interview went well. First, <u>the interviewer asked me how I had started listening</u> to podcasts. I replied that I'd been bored with all my music and had looked up the available podcasts on my way to the metro station. Then we talked about my podcast listening habits. I said that each day, as I was walking to the metro, I listened to a news podcast. And then I mentioned all the different kinds of podcasts I listen to. He asked me if I listened to podcast series. I told him that I loved them. I also said that podcasts could be useful for my job. I told him that I'd worked for a charity organisation for the past four years and I'd picked up some really helpful ideas by listening to podcasts.

See you soon,
Andrea

b What did Andrea and the interviewer actually say? Complete the sentences in direct speech.

1 Interviewer: 'How _____ you _____ listening to podcasts?'
2 'I _____ bored with all my music, so I _____ up the available podcasts on my way to the metro station,' replied Andrea.
3 'Each day, as I _____ to the metro station, I _____ to a news podcast,' said Andrea.
4 Interviewer: '_____ you _____ to any podcast series?'
5 'I _____ them,' Andrea replied.
6 'Podcasts _____ useful for my job,' Andrea told the interviewer.
7 'I _____ for a charity organisation for the past four years. I _____ some really helpful ideas by listening to podcasts,' said Andrea.

c ▶ 08.03 Listen and check your answers.

d Underline the correct words in the rules.

1 When we report what someone has said or written, we often change the tense of the direct speech *backwards / forwards* in time.
2 We use *question word order / normal word order* in reported questions.
3 We often don't change the tense when we report things that are *still true / no longer true*.

e Write the tense we use for reported speech.

Direct speech	Reported speech
present simple	_____
past simple	_____
present continuous	_____
present perfect	_____
can	_____

f ≫ Now go to Grammar Focus 8A on p. 158.

g Work in pairs. Write a story using reported speech and questions.

1 Write the first two sentences. Begin like this and continue using reported speech:
My friend called me a few weeks ago with some news. He/She said …
2 Pass your sentences to another pair. Read the sentences you received and add another sentence. Begin:
I asked him/her …
3 Pass your sentences to another pair. Read the sentences you received and add another sentence. Begin:
He/She said …
4 Pass your sentences to another pair. Read the sentences and add a final sentence.

h 💬 Check that the reported speech is correct. Then read your story to the class.

5 SPEAKING

a 💬 Work with a partner. Look at the opinions about podcasts. Do you agree with them? Why / Why not?

1 Podcasts have completely changed the way we share information. They're a useful way to show people a different point of view.
2 Podcasts are a very valuable tool in education because you can learn so much from them.
3 On podcasts, you just have ordinary people saying anything they like. Some of the opinions they express are too strong.
4 Podcasts just feed people more and more information and stop them from thinking for themselves.
5 Podcasts are a fantastic form of entertainment that you can take with you almost anywhere.

b 💬 Work in small groups and discuss the opinions.

1 SPEAKING AND READING

a 💬 Discuss the questions.

1 Do you read online reviews for any of these things?
   - restaurants, cafés or clubs
   - places to go on holiday
   - things to buy (e.g., computers, films, phones, cars)
2 How much do you trust online reviews? Explain your answer.

b 💬 Read the review of The Shed at Dulwich and look at the photo. What is the reviewer's opinion of the restaurant? Would you like to eat there? Why / Why not?

c 💬 Now read *The restaurant that wasn't there* and look at the photos on p. 131. How is the restaurant different from the review?

The Shed at Dulwich ★★★★★
Reviewed 16 May

If you enjoy creative, exciting food, then you'll love The Shed! My husband and I occasionally take a trip to London from our home in the country. We both love food and we love to try new places. We came across The Shed at Dulwich on the Internet. They don't take reservations online, so I had to phone. It took over a week of phoning to get through to them and finally book a table, but we weren't disappointed. The whole experience was wonderful. The portions were quite small, but the food was perfectly cooked and our waiter made us feel really special. All their food is organic and comes from their own gardens, so the menu changes according to the season – a wonderful idea! We'll certainly go back!

The restaurant that wasn't there

Have you ever been fooled by fake reviews online? Have you gone to a restaurant with five-star reviews only to find the food was terrible when you got there? And have you ever wished you could do something about it? Well, that's what London journalist Oobah Butler did. He managed to make his own garden shed into a five-star-rated restaurant, complete with a fake website and fake reviews.

Butler had always been concerned that online restaurant reviews might not always be genuine and that some of the people who wrote them had never actually eaten in the places they reviewed. Then one day in April, while sitting in his garden shed at home, he had an idea: if people were happy to believe anything they read online, maybe it would be possible not just to fake a restaurant review but to fake a restaurant itself. So he set out to make his garden shed into a top-rated London restaurant.

He created a website for The Shed at Dulwich, gave his street as the address (but no house number) and called it a 'reservation-only restaurant'. Then he made up an attractive menu with each dish named after a particular feeling – Love, Happy, Comfort and so on. He also took photos of the dishes, using things he found around the house – a kitchen sponge covered in coffee grounds, dishwasher tablets and shaving cream – all beautifully arranged on plates to look like expensive dishes. And then he submitted his restaurant to online review sites and waited.

Setting up the website was easy, but becoming well known was going to be a little more difficult. He started out ranked at 18,149, so he needed some convincing reviews, and these needed to be written by real people in different places to avoid the anti-spam technology used by review websites. So he contacted all his friends and acquaintances and asked them to write reviews.

To his surprise, a few weeks later people started phoning to make reservations. As the restaurant didn't exist, he had to reply that they were fully booked for weeks in advance, and this made the restaurant appear even more popular. Over the next month, the phone kept ringing, and he also had enquiries from people who were interested in working at The Shed and from companies who wanted to send him free samples of products.

Six months later, The Shed was ranked number 30 online out of all London restaurants, and he was receiving enquiries by phone and email from all over the world. Then in November, he found out that The Shed was London's top-rated restaurant.

He wasn't sure what to do next, but at this point he felt that it wasn't worth pretending any longer. So he decided to make his shed into a real restaurant. He put out a few chairs and tables and held an opening party for selected guests, serving microwaved meals bought from a local supermarket. The guests seemed to enjoy eating their microwaved food, and one couple even asked if they could come again.

So perhaps they really did think it was the best restaurant in London!

d Read the article again and make notes in answer to these questions.

1 What gave Oobah Butler the idea? *sitting in her garden*
2 How did he keep the location secret? *nev can go there*
3 How did he get positive reviews? *friends before*
4 What was unusual about the menu? *dish with emote*
5 How did he create the dishes pictured on the website? *with*
6 At what point did he open the restaurant? *when is tab dish necessary*
7 What kind of food did he serve?
microwaled food from local Super.

e 💬 What do you think about this story? Decide which comment(s) you agree with. Explain your answer(s).

1 This shows that online reviews are a waste of time.
2 It's easy to deceive people online, so you should be careful what you read.
3 What Oobah Butler did was wrong and he should feel bad about it.
4 Some people waste a lot of money on things just because they are fashionable.

2 GRAMMAR Verb patterns

a Match the verb patterns in sentences 1–4 with rules a–d.

1 ☐ **Setting up** the website was easy.
2 ☐ At this point he felt that it wasn't worth **pretending** any longer.
3 ☐ The guests seemed to enjoy **eating** their microwaved food.
4 ☐ He also had enquiries from people who were interested in **working** at The Shed.

We use verb + *-ing*:
a after prepositions
b after certain verbs (e.g., *keep, start, love*)
c after some expressions (e.g., *it's worth, it's no use*)
d as the subject of a sentence

b Match the verb patterns in sentences 1–4 with rules a–d.

1 ☐ People are happy **to believe** anything they read online.
2 ☐ Oobah Butler managed **to make** his garden shed into a five-star-rated restaurant.
3 ☐ They needed to be written by real people in different places **to avoid** anti-spam technology.
4 ☐ He wasn't sure what **to do** next.

We use an infinitive:
a after question words
b after certain verbs (e.g., *want, plan, seem, decide*)
c after certain adjectives (e.g., *difficult, good, important*)
d to show purpose

c ≫ Now go to Grammar Focus 8B on p. 158.

d Write the correct form of the verbs in brackets. Then choose an ending or add your own idea to make it true for you.

1 I enjoy *shopping* (shop) *for clothes* / *with friends* / …
2 I'm planning *to get* (get) *a new phone* / *new shoes* / …
3 It's difficult *to ch* (choose) *clothes* / *music* / … for other people.
4 I know how *to write* (write) *a good review* / *blog* / …
5 I think it's worth *spending* (spend) a lot of money on a(n) *meal in a restaurant* / *good haircut* / … .
6 I'm not interested in *heari* (hear) about *people's problems* / *new shops and restaurants* / …
7 I often *walk around the shops* / *look online* / *to look* (see) if there's anything I want *to buy* (buy).
8 *Going* (go) to *language classes* / *the gym* / … is a good way to meet new people.

e 💬 Compare your sentences in 2d. Can you find anyone who has four or more statements that are the same as yours?

3 LISTENING

a 💬 You are going to hear an expert on digital marketing talking about fake reviews. What do you think he will say about these topics?

• whether you can trust reviews
• how hotels and restaurants get positive reviews
• how review sites fight against fake reviews

b ▶ 08.07 Listen to the interview. Did the expert talk about any of the things you mentioned?

c ▶08.07 Listen again and decide if the sentences are true (*T*) or false (*F*). Correct the false sentences.

1 Nearly all customers read online reviews.
2 Most people are influenced by positive reviews. ~~T~~ F
3 If a customer promises to write a positive review, they usually write it. F
4 'Opinion spam' means that someone is paid to write a fake review. T
5 If Amazon finds a fake reviewer, it always takes legal action. T
6 TripAdvisor employs teams of people to identify fake reviewers. F
7 The expert says it's best to read the negative reviews instead of the positive ones. F
8 Fake reviews usually have fewer personal details than genuine ones. F

d 💬 Work in a small group. Discuss the questions.

1 What do you think of the expert's advice? Do you read reviews in the way he suggests?
2 When was the last time you did the following?
• wrote a review about a place or a product
• thought of writing a review, but forgot or decided not to

4 VOCABULARY Reporting verbs

a Complete the sentences from the interview. Which verbs from the box do you think the expert used?

advise   ask   were offering   persuade   promise
recommend   threaten   warn

1 You can _persu_ customers to give you a good review. ask
2 Customers usually _prom_ to write a good review and then they forget all about it.
3 You can't really _ask_ a customer to write a review for _persu_ you – it's up to them.
4 They found websites that _were off_ to write 10 positive reviews for $85.
5 They can _warn_ them not to continue.
6 They can _threa_ to take them to court.
7 I would certainly _rec_ reading both the good and the bad reviews. _comm_
8 And I'd also _advice_ people to read the review carefully to see what they really say.

b ▶08.08 Listen to the sentences and check what the expert actually said.

c Write the verbs from 4a in the table.

Verb + *to* + infinitive	Verb + object + *to* + infinitive	Verb + verb + *-ing*
offer ~~admitted~~ promise were offering threaten agree, refuse	ask persuade warn advise remind	recommend suggest admit

d Read these examples. Add the verbs in their infinitive form to the table.

1 Because there was no hot water, the hotel **agreed** to give us a 10% discount.
2 We liked the hotel so much that I **suggested** staying another night.
3 The food was so bad that I **refused** to pay for it.
4 Twice I had to **remind** the waiter to bring me some water.
5 My colleague **admitted** to stealing from the office.
   ↳ exception

e ≫ Now go to Vocabulary Focus 8B on p. 141.

5 SPEAKING

a You're going to talk about an experience you've had. Make notes about one of the topics below.

• A time when you recommended something to someone (e.g., a restaurant or a film) or someone recommended something to you
• A time when someone warned you not to do something
• A time when you admitted making a mistake. What had you done? How did you feel? How did other people react?
• A time when you refused to do something. What did you refuse to do? Why did you refuse to do it?
• A time you or someone else promised to do something but didn't do it. What was it?

b 💬 Take turns to talk about your experience for at least a minute. Has anyone in your group had a similar experience?

I recommended my favourite restaurant to a colleague. He went there for dinner and later I found out that …

Something similar happened when I went to a coffee shop that my brother recommended. While I was there, …

8C EVERYDAY ENGLISH
On the whole, I prefer taking action shots

1 LISTENING

a 💬 Discuss the questions.

1 Have you had any good news to share recently? Have you been told any good news? What was it?
2 How do you usually share your good news – by text, online, in person?

b 💬 Look at the photo. What do you think is happening? How do you think Becky is feeling?

c ⏯ 08.09 Watch or listen to Part 1. Answer the questions.

1 What does Becky ask questions about in the interview?
2 How does Becky think the interview went?

d ⏯ 08.09 Watch or listen to Part 1 again. Complete each sentence with one or two words.

1 Rachel is worried that there's not enough _____ in the area for two florists.
2 Becky prefers taking _____.
3 The course can include a _____ in a local gallery.
4 There are normally two _____ a year.
5 Becky found her interview more _____ than she was expecting.
6 They will tell her _____ whether she got a place.

e 💬 Discuss the questions.

1 Do you think Rachel is right to be worried about the new florist's in her area? Do you know of an area in your town/city with lots of the same types of shops/restaurants?
2 Would you like to do the photography course that Becky has applied for? Why / Why not?

2 USEFUL LANGUAGE Generalising

a ▶ 08.10 Listen and complete the sentences with the phrases in the box.

generally   normally   on the whole   tends to   typically

1 But I think, _____, I prefer taking action shots.
2 It _____ either be working at a local gallery on a photography exhibition, or working with a professional photographer as an assistant.
3 The placement _____ lasts two weeks.
4 Yes, _____, each class has two opportunities to go on study visits per year.
5 Well, _____ they don't tell you during the interview …

b <u>Underline</u> the phrases for generalising in these sentences.

1 It can be difficult to relax at the end of the day. I find my yoga class really helpful for that.
2 As a rule, I'm not very good at interviews – I get too nervous.
3 I don't usually spend much time worrying about things that haven't happened yet.

c Are the sentences in 2b true for you? If not, change them to make them true.

3 CONVERSATION SKILLS Being vague

a Replace the words in **bold** with the words in the box.

a couple of   sort   that sort of thing

1 I prefer taking action shots – sport and **stuff like that**.
2 You have **a few** portraits in your portfolio.
3 I'm not very good with that **kind** of thing.

b Complete the second sentence in each pair using vague language so that it means the same as the first sentence. More than one answer might be possible.

a couple of   that sort/kind of thing
things/stuff like that

1 I like swimming, playing tennis and jogging.
I like swimming and _____ .
2 Everything went well except for one or two problems.
Everything went well except for _____ problems.
3 I'm going to the supermarket. I need some milk, eggs, bread and cheese.
I'm going to the supermarket. I need some milk and _____ .

4 LISTENING

a 💬 Look at the photos. Discuss the questions.

1 What news do you think Tina has about the new shop?
  a The builders have stopped work.
  b It's going to be a clothes shop.
  c It has closed down.

2 What news do you think Becky might receive?
  a She's got a new job as a photographer.
  b She's got some money to help her do the course.
  c She's got a place on the photography course.

b ■ ▶ 08.11 Watch or listen to Part 2 and check your ideas.

5 PRONUNCIATION
The sounds /h/ and /w/

a ▶ 08.12 Listen to these sentences. What sounds do the underlined words begin with?

1 Pretty well, I think, on the whole.
2 What was the question?
3 I was there for around two hours.

b ▶ 08.13 Match the words in the box with the sound each word begins with. Listen and check.

white   honest   hotel   wrap   who   work

• /h/ e.g., happy:
• /w/ e.g., water:
• first letter silent:

c ▶ 08.14 Listen to the following sentences. Choose the word you hear.

1 You can eat / heat the food up in the microwave.
2 He wrote on the board invite / in white.
3 A few weeks ago, she lost her earring / hearing.
4 The man you are looking for is the one in the west / vest.
5 I hate / ate the food that my daughter cooked.

6 SPEAKING

💬 Ask your partner for advice on one of these topics:

• a course you would like to do
• a local restaurant for a special occasion
• an area of your town/city to live in

> I'd like to take my sister out for her birthday to that new French restaurant.

> I've heard that it's quite expensive. But, on the whole, the food is very good.

✓ UNIT PROGRESS TEST

CHECK YOUR PROGRESS

You can now do the Unit Progress Test.

1 LISTENING AND SPEAKING

a 💬 Look at the three photos of air travel below. What is happening in each photo?

b 💬 In your opinion, what are the best and worst things about air travel?

c You are going to listen to someone talking about a news story. Some of the key words from the story are in the box. What do you think happened?

> 11-year-old boy   Manchester   mother   shopping
> airport   security   plane   Rome   complained

d 💬 Compare your stories with other students.

e ▶ 08.15 Listen to the story. How close was it to your story?

f Do we know if these statements are true? Write true (T), false (F) or don't know (DK).

1. ☐F The speaker read the story in a newspaper.
2. ☐ The boy was alone in the shopping centre.
3. ☐DK His mother went to the airport to look for him.
4. ☐ The boy spoke to the children in the other family.
5. ☐ The boy didn't have a boarding pass.
6. ☐ They didn't count the passengers before they took off.
7. ☐ The airline offered the mother a free flight in the future.
8. ☐ It's the first time something like this has ever happened.

g ▶ 08.15 Listen again and check your answers.

h 💬 Discuss the questions.

1. Do you think something like this could happen in your country?
2. Do you think airport security in your country is
   a too strict?
   b not strict enough?
   c about right?

2 READING

a Look at the headline of a similar news story below. What do you think happened? Choose a or b.

1. a He drove the car himself.
   b He was a passenger in the car.
2. a He flew the plane himself.
   b He was a passenger on the plane.

b Read the story quickly and check your answers to 2a.

c Read the story again. Make notes about things that are the same as in the story you listened to.

13-YEAR-OLD BOY DRIVES TO AIRPORT AND FLIES ACROSS THE USA

Kenton Weaver is 13 years old and has no photo ID. But that didn't stop him from taking his father's car in the middle of the night, driving more than 20 miles to a Florida airport and taking two connecting flights to San José, California. 'I really enjoyed it,' said Kenton.

Kenton's mother, Kim Casey, lives just half an hour from San José airport in Fresno, California, but the boy's father, Dean Weaver, thinks it was the journey itself that interested the boy. According to Dean, his son is fascinated by aeroplanes. 'He'll do anything to go to an airport,' Dean said. 'He wants to be a pilot.'

Kenton did not own a credit card, passport, driving licence or photo ID of any kind. Yet he was able somehow to buy a plane ticket, go through airport security, fly to Chicago and catch his connecting flight to San José without any problems. His father said it is possible Kenton used the numbers from one of his own credit cards to buy the ticket online.

3 WRITING SKILLS Summarising information

a Read a summary of the news story. Which words in **bold** tell us … ?

1 that the person is reporting a story they read or heard about somewhere

2 that the person is commenting on what happened

There was an **incredible** story in the newspaper last week. **Apparently,** a 13-year-old boy took his father's car, drove it to the airport and then took two flights from Florida to California to see his mother, who lives there. **Amazingly,** he did all this without a credit card, ID or driving licence. **It seems that** he used his father's credit card number to buy the plane ticket online and no one asked him any questions. **Fortunately,** they found him and everything was all right in the end.

b ▶08.15 Listen to the story in 1e again. Write down any more words used to comment on the story.
of course, incredibly, I guess, ---

c Compare the sentences below with the highlighted sentence in the summary in 3a. Answer questions 1–4.

A boy of 13 took his father's car. The boy drove it to the airport. The boy took two flights from Florida to California. The boy flew there to see his mother. His mother lives in California.

1 How many sentences are in 3c?
2 What words are added to connect these sentences in 3a?
3 What words are left out or changed in the summary in 3a? Why?
4 Why is the summary in 3a better than the sentences in 3c?

d Here is a different summary of the same news story. Connect the sentences to make four or five sentences. Use the words in the box to help you (you can use the words more than once).

and   before   but   who   with

who
I read an incredible news story about a boy.
Apparently he flew alone from Florida to California.
He was only 13.
He managed to fly alone across America.
He even changed planes in Chicago.
He bought a ticket online.
He used his father's credit card number.
No one at the airport asked him any questions.
He even took his father's car.
He parked it in the airport car park.
He got on the plane.

e 💬 Work in pairs and compare your summaries. Are they the same?

4 WRITING An email about a news story

a 💬 Work in pairs. Choose one of the headlines below or a story in the news at the moment. Discuss and make notes about what happened.

POLICE FIND MISSING GIRL

Tiger escapes from ZOO

MAN JUMPS FROM PLANE – and SURVIVES

SURFER ESCAPES SHARK ATTACK

b Work in pairs. Write an email to a friend, summarising the story in a few sentences. Include words or phrases to comment on the story.

c 💬 Work with another pair. Read each other's emails and answer the questions.

1 Is the information clear and in a logical order?
2 Is the amount of information right?
3 Are there too many or too few sentences? Are they connected in the best way?
4 Can you improve the summary?

d 💬 Tell another pair about your news story.

UNIT 8
Review and extension

1 GRAMMAR

a Read the text and <u>underline</u> the correct answers.

'Internet users worry about [1]*to lose / losing* private information online, but they don't mind [2]*to see / seeing* advertisements that are personally directed at them.' That's what the Digital Advertising Alliance discovered when they conducted a survey [3]*to find out / finding out* how consumers feel about targeted advertising. Only 4% said they didn't like the idea of [4]*to get / getting* targeted advertising.

Consumers seem [5]*to understand / understanding* that adverts make it possible [6]*to have / having* free websites: 75% of people said that they didn't want [7]*to pay / paying* for websites with no advertising on them.

b Complete the reported speech.

1 'I'll never go to that hairdresser again,' you said.
You said *you wouldn't* to that hairdresser again.
2 Kim asked Dev, 'What are you going to buy?'
Kim asked Dev *what she was going* to buy.
3 The editor said to me, 'You may need to rewrite this story.'
The editor told me *that I might need* this story.
4 The interviewer asked me, 'Have you ever written a blog?'
The interviewer asked me *if I had ever written* a blog.

2 VOCABULARY

a Complete the sentences with a suitable noun. Sometimes more than one answer is possible.

1 You know so much about politics. You should create your own *podcast* about it.
2 I'm really excited about this project. We brainstormed some amazing *ideas* in the meeting today.
3 If you're worried, you should have a *talk* about it with your manager.
4 I watched a really funny *episode* of that new comedy series last night. Did you see it?
5 I spend too much time checking my *newsfeed* on social media, but I love to stay up to date with what's happening.

b Write a sentence with each of the reporting verbs below.

1 advise
2 warn
3 threaten
4 recommend
5 promise

3 WORDPOWER *in / on* + noun

a Look at the phrases in the box and <u>underline</u> the cor words in the rules.

in a magazine   in capital letters   in cash
in the photo   on a website   on the label

1 We use *in / on* + flat surfaces like *wall*, *page* and *screen*.
2 We use *in / on* + *film*, *photo* and *picture* (when we talk ab what they show).
3 We use *in / on* + the Internet, the radio, TV, Facebook and Twitter.
4 We use *in / on* + written and printed material (e.g., *the newspaper*, *a sentence*, *an email*).
5 We use *in / on* with sizes (e.g., *12*, *medium*), currencies (e.g., *pounds*, *dollars*, *euros*) and before *stock*.

b Complete the sentences with *in* or *on*.

1 What can you see *in* the picture?
2 I've got some photos of Paul *on* my phone.
3 The answer was *in* the first paragraph.
4 Was it strange to see your name *in* print?
5 The full article is *on* page 4.
6 They were talking about his new film *on* the radio.
7 Did you pay *in* cash?
8 How much is £30 *in* euros?
9 The words 'Not for sale' were *on* the sign.
10 **A** I'm looking for these shoes *in* size 9.
   B I'm afraid we don't have them *in* stock at the moment.
11 Your seat number is *on* the ticket.
12 If you write *in* pencil, it doesn't matter if you make a mistake.

c 💬 Take turns to test each other on the phrases.

> The Internet?

> On the Internet.

> Pencil?

> In pencil.

✪ CAN DO OBJECTIVES

- Talk about films and TV
- Give extra information
- Recommend and respond to recommendations
- Write an article

ENTERTAINMENT

UNIT **9**

GETTING STARTED

a 💬 Look at the photo and answer the questions.

1 Who are these people?
2 What are they doing and why?
3 What do you think the people watching think of the performance? Why?

b 💬 Are there similar street entertainers in your area? Do you like them?

c 💬 What other kinds of street entertainers can you think of? Which ones do you like or not like?

103

9A BINGE WATCHING HAS BEEN CRITICISED BY DOCTORS

1 LISTENING

a 💬 Trailers are adverts for films or TV series that are coming soon. Discuss the questions about trailers.

1 Do you watch trailers for films and TV series? Why / Why not?
2 Do trailers usually make you want to watch the film or series? Why / Why not?
3 Think of a time you watched a film / TV series because you liked the trailer. Were you pleased or disappointed? Explain your answer.
4 Which of these things make a good trailer? Are any other things important?
☐ a lot of short scenes
☐ one or two longer scenes
☐ only scenes with music – no talking
☐ a description of what the film or series is about

b ▶ 09.01 Listen to Ava and Lucas talking about trailers. Answer the questions.

1 Who was disappointed? _____
2 Who talks about some research? _____
3 What organisations use the research? _____

c ▶ 09.01 Listen again and answer the questions.

1 What does Ava think is a key problem with trailers?
2 Why is she surprised that they are expensive to make?
3 How did researchers check the facial expressions of people watching trailers?
4 What did this tell the researchers?
5 How did they use this information?
6 What are two important features of a successful trailer?
7 Who isn't worried about the way film companies make trailers? Why not?

d 💬 Think of a trailer you have seen recently. Did it follow the structure Lucas describes? Did it make you want to watch the film or TV series? Why / Why not?

2 VOCABULARY -ed / -ing adjectives

a Underline the correct adjectives to complete the sentences.

1 I watched this true crime programme last night – it was really *disappointing / disappointed*.

2 They make TV series and films look a lot more *interesting / interested* than they are.
3 So, from the facial expressions, they could work out whether the people were *amusing / amused* or *fascinating / fascinated* or *boring / bored*.
4 But it also meant film companies could use the information to come up with a model for making really *motivating / motivated* trailers.
5 It's a bit *depressing / depressed* – more algorithms to make us do things.
6 And I'm always *interesting / interested* in finding out about the latest marketing trick.

b Look at the two examples.

I found the film **boring**.
I was so **bored** by the film that I fell asleep.

Which adjective in **bold** ... ?

1 describes how the speaker felt _____
2 describes what the film was like _____

c ▶ 09.02 **Pronunciation** Listen to the -ed adjectives. How is the final -ed pronounced in each one? Complete the table with the words in the box.

disappointed   interested   amused
fascinated   bored   motivated   depressed

/d/	/t/	/ɪd/

d Complete the sentences with the -ed or -ing adjective form of the verbs in the box.

amuse   depress   disappoint   fascinate   interest   motivate

1 Nicole and I are going to a concert next week. Are you _____ in coming, too?
2 Some people find winter sad and _____, but I like it.
3 That new restaurant was a little _____ – the food wasn't nearly as good as the review said.
4 I thought Chiara would laugh at my joke, but she wasn't _____.
5 My test scores were high, so I feel very _____ to keep studying hard.
6 The book tells an absolutely _____ story of growing up in New York. It was an amazing read!

e Make notes about these topics.

• a time you felt disappointed
• a book or film that you found interesting
• a film or TV series that you find amusing
• something you find motivating to work/study hard for
• something you think is boring
• what you do when you feel depressed

f 💬 Take turns to tell each other about each topic. Ask your partner questions about their ideas.

3 READING

a 💬 Discuss the questions.

1 Do you sometimes watch three or more episodes of a TV series one after the other? Why / Why not?

2 What are some of the advantages and disadvantages of watching TV in this way?

b Read the article. What advantages and disadvantages does it mention? Were they the same as your ideas in question 2?

c 💬 Read the article again and make notes for each category below. Compare your ideas with your partner.

1 I didn't know about this.

2 I agree with this.

3 I don't agree with this.

4 This is something I've done or felt.

To BINGE or not to BINGE ...

Last week, a new TV series was uploaded to your streaming service and it's great. Two nights ago, you watched the first episode, and then last night you watched episode two. It ended with a really exciting cliffhanger* and you didn't know what was going to happen next – you just had to watch the next episode. And then the next. Then suddenly it was 1.30 am, and today you're sitting at work feeling exhausted. Sound familiar? Admit it – you've been binge watching.

In the past, TV viewing was controlled by what was on the TV channels. But things have changed with the growth of streaming services like Netflix and Amazon Prime. Instead of waiting a week for each new episode of a TV series to become available, we can now get them all at once and watch as many episodes as we like. In particular, young people are attracted to TV series they can binge on. In a recent study in the USA, 76% of adults between the ages of 18 and 29 admitted cancelling other plans in order to stay up all night and binge watch a series.

So why do we do it? The simple answer is that it makes us feel good. When we binge watch, we get a sense of enjoyment due to the fact that dopamine, a natural feel-good hormone, is released into our brains. Binge watchers say that a good TV series is a great way to relax and escape from some of the stress of our day-to-day lives. They also like the fact that episodes are long and are a pleasant change from the kind of bite-sized entertainment that is found on social media.

However, binge watching has been criticised by doctors and other health experts. They say it encourages lack of activity, which can lead to poor fitness and problems with weight. They also say it can have a negative effect on our sleep. So, having stayed up until 1:30 am watching your favourite series, you then have trouble getting to sleep. Finally, binge watching can cause psychological problems. Some viewers talk about a sense of loneliness and emptiness when a series ends, and they say that binge watching is an addictive behaviour.

*cliffhanger a film, TV programme or story that is exciting because the ending is uncertain until it happens

The experts say that many of the harmful effects of binge viewing can be reduced by following some simple rules:

- Set a daily time limit on the number of hours you watch TV and stick to it.
- Choose a room where you watch TV and only watch it there, but don't choose your bedroom – that's for sleeping.
- Watch an episode from three different series and not the same one – if you think you need to watch three episodes in an evening.
- Take a break between episodes and do something different for 10 minutes.
- Stop watching anything 30 minutes before you go to bed.

Many TV streamers don't believe that binge watching is harmful. They say it's like reading a book you can't put down, and that's never been considered a health problem. You get lost in the story and you have to keep going. These TV series are also like books because to really appreciate them, you need to stay with the story and feel they are part of your life.

Whether you see binge watching as harmful or harmless, the opportunity to stream your favourite programme on demand isn't going away any time soon. More and more series are being made by a wider range of streaming companies. The writing and the production quality are improving all the time. These programmes are made to pull us in and keep us in front of our TVs.

4 GRAMMAR The passive

a Look at the examples of the passive in **bold** and underline the correct words to complete the rules.

Last week, a new TV series **was uploaded** to your streaming service.
Young people **are attracted** to TV series they can binge on.

We often use the passive when:
1 we *know* / *don't know* who did an action
2 it's *obvious* / *not obvious* who did an action
3 it's *important* / *not important* who did an action

The first episode **was directed by** Martin Scorsese.
The whole episode **was filmed with** a smartphone camera.

4 We can use *by* / *with* + noun after a passive verb to say what was used to do the action.
5 We can use *by* / *with* + noun after a passive verb to say who/what did the action.

b Read the sentences. Underline the passive verbs and circle the active verbs.

1 In the past, TV viewing was controlled by TV channels.
2 Some viewers talk about a sense of loneliness and emptiness when a series ends.
3 Dopamine, a natural feel-good hormone, is released into our brains.
4 Seventy-six percent of adults between the ages of 18 and 29 admitted cancelling other plans in order to stay up all night and binge watch a series.
5 However, binge watching has been criticised by doctors and other health experts.
6 Finally, binge watching can cause psychological problems.
7 The experts say that many of the harmful effects of binge viewing can be reduced by following some simple rules.
8 More and more series are being made by a wider range of streaming companies.
9 The writing and the production quality are improving all the time.

c Which of the passive forms are … ?

1 ☐ present simple   4 ☐ present perfect
2 ☐ present continuous 5 ☐ a modal verb
3 ☐ past simple

d Now go to Grammar Focus 9A on p. 160.

e ≫ Communication 9A 💬 You are going to read about video and audio streaming services. Student A: Read the text below and choose the correct form of the verbs to complete the sentences. Student B: Go to p. 131. Read the text and choose the correct form of the verbs to complete the sentences.

Student A

Video streaming facts and figures
Video *has streamed* / *has been streamed* since the early 1990s. It *started* / *was started* by a company called Starlight Networks. Now the largest streaming site in the world is YouTube, which *has* / *is had* over two billion users worldwide. The global video streaming service *values* / *is valued* at about $160 billion. An average YouTube viewer *spends* / *is spent* 40 minutes a day watching streamed video.

f 💬 Work in pairs. Share the information you learned about streaming services.

5 SPEAKING

a You are going to recommend a film or TV programme that you like. Make notes on as many of the questions as you can.

- What is it called?
- What kind of film or programme is it?
- What happens? Who are the main characters?
- When and where is it set?
- Who directed it?
- Is it based on a book or a true story?
- Who is in it – any famous actors or celebrities?
- Does it have special effects?

b Write three reasons why you like this film or TV programme.

c 💬 Take turns to recommend your film or TV programme. Have you watched the films or TV programmes you hear about? If so, do you like them, too? If not, would you like to watch them? Why / Why not?

9B | I WENT TO A CONCERT THAT CHANGED MY LIFE

Learn to give extra information

G Defining and non-defining relative clauses
V Music; Word-building (nouns)

1 VOCABULARY Music

a 💬 What's happening in the photos below? Match the words to photos 1–3.

audience	DJ	festival	guitar	musician
orchestra	perform	play live

b ▶09.04 Listen to four clips of music and <u>underline</u> the correct words.

1 They are playing *live* / *in a recording studio*.
2 You can hear a *DJ* / *musician*.
3 Someone is *performing* / *enjoying* a piece of music.
4 You can hear *a choir* / *an orchestra*.

c 💬 Discuss the questions. Use a dictionary to check the words in **bold**.

1 When and where did you last listen to a song?
2 What are your favourite **albums** and your favourite **tracks**?
3 Do you like making **playlists**?
4 When and where did you last sing or play a musical **instrument**?

2 LISTENING

a 💬 How many different musical experiences can you think of? Write a list.

going to concerts, singing in a choir …

b 💬 Compare your lists. Which of these experiences do you like taking part in or going to? Why?

c ▶09.05 Listen to three people talk about musical experiences that changed their lives. Match the speakers with photos a–c.

Annie _____   Jeff _____   Erica _____

d ▶09.05 Listen again and make notes in the table.

	What kind of music do they talk about?	What or where was the event?	How did it change their life?
Annie			
Jeff			
Erica			

e 💬 Talk about which of the musical experiences you would like to have. Explain your answer.

3 GRAMMAR Defining and non-defining relative clauses

a Look at the <u>underlined</u> relative clauses in the sentences. Circle the noun phrase which each relative clause tells you more about.

A. *Defining relative clauses*
1 Samba is (a kind of Brazilian music) <u>which also has African rhythms</u>.
2 It's a drum <u>you play with your hands</u>.
3 I was sitting next to one of the people <u>who was in my group</u>.
4 They were all about the place <u>where he grew up</u>.

B. *Non-defining relative clauses*
5 I was with my brother and a friend of his, <u>who was older than me</u>, and we were listening to Jay-Z.
6 I started noticing the words, <u>which were really different from the songs I normally listened to</u>.

b Answer the questions.

1 Which kind of relative clause, defining (*D*) or non-defining (*ND*), ... ?
☐ defines what the noun phrase means and makes it more specific
☐ only adds extra information about the noun phrase
☐ has a comma before it, and sometimes after it
☐ has no comma before it
2 Where does a relative clause come in a sentence?
a immediately after the noun phrase it refers to
b always at the end of the sentence.
3 Make a list of the relative pronouns in 3a.
which, _____, _____

4 Look at the sentence and complete the rule.
It's a drum (which) you play with your hands.
In *defining* / *non-defining* relative clauses, you can leave out the pronoun if it is the *subject* / *object* of the relative clause.

c ▶ 09.06 **Pronunciation** Listen to the sentences. In which sentence do you hear a pause before the relative pronoun in **bold**?
1 People **who** sing a lot always seem happy.
2 Carly, **who**'s a fantastic singer, works in a café during the day.

d ≫ Now go to Grammar Focus 9B on p. 160.

e 💬 Take turns to describe the words in the box using a sentence with a defining relative clause. Guess which word your partner is describing.

| album | audience | choir | concert | DJ | festival |
| guitarist | musician | orchestra | playlist | track |

> It's something that you can download.
>
> An album?
>
> No, it's something that you can find on an album.
>
> A track!

f Add a non-defining relative clause to each of these sentences. Use *who*, *which* or *where*.
1 The concert at the Town Hall, ... , was a bit disappointing.
2 He learned the guitar from his uncle, ...
3 There's a good café near here called *The Music Room*, ...
4 They decided to sell their piano, ...

g 💬 Work in small groups. Read out only the relative clause you added. Can the others guess which sentence it goes with?

The THREE BEST MUSIC FESTIVALS *you've probably never heard of*

FUJI ROCK FESTIVAL, Japan

A celebration of rock and electronic music at the foot of Mount Fuji

This is Japan's largest outdoor music event. It's held every year at the Naeba Ski Resort. You can enjoy the beauty of the forests and rivers as you walk (often a very long way!) from one stage to another. This is one of the world's safest and most environmentally friendly festivals, which is probably why everyone's happiness and creativity levels are so high!

Past performers include: Kendrick Lamar, Gorillaz, Janelle Monáe.

ROSKILDE, Denmark

A rock festival that gives all its profits to charity

Here, you can enjoy performances of rock, punk, heavy metal, hip-hop and indie by musicians from around the world. The organisers donate all the money they make to projects for the development of society and culture.

Don't forget that summer days are long in Denmark. It doesn't get dark until 11 pm, and it starts getting light at 3:30 am.

Past performers include: Metallica, Bruce Springsteen, Rihanna

4 READING AND VOCABULARY
Word-building (nouns)

a 💬 Discuss the questions.

1 Have you ever been to a music festival?
2 If so, what kind of music was there? Did you enjoy it? Why / Why not?
3 If not, do you know of any music festivals you would like to go to? What are they like?

b Read *The three best music festivals you've probably never heard of*. Which festival would you rather go to? Why?

c Read the article again and match the comments with the festivals. Write Fuji Rock Festival (*F*), Roskilde (*R*) or Comunité Festival (*C*).

1 ☐ 'Even the toilet paper is made from recycled cups from last year's festival!'
2 ☐ 'I'm glad I took a good pair of walking boots with me.'
3 ☐ 'The nights were so short!'
4 ☐ 'I was happy to get away from huge crowds of people.'
5 ☐ 'It's really nice to know that all the money goes to good causes.'
6 ☐ 'The water was so clear!'

COMUNITÉ FESTIVAL, Mexico
Eco-friendly festival in the Mexican jungle

This is a small-scale festival where you can enjoy Latin American, electronic and dance music in the jungle atmosphere of the Gulf of Mexico. If it gets too hot, just dive into one of the natural freshwater pools around the site, or head off to a nearby beach. The festival is held every January and some of the money goes towards protecting coral reefs in the Caribbean.

Past performers include: James Holden, Auntie Flo, Kaitlin Aurelia Smith

d Complete the table with words from the article.

Adjective	Noun		Verb
beautiful	1		
	2		celebrate
charitable	3		
creative	4		create
cultural	5		
	6		develop
happy	7		
musical	8	(person)	
organised	9	(person)	organise
	10	(person)	perform
	11		

e ▶️ 09.08 **Pronunciation** Listen to the words in 4d. Notice how the stress sometimes changes position as we change the form of the word. Mark the stress on each word.

f ▶️ 09.08 Listen again and practise saying the words.

g Write the noun forms of the words. Use one suffix from the box for each pair of words, and make spelling changes if necessary.

-ance/-ence -(a)tion -er/-or -ist -ity -ness -ty

1 loyal, honest: loyalty, _____
2 fit, sad: _____ , _____
3 able, responsible: _____ , _____
4 design, act: _____ , _____
5 appear, patient: _____ , _____
6 piano, guitar: _____ , _____
7 locate, relax: _____ , _____

h 💬 Talk about which of the qualities in the box are important for the people 1–4. Which qualities are not needed? Say why.

beauty creativity honesty intelligence
kindness musical ability responsibility

1 a pop singer 2 a friend 3 a teacher 4 a politician

5 SPEAKING

a You are going to talk about an interesting or exciting experience in your life that involved music. Make notes on the questions below.

1 What happened?
2 When was it?
3 Who was with you?
4 Why was it important?
5 Why have you remembered it?

b 💬 Take turns to talk about your experiences and ask follow-up questions.

> I went to hear a band I've been a fan of for years ...

9C EVERYDAY ENGLISH
It's meant to be excellent

1 LISTENING

a 💬 Discuss the questions.

1 How often do you have an evening out with friends? What do you usually do?
2 How easy is it to organise an evening out with your friends? Do you all have the same interests? Do you ever disagree on what you want to do?
3 Which of the activities in the box do you enjoy?

> a meal in a restaurant   a horror film
> a meal at a friend's house   a pop concert
> a play at the theatre

b 🎥 ▶ 09.09 Watch or listen to Part 1. Which activities are mentioned? What do they decide to do in the end?

c 🎥 ▶ 09.09 Watch or listen to Part 1 again. Who … ?

1 suggests going to a jazz club *Becky / Mark*
2 suggests going to a classical music festival
   Becky / Rachel
3 doesn't like classical music *Becky / Tom*
4 suggests a local rock band *Tom / Rachel*
5 hasn't seen a rock band for 10 years *Rachel / Mark*

2 USEFUL LANGUAGE
Recommending and responding

a 🎥 ▶ 09.09 Watch or listen to Part 1 again and tick (✓) the phrases you hear.

1 ☐ That's a great idea!
2 ☐ It's meant to be excellent.
3 ☐ It was highly recommended by …
4 ☐ It's supposed to be really good.
5 ☐ I'm not a big fan of classical music.
6 ☐ Why don't we go and see that local band?
7 ☐ They've had great reviews.
8 ☐ I think you'd love it.
9 ☐ I doubt Mark would be interested.
10 ☐ It sounds really interesting, but …

b Which phrases in 2a … ?

1 give a recommendation or opinion
2 respond to a recommendation

c 💬 Work in groups of three. Use the diagram below to have a conversation.

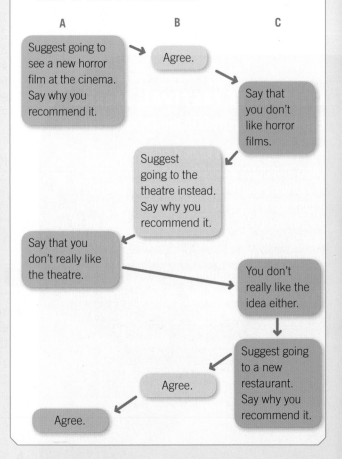

A | B | C

- **A:** Suggest going to see a new horror film at the cinema. Say why you recommend it.
- **B:** Agree.
- **C:** Say that you don't like horror films.
- **B:** Suggest going to the theatre instead. Say why you recommend it.
- **A:** Say that you don't really like the theatre.
- **C:** You don't really like the idea either.
- **A:** Suggest going to a new restaurant. Say why you recommend it.
- **B:** Agree.
- **C:** Agree.

3 PRONUNCIATION Showing contrast

a ▶ 09.10 Listen to the following sentence. Which word is stressed?

Tom likes classical music.

b ▶ 09.11 Listen to these conversations. Decide which word is stressed more in each sentence.

1 **A** You like classical music, don't you?
B No. Tom likes classical music. I like rock music.
(= It's Tom who likes classical music, not me.)
2 **A** Does Tom like pop music?
B No, Tom likes classical music.
(= It's classical music that Tom likes, not pop.)

> When we want to show a contrast (emphasise that something is different), we stress that word more.

c 💬 Work in pairs. Take it in turns to ask the questions and reply, showing contrast by stressing a word.

1 Did you buy the red shoes? (blue)
2 Did you go to the cinema with John? (theatre)
3 Did you see John? (Chris)

4 CONVERSATION SKILLS
Asking someone to wait

a ▶ 09.12 Listen to part of the conversation between Rachel and Becky. Complete the sentences.

1 **Rachel** Wait a _____, I'll just ask Mark.
2 **Becky** _____ on, Tom wants to say something.

b Complete the table with the words in the box.

check   hang   please   second   wait

¹ _____ on Just ² _____	a minute / a ³ _____ / a moment.
One moment, ⁴ _____.	
Let me ⁵ _____ (for you).	

c Which expression is more formal?

d 💬 Work in pairs. Follow the instructions and have a conversation.

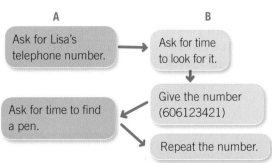

5 LISTENING

a 💬 Tom told Mark to wear something cool. Look at the clothes below.

Which do you think is the coolest? Which do you think Mark will wear?

b 🎥 ▶ 09.13 Watch or listen to Part 2 and check your ideas. What do the others think of Mark's clothes?

c 💬 Discuss the questions.

1 Do you usually spend a lot of time choosing what to wear when you go out? Why / Why not?
2 What kind of clothes do people in your area wear when they go out for the evening (e.g., to a restaurant, to the cinema, to the theatre)?

6 SPEAKING

≫ **Communication 9C** 💬 You're going to have a conversation about what to do today.
Student A: Read the information below. Student B: Go to p. 131.

> **Student A**
> You want to arrange an afternoon with Student B.
> • You would like to go to an exhibition of modern art.
> • You've just eaten, so you don't want to go out for a meal.
> • Someone gave you an advert for a photography exhibition. You have the advert in your bag.

We could go to the modern art exhibition. It's meant to be really interesting.

That sounds OK, but I'm not a big fan of modern art.

☑ UNIT PROGRESS TEST

→ **CHECK YOUR PROGRESS**

You can now do the Unit Progress Test.

9D | SKILLS FOR WRITING
I like going out, but …

Learn to write an article
Ⓦ Contrasting ideas;
The structure of an article

a

1 SPEAKING AND LISTENING

a 💬🗨 Look at photos a–e. If you could win free tickets to go to one of the events, which would you choose? Why?

b ▶09.14 Listen to Anna and her friend Camila. Answer the questions.

1 Who has tickets to the Kendrick Lamar concert?
2 Who doesn't want to go?
3 Why doesn't she want to go?

c Make notes about the topics below. What are the positive and negative points of these ways of listening to music?

- live performances (concerts, etc.)
- recorded performances (albums, films, etc.)

d 💬🗨 Discuss your opinions. Do you prefer live or recorded music? Why?

2 READING

a Read Julia's blog, *Why I prefer to stay at home*. What is her main point?

1 Films are too expensive and it's cheaper to stay at home.
2 It's more comfortable and convenient to watch films and TV series at home.
3 Films are less satisfying than TV programmes.

b Read the blog again and answer the questions.

1 What annoys Julia about cinema audiences?
2 Why were the couple sitting behind her rude?
3 What does she do if she finds a film boring?
4 Why is the length of a TV series sometimes a good thing?

≡ ⌂   💬 ↻ ☰ ✉

Why I prefer to stay at home

1 What was your last experience at the cinema like? I remember the expensive tickets, the long queues and the uncomfortable seats. Does this sound familiar? I love going out to see my friends and going to parties. I like having fun. However, I don't really enjoy going to the cinema any more.

2 To me, the main problem with going to the cinema is the audience. Although many people say that seeing a film at a cinema is a good chance to go out and be sociable, I really hate listening to other people's comments. The last time I went to the cinema, there was a couple behind me who commented loudly on everything. They laughed at everything in the film, really loudly – even at things that weren't funny! I politely asked them to be quiet. Despite this, they continued as if they were watching their own TV. If I watch something at home, I can invite my friends and spend time with people I know and like rather than sitting near noisy strangers.

3 Another reason for staying at home is convenience. I like to watch films and TV programmes when I want to watch them, not at specific times. In spite of my love of films and TV programmes, I don't enjoy all of them. If I'm at home, I can stop the film and watch something else, or I can skip through the boring bits. For example, I was really disappointed with a film I saw last night – so I just turned it off!

4 While I watch a lot of films, I also watch a lot of TV series online now. I really enjoy watching a whole series. It gives characters time to develop in interesting and unexpected ways. In fact, there are so many great TV series to watch, I've hardly got time to go out to the cinema.

5 So these days, when my friends invite me to the cinema, I usually say, 'No, thanks.' I really do prefer to watch films and TV programmes at home. I can choose what I want to watch, I can choose the time when I want to watch it and I can choose who I watch it with. The question really is: why should I go out?

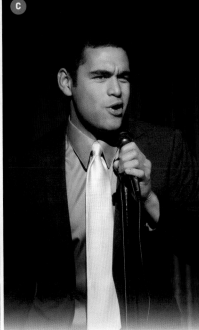

3 WRITING SKILLS Contrasting ideas; The structure of an article

a In the example below, *however* introduces a contrast. Find more examples of expressions used to contrast ideas in Julia's blog.

I like having fun. **However**, I don't really enjoy going to the cinema any more.

b Complete the rules and examples with the words in the box. Use each word twice.

| although | despite | however | in spite of | while |

- *I enjoy films.* ¹_____*, I think I prefer TV series.*
  We can use ²_____ at the beginning of a sentence. It contrasts with an idea in the previous sentence.

- ³_____ / ⁴_____ *cinemas have become more comfortable, they're not as comfortable as my sofa.*
  We can use ⁵_____ and ⁶_____ to introduce a contrasting idea. They are followed by a clause with a verb.

- *The price of a cinema ticket has gone up recently.*
  ⁷_____ / ⁸_____ *the cost, I still love going to the cinema.*
  We can use ⁹_____ and ¹⁰_____ to introduce a contrasting idea. They are followed by a noun or pronoun.

c Match ideas 1–6 with a contrasting idea a–f. Connect the ideas using the words in brackets in the correct position. Write only one sentence, if possible.

1 ☐ I was given two free tickets to a jazz concert (However)
2 ☐ music is something we normally listen to at home (Although)
3 ☐ TV screens have got bigger and bigger (Although)
4 ☐ the beat is very important in hip-hop music (While)
5 ☐ the convenience of watching a film at home (In spite of)
6 ☐ my love of special effects (Despite)

a the words are just as important.
b I don't like that kind of music, so I'll give them away.
c there's nothing like the big screen at a cinema.
d I still want films to have a good story and good acting.
e it's always interesting to watch musicians perform.
f I prefer to see films at a cinema.

d Look at paragraphs 2–4 in Julia's blog. What is the main idea of each paragraph? Choose a or b.

Paragraph 2:
a cinema audiences   b being polite in cinemas
Paragraph 3:
a boring films   b the convenience of staying at home
Paragraph 4:
a the length of TV series   b an alternative to watching films

e 💬 Discuss the questions about Julia's blog.

1 Is the main idea mentioned at the beginning or in the middle of the paragraph?
2 Does Julia sometimes use examples?
3 How does Julia get the reader's attention in paragraph 1, the introduction?
4 In paragraph 5, the conclusion, does Julia introduce new ideas? Why / Why not?

4 WRITING An article

a You are going to write an article about a kind of entertainment you love or hate. Choose one of the topics below or your own idea. Then make notes about questions 1–4.

- music concerts in stadiums or in small clubs
- watching sport in a stadium or live on TV
- classical music or pop music

1 What's your opinion about this topic?
2 What experience do you have with it?
3 What other things do you know about it?
4 What do other people often say about it?

b 💬 Compare your ideas with a partner.

c Plan your article. Follow these instructions:

1 Write down the main ideas of the article.
2 Write down different points for each idea.
3 Think of any examples from your experience.

d Write your article. Make sure you write an introduction and conclusion. Remember to use words or phrases to show contrast.

1 GRAMMAR

a Read the text and <u>underline</u> the correct words.

Can you imagine a film [1]*who / that* had no music? It would be very boring. Here are two talented film composers [2]*what / that* everyone should know about.

John Williams [3]*sees / is seen* as one of the greatest film composers of all time. He [4]*has nominated / has been nominated* for more awards than anyone else, apart from Walt Disney. Williams, [5]*whose / who* music can be heard in the *Harry Potter* and *Star Wars* films, is most famous for working with director Steven Spielberg.

The music for *The Lion King*, *Gladiator*, the *Dark Knight* trilogy and more than 150 other films was written [6]*with / by* German pianist and composer Hans Zimmer. But when he was younger, Zimmer wrote jingles, [7]*which / that* are short songs used in advertising.

b Complete the second sentence so that it means the same as the first sentence (or pair of sentences). Use three words in each gap.

1 The film was based on a book. I loved it when I was a child.
The film was based on a _____ when I was a child.

2 That's the place. The final scene was filmed there.
That's the place _____ scene was filmed.

3 *The Empire Strikes Back* is the second film in the *Star Wars* series. *The Empire Strikes Back* came out in 1980.
The Empire Strikes Back, _____ in 1980, is the second film in the *Star Wars* series.

4 People are forgetting many traditional folk songs.
Many traditional folk songs _____ .

5 They were recording the concert when I was there.
The concert _____ when I was there.

2 VOCABULARY

a Read the text and complete the adjectives with the correct ending, *-ed* or *-ing*.

I stayed at home and binge watched a new animal documentary series this weekend. It was [1]fascinat _____ . I've always been [2]interest _____ in nature, and I wasn't [3]disappoint _____ . The final episode was a bit [4]bor _____ , though. It was all about plastic pollution. I mean, I know it is important to get that message out there, but it was quite [5]depress _____ to watch. I suppose I am more [6]motivat _____ to recycle; it's just that I prefer episodes that are [7]excit _____ and dramatic.

b Complete the sentences with noun forms of the words in brackets.

1 The festival is a _____ of music from different cultures. (celebrate)

2 We'd like to thank the _____ for all their hard work in preparing the show. (organise)

3 This film shows the _____ of the Pacific Islands. (beautiful)

4 The _____ are preparing for their _____ this evening. (music; perform)

3 WORDPOWER *see, look at, watch, hear, listen to*

a Match questions 1–8 with responses a–h.

1 ☐ Amy! Amy! Why isn't she answering?
2 ☐ What's that noise?
3 ☐ Have you found another painting?
4 ☐ Are they dancing?
5 ☐ What's that light in the sky?
6 ☐ Do you **see** what I mean?
7 ☐ Are you going to **see** the doctor?
8 ☐ Have you **seen** the latest Marvel film?

a Yes, I have an appointment tomorrow.
b I don't **see** anything.
c No, I don't understand.
d Yes, I **watched** it with Brendan.
e I don't **hear** anything.
f She's **listening to** music.
g Yes, come and **look at** it! It's amazing!
h Yes, come and **watch**.

b Add the words in **bold** in 3a to the table.

1	pay attention to something because of its appearance (e.g., a photo, a flower)
2	pay attention to something because of the movement (e.g., a film)
3	be able to recognise sights
	watch something that's moving, or attend some entertainment event
	understand
	visit
4	be able to recognise sounds
5	pay attention to sounds

c 💬 <u>Underline</u> the correct words. Then discuss the questions.

1 How often do you *watch / look at* old photos of yourself?
2 When did you last *see / watch* the dentist?
3 What music do you *listen to / hear* when you're in a bad mood?
4 *Watch / Look* out of the window. What can you *see / look a*
5 *Listen / Hear*. What can you *listen / hear*?
6 If you *listened to / heard* a strange noise in the night, would you go and *watch / see* what it was?
7 What is the worst film you've ever *seen / looked at*?

CAN DO OBJECTIVES

- Talk about new things it would be good to do
- Talk about imagined past events
- Talk about possible problems and reassure someone
- Write an email with advice

UNIT 10

OPPORTUNITIES

GETTING STARTED

a 💬 What kind of event can you see in the photo? How are these events similar or different in your country?

b 💬 Ask and answer the questions.

1 What opportunities can going to university give you?
2 What opportunities have you had in your life? For example, think about education, travel, meeting people and work.

3 Describe a time when you did something that you found scary or difficult (e.g., skydiving, giving a speech or performing in a show). How did this experience make you feel? Explain your answer.

10A | IF I WAS FITTER, I'D DO IT!

1 SPEAKING

a 💬🔊 Look at photos a–c.

1 What is happening (or going to happen) in each photo?
2 How are the people in each photo feeling?

b Add more sports in these categories.

- winter sports: skiing, …
- ball sports: tennis, …
- water sports: surfing, …

c 💬🔊 Discuss the questions.

1 Which of the sports on your lists in 1b have you tried?
2 Which do you think are the most …?
   - fun
   - exciting
   - dangerous
   - difficult
3 Would you like to try any new sports? Which would you like to try?

2 VOCABULARY Sport

a 💬🔊 Check the meanings of the words in **bold**. Then match the sports in the pictures below with sentences 1–5. Sometimes more than one answer is possible.

1 It's an **extreme** sport.
2 It's a really good **workout**.
3 You win **points** when your opponent **misses** the ball.
4 You usually lose a game if you hit a lot of bad **shots**.
5 The **training** is very difficult.

b 〉〉 Now go to Vocabulary Focus 10A on p. 142.

table tennis

snowboarding

volleyball

wrestling

diving

a ski jumping

b tennis

c surfing

3 LISTENING

a 💬🔊 Look at the photos below and discuss the questions.
   1 What are these activities? Have you tried them or would you like to?
   2 What do you think is the most fun about them?

b ▶10.02 Listen to Gina and Libby talking about scuba diving and The Color Run. Then answer the questions.
   1 Why do they like each sport?
   2 What do they agree to do at the end?

c 💬🔊 ▶10.02 Listen again and discuss the questions.
   1 Where did Gina try scuba diving?
   2 How much training did she do?
   3 Why was she scared at first?
   4 How long is the run that Libby's going to do?
   5 How is it different from normal runs?

d Which of the two sports sounds more exciting/ dangerous? Which would you rather try? Why?

e 💬🔊 Write down all the reasons why you like your favourite sport. Work with someone who likes a different sport and tell them why you like your favourite.

> Of course, football is the greatest game in the world. People in every country love it, and …

4 GRAMMAR Second conditional

a Look at these second conditional sentences and underline the correct words to complete the rules.
   • Was it scary? I think if I went, I'd be terrified!
   • If I was a bit fitter, I would definitely do it.

   > 1 We use the second conditional to talk about *things we will probably do in the future* / *things we imagine, but are not real*.
   > 2 To form the second conditional, we use *If + past simple / present simple*, *would / will* + infinitive.

b ▶10.03 Pronunciation Listen to the pronunciation of *would* in each of the sentences. Is it strong (stressed) or weak (not stressed)? Write strong (*S*) or weak (*W*).
   1 ☐ If you went, you would absolutely love it.
   2 ☐ I wouldn't do a full marathon – I'm not fit enough!
   3 ☐ It would be great if there was a big group of us going.
   4 ☐ Would you like to try?
   5 ☐ Yes, I would, but … .
   6 ☐ If I was a bit fitter, I would definitely do it.

c ▶10.03 Listen again and repeat the sentences.

d ≫ Now go to Grammar Focus 10A on p. 162.

e Tick (✓) the sentences that are true for you. Then write a second conditional sentence for each one saying what you would or might do if things were different.
   ☐ I can't run long distances.
   ☐ I'm not very tall.
   ☐ I don't live in a country that gets a lot of snow.
   ☐ I can't afford a personal fitness trainer.
   ☐ I'm scared of heights.
   ☐ I'm not very fit.
   ☐ I'm not an Olympic champion.

   If I could run long distances, I'd enter a big marathon and raise money for charity.

f 💬🔊 Compare your sentences in 4e.

5 VOCABULARY Adjectives and prepositions

a Some adjectives are followed by a preposition. Complete each sentence with a preposition.

1 I was a bit worried _____ it before we went into the water for the first time.
2 It sounds perfect _____ me!
3 And it's popular _____ all kinds of people.

b ▶ 10.05 Listen and check your answers.

c Underline the correct prepositions.

1 ☐ I don't like extreme sports – I'm afraid *about* / *of* hurting myself.
2 ☐ I'm not scared *of* / *to* spiders.
3 ☐ I am very proud *of* / *about* my little sister.
4 ☐ I think that having good friends is essential *of* / *for* a happy, healthy life.
5 ☐ I'm very interested *in* / *about* health and fitness.
6 ☐ I'm worried *of* / *about* my football team's performance at the moment.
7 ☐ I'll never get tired *in* / *of* visiting new places.
8 ☐ I've found a sport that is right *for* / *in* me.
9 ☐ I think the quality of women's tennis is similar *to* / *from* men's.

d Tick (✓) the sentences in 5c that are true for you. Change the others so that they are true for you.

e Look at adverts a–c below. Fill in the gaps with the correct prepositions for the adjectives in bold.

6 SPEAKING

a Make notes about what you would do if you had one of the opportunities below.

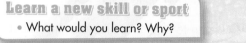
Learn a new skill or sport
• What would you learn? Why?

Go on a free trip with a friend to anywhere in the world
• Where would you go? Why?
• Who would you take?

Meet a famous person
• Who would you choose?
• What would you say or ask?

Travel in time
• What year would you travel to? Why?
• What would you do when you were there?

b 💬 Compare your ideas. Would you like to do the things your partner would like to do?

Dance Yourself Fit

Are you **worried** ___ being unfit, but **afraid** ___ joining a gym? Fitness is **essential** ___ good health and happiness – but what can you do if you don't like sport? That's simple – get dancing!

We're very **proud** ___ our team of qualified dance instructors.

Become a GUIDE RUNNER

If you want to keep fit and you're **interested** ___ helping people too, why not become a guide runner? Running is **popular** ___ blind people, but many of them need a guide runner for support. Just let us know your level of fitness and where you live. You'll even get automatic entry into any races!

Body Training Adventure Programme

Are you **tired** ___ the usual exercise classes? Do you need something more exciting and challenging?

Join our intensive fitness training programme for all ages and abilities. It's **similar** ___ an army-style boot camp but with an added emphasis on fun and teamwork.

Activities include rock climbing, mountain biking and boxing.

10B MAKING THE MOST OF OPPORTUNITIES

1 SPEAKING

a 💬 Discuss the questions.

1 Do you think luck is important in life? Why / Why not?
2 Have you ever had really good or really bad luck? What happened?
3 Can people do anything to make themselves 'luckier'? Think of three things.

2 READING

a 💬 Look at the photos, which show details of three true stories about good luck. Can you guess what the three stories might be about?

b 💬 Compare your ideas with other students. Are your ideas the same or different?

c Read *Searching for serendipity* quickly. Were your ideas in 2a correct?

Searching *for* serendipity

HOME | NEWS | YOUR STORIES | LOG IN

Are you making the most of life's opportunities?

I had my own business but needed a website. My friend Wendy gave me the email address of a designer named Mark. Unfortunately, Wendy's handwriting is awful, so I sent the email to the wrong person. Someone named Matt replied. Obviously, there had been a mistake. He said he wasn't actually a designer – he was a teacher – but he could help me if I wanted!

Matt seemed nice. And anyway, I didn't have anyone else to help me, so I decided to write back to him. In the end, Matt worked on my website for free. He did a great job and my business started to go really well. Meanwhile, we got to know each other via email. And ten months later, we met. We fell in love immediately, and a year later, we got married. If Wendy had had better handwriting, my business wouldn't have been such a success, and I certainly wouldn't have met Matt!

ANNA

Two years ago, Anna Frances had some very good luck when her colleague gave her some wrong information.

So was Anna just lucky? Or did she make her own luck? Why do these lucky accidents seem to happen to some people and not to others? And is there any way to make yourself more lucky? Well, it seems that the secret of happiness is to make the most of the opportunities that life gives us. We need to be open to serendipity – the random events that lead to happy, sometimes life-changing, results.

Dr Stephann Makri is working on a project about serendipity at City University, London. He thinks that serendipity is more

than an accident and that we can all have more 'luck' if we learn to pay attention to life's opportunities. He has noticed that many people's good-luck stories share the same basic pattern. First, people notice that there is an opportunity. Then they take action to make the most of it. For example, if you imagine meeting an old friend in the street who will later introduce you to the love of your life, several things have to happen. First, you have to notice the friend. Then you have to stop and talk to them, even though you might be busy. Finally, you need to be ready to follow up on whatever comes out of the conversation. So, it might be luck that leads you to walk towards your friend on the street – but the rest is up to you!

More serendipity stories ...

TOM
After university, I didn't have a job. I subscribed to a job website and got a lot of emails from them every day. I usually deleted them. One day, I was feeling particularly annoyed by all the emails, so I opened one of them to click on the 'unsubscribe' link. But I spotted an interesting job. It was in New York and I didn't really have the experience they wanted, but I decided to apply. I didn't get the job, but they emailed me two weeks later to say they had another job I could apply for. I got it and I ended up working in New York City, where I met my girlfriend, Paula. None of it would have happened if I had deleted the email.

CARLA
My mum, Betty, is 71. There's a café in town that I like, and I persuaded my mum to come with me, just to get out of the house. She didn't want to come at first, but when we got there, she really liked the café. While we were there, she started chatting with some bikers. My mum said she had always wanted to ride a motorcycle! I was shocked! Kenny, one of the bikers, offered to take us both out with the rest of the group. To my amazement, my mother said yes! I was really worried, but my mum loved the experience!

d Complete the sentences with the names in the box.

Anna	Betty	Carla	Kenny	Matt	Tom

1 _____ failed at first, but was right to take a chance.
2 _____ did an activity she'd always wanted to do.
3 _____ was surprised by someone else's behaviour.
4 _____ did some work for someone, even though it wasn't his job.
5 _____ made contact with the wrong person.
6 _____ did something kind for someone the first time they met.

e 💬 Discuss the questions.

1 Which person do you think was the 'luckiest'?
2 Do you agree that people make their own luck? Why / Why not?
3 Do you make the most of life's opportunities in a similar way to the people in the stories? Explain your answer.

3 VOCABULARY Expressions with *do*, *make* and *take*

a Underline the correct answers to complete the summary of Dr Makri's ideas.

> Can we ¹*take / make / do* our own luck? Dr Makri has been ²*doing / making / taking* research into serendipity and he believes we can. The secret lies in ³*doing / taking / making* advantage of an opportunity when it comes our way. If you see an opportunity in a chance event, you should ⁴*take / make / do* action and ⁵*take / have / make* the most of that opportunity.
>
> Everyone can be 'luckier'. If you get out and meet people, you'll have more chance encounters. Be brave and ⁶*take / make / do* risks in order to act freely when an opportunity comes your way.

b ≫ Now go to Vocabulary Focus 10B on p. 143.

4 GRAMMAR Third conditional

a Underline the correct words. Then check your answers in the article on p. 120.

If Wendy ¹*had / had had / would have had* better handwriting, my business ²*wasn't / hadn't been / wouldn't have been* such a success, and I certainly ³*didn't meet / hadn't met / wouldn't have met* Matt.

b Answer the questions.

1 Did Wendy have good handwriting? Was Anna's business successful? Did she meet Matt?
2 When do we use the third conditional? Choose a or b.
  a to talk about the results of real past events
  b to talk about an imagined past event and its likely result
3 What is the correct form of the third conditional?
  a *If + past simple, would + past participle.*
  b *If + past perfect, would have + past participle.*

c ▶10.06 Listen and match conversations 1–4 with pictures a–d below.

Conversation 1 ☐   Conversation 3 ☐
Conversation 2 ☐   Conversation 4 ☐

d ▶10.07 **Pronunciation** Listen to the sentences below. Which words are stressed in each sentence?

1 I would have won easily if I hadn't hurt my arm.
2 I wouldn't have bought it if I'd known it was in such bad condition.
3 If you hadn't pushed me, that car would have hit me!
4 I wouldn't have discovered the truth if I hadn't read her letters.

e ▶10.07 Listen again and practise saying the sentences.

f ≫ Now go to Grammar Focus 10B on p. 162.

g Write sentences using the third conditional about these people from the article on p. 120.

Anna   Wendy   Matt   Tom   Betty   Carla   Kenny

If Anna had used the correct email address, she might not have fallen in love with Matt.

h 💬 Compare your sentences.

5 SPEAKING

a You're going to tell the story of a past event that made your life better. Make notes about one of the topics below.

- a good friend, and how you met them
- a sport or hobby, and how you started doing it
- an accident, and how it happened
- a job, and how you got it
- a school, and why you went there
- a big decision, and how you made it

Think about the important events in your story. What were the consequences of what happened? How would your life have been different if you had done something differently?

b 💬 Take turns to tell your stories. Ask each other questions to find out more about what might have happened if things had been different.

> What would have been different if you hadn't gone to that school?

> I wouldn't have met my best friend, Gabriela.

10C EVERYDAY ENGLISH

You've got nothing to worry about

1 LISTENING

a 💬 Discuss the questions.

1 When was the last time you were very nervous?
2 What situations make you nervous (e.g., public speaking, flying, starting a new job)? What do you do to calm down?

b 📹 ▶ 10.09 Watch or listen to Part 1. What do you think Tom and Mark are talking about?

c 📹 ▶ 10.10 Watch or listen to Part 2 to check.

2 USEFUL LANGUAGE
Talking about possible problems and reassuring someone

a 📹 ▶ 10.10 Watch or listen to Part 2 again and complete the sentences.

1 You've got _____ to worry about.
2 I'm _____ it'll be OK.
3 You don't _____ it's a bit boring?
4 I'm still _____ that something will go wrong.
5 What _____ she says no?
6 She's _____ not going to say no.

b Add the sentences in 2a to the table.

Talking about a problem	Reassuring someone
	You've got nothing to worry about.

c 💬 Think of (real or invented) worries you might have about these situations. Talk to your partner. Reassure them about their worries.

- do badly in an exam
- public speaking
- a stressful day at work
- a difficult journey

> I'm worried that I will forget what to say.

> You'll be fine!

3 PRONUNCIATION
Sounding sure and unsure

a ▶ 10.11 Listen to this extract from the conversation. Does Tom sound sure or unsure?

Mark So, where are you taking her?
Tom I've booked a table at *Bella Vita*. It's the place where we went on our first date.

b 📹 ▶ 10.10 Now watch or listen to Part 2 again. Does Tom sound sure or unsure all the way through?

c ▶ 10.12 Listen to the following sentences. Do you think speaker B is sure or unsure?

1 **A** Do you think Rachel wants to go to a restaurant?
  B I think so, yes.
2 **A** Does Rachel like pizza?
  B I think so, yes.
3 **A** When did you meet her?
  B About two years ago.
4 **A** Where did you go on your first date?
  B We went to *Bella Vita*.

4 LISTENING

a  Tom and Becky are in the restaurant. What might happen? Talk about the ideas below. Which one do you think is most likely? Why?

1 Tom is too nervous and doesn't ask Becky to marry him.
2 Becky asks Tom to marry her before he can ask her.
3 Becky is very surprised and says yes.

b 🎥 ▶ 10.13 Watch or listen to Part 3 and check.

c Are the statements true (*T*) or false (*F*)?

1 Becky and Tom both think that they went to this restaurant for their first date.
2 Tom tried to phone Becky earlier.
3 Becky wants to talk to Tom about their plans for the weekend.
4 Becky was expecting Tom to ask her to marry him.
5 Becky says she will marry Tom.

5 CONVERSATION SKILLS
Changing the subject

a ▶ 10.14 Listen and complete the sentences.

1 **Becky** That _____ me, I need to book the restaurant for the office party.
2 **Tom** So anyway, as I was _____, you've really changed my life.

b Look again at the sentences in 5a. Who is starting a completely new subject, and who is returning to a previous subject?

c Look at the phrases in **bold**. Are they ways to change the subject or return to a previous subject?

1 **Speaking of** cafés, have I told you about the place we found last week?
2 **By the way**, did you see that new comedy programme last night?

d 💬 Work in pairs.

Student A: You want to talk about your weekend. Talk to Student B. Can you keep the conversation on the same subject?

Student B: You don't want to hear about Student A's weekend. Try to change the subject and talk about other things (e.g., a film you've seen recently, someone you saw today).

> I went to see a film this weekend.

> Oh, speaking of films, did you see that *La La Land* is on TV tonight?

6 SPEAKING

>>> **Communication 10C** 💬 Student A: Read the information below. Student B: Go to p. 131.

Student A
You want to talk to Student B about a trip abroad you are going to take (where are you going?).
You are worried because:

• you are scared of flying (what might happen?)
• you are nervous about communicating in a different language (what problems might this cause?)
• you are not very good at trying new food (what food might you have to try?).

Make notes. Then have the conversation. Reassure Student B when they try to talk about a big presentation they have to give, but try to bring the conversation back to your trip.

> Anyway, as I was saying, I'm really nervous about what might happen.

✅ UNIT PROGRESS TEST

→ CHECK YOUR PROGRESS

You can now do the Unit Progress Test.

10D SKILLS FOR WRITING
I think you should go for it

1 SPEAKING AND READING

a 💬 Read the advert on the right for an organisation called NowVolunteer and discuss the questions.

1 What kind of organisation do you think NowVolunteer is? What kinds of programmes do you think they offer, and where?

2 What kinds of people do you think join a NowVolunteer programme and why?

3 Do you think volunteers have to pay money to work on a programme?

b Read the web page below quickly and check your answers to 1a.

🌐 NowVolunteer

Join one of our programmes. See the world, help other people, develop new skills.

HOME   PROJECTS   JOIN US   🌐 NowVolunteer

Volunteering. Adventure. Experience.

Do you want to have the adventure of a lifetime and make new friends from around the world? NowVolunteer is a volunteer organisation that gives young people the opportunity to travel, have fun and help people.

And we can help your career, too. Companies want to know about your experience, not just about your qualifications. So join us to improve your CV.

See our volunteer profiles to see what people say about their experiences.

🎖 Unique, award-winning programmes

We organise specialised programmes in 50 countries. You can work with children, help local communities, work on environmental projects, learn a new skill ... and, at the same time, have a great travel experience.

💼 We arrange everything for you

Just choose a programme and we'll take care of the details. All you need to do is raise $500 for our programmes before you go. We'll provide free accommodation while you're volunteering.

2 LISTENING AND SPEAKING

a You're going to hear Greg talking about his experience with NowVolunteer. Look at the photo below. What do you think he might say about his trip?

Greg from Auckland, New Zealand worked on a community health project in Madagascar.

b ▶ 10.15 Listen to Greg. Does he mention any of your ideas from 2a?

c ▶ 10.15 Listen again and make notes in the table.

1 What he studied	
2 Reason for going	
3 How he raised money	
4 What he did	
5 What happened next	

d 💬 Discuss the questions.

1 Would you like to join the same programme as Greg? Why / Why not?

2 Do you know anyone who has done volunteer work like this? If so, what was their experience like?

3 Have you ever worked for no money? If so, did you enjoy it?

124

3 READING

a Grace is in her last year at university, studying marketing. She emailed her friends asking for advice. Read her email and answer the questions.

1 What two programmes is Grace interested in?
2 What might be a problem for her?

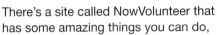

Hi, everyone!

I've been thinking about what to do next year and I thought I'd take a year off and do some volunteer work.

There's a site called NowVolunteer that has some amazing things you can do, like looking after elephants in Thailand or teaching English in Nepal. The only problem is you have to raise $500 for them first, but then they give you training and pay for your accommodation.

What do you all think? Am I onto a great idea here or should I just forget it and start looking around for jobs?

Replies, please! ;-)
Grace

b ≫ **Communication 10D** Work in pairs. Student A: Go to p. 130 and read Amanda's reply. Student B: Go to p. 132 and read Laura's reply. Do they think Grace should do volunteer work? What reasons do they give?

c Tell your partner about the reply that you read. Who do you agree with?

4 WRITING SKILLS Advising a course of action

a Look at these expressions from the emails Amanda and Laura wrote. Then answer the questions.

1 I think you should …
2 If I were you, I'd …
3 I'm fairly sure you'd …
4 I think you'd have a good time, but …
5 It would definitely …
6 I'm just suggesting that …
7 Maybe it would be better to …

Which expressions … ?

- only give advice
- also imagine what could happen

b Compare Amanda's and Laura's emails. Who uses more 'careful' language? Why?

a because she's advising a friend to do something she wants to do
b because she's advising a friend not to do something she wants to do

c Which of these does Laura use?

a adverbs to express uncertainty (*maybe, perhaps*)
b modal verbs to express obligation (*should, must*)
c modal verbs to express uncertainty (*might, could, would*)
d expressions of certainty (*I'm sure, definitely*)
e expressions of uncertainty (*I think, I'm not sure*)

d Rewrite these sentences using the words in brackets to make the advice more 'careful'. Make any other changes necessary.

1 Write to them and ask where they spend the money. (If I)
2 Look for a job with a marketing company in Thailand. (better)
3 It won't be very interesting. (not sure)
4 You'll meet a lot of interesting people. (think)
5 Look at the alternatives. (suggesting)

5 WRITING An email with advice

a Think of an alternative to your present lifestyle or job – something you'd like to do for a year. Write an email asking other students if they think it's a good idea.

b Work in pairs. Read your partner's email and write a reply. It can be positive and enthusiastic (like Amanda's) or more careful (like Laura's).

c Read your partner's reply to your email. Do you think it's good advice? Why / Why not? Does the advice use appropriate expressions?

UNIT 10
Review and extension

1 GRAMMAR

<u>Underline</u> the correct words.

1 **A** We lost really badly.
  B I know. We would *scored* / *have scored* a lot more points if we *did* / *'d done* more training over the last few weeks.

2 **A** Are you going to accept the offer?
  B I can't decide. What *would* / *did* you do if you *were* / *had been* me?

3 **A** If I *didn't miss* / *hadn't missed* the train, I'd never *met* / *have met* my wife, Jasmine.
  B That's so romantic!

4 **A** Hey! Was that a golf ball? Where did it come from?
  B I don't know, but you were very lucky. It *could have* / *could* hit you!

5 **A** Yusuf gets so disappointed when he doesn't win.
  B If he *wasn't* / *couldn't be* such a competitive person, he wouldn't play as well as he does.

6 **A** Why didn't you call me?
  B Well, I *would* / *wouldn't* have if I *had* / *hadn't* left my phone at the office.

2 VOCABULARY

a Complete the sentences with the words in the box.

about	net	of	opponent	point	track	workout

1 It's a fun game and a great _____ , too.
2 He'll win the match if he scores one more _____ !
3 You won the game! I'm so proud _____ you!
4 You have to hit the ball over the _____ .
5 You won last time, but this time your _____ may beat you!
6 How many times did you run around the _____ ?
7 Are you worried _____ the tennis match tomorrow?

b Complete the questions with the correct form of *make*, *do* or *take*.

1 What sports do you _____ ?
2 Do you know anyone who _____ a lot of risks?
3 How often do you _____ a break when you're studying?
4 Do you _____ the most of your free time? Why / Why not?
5 Should scientists _____ more research into medicine or space travel?
6 Have you ever _____ friends with someone from a different country? Who?
7 Have you ever had to _____ an important decision?

c 💬 Ask and answer the questions in 2b.

3 WORDPOWER Easily confused words

a Match the sentence halves.

1	☐ If you need money,	a	I can **lend** you some.
2	☐ I need some money,	b	so I'll have to **borrow** som

3	☐ Go on! Don't **miss**	a	points if you run with the ball.
4	☐ You'll **lose**	b	this opportunity! It'll change your life!

5	☐ **Take** some water	a	when you come to the gyr
6	☐ **Bring** some energy drinks	b	when you go running.

7	☐ If you want to take part,	a	**raise** your hand.
8	☐ If you have work experience,	b	your chances of getting a job will **rise**.

9	☐ They **robbed**	a	the money from a bank.
10	☐ They **stole**	b	a bank.

11	☐ Where are you working?	a	I'm **currently** working at home.
12	☐ Do you work at a bank?	b	**Actually**, I work at a schoo

b <u>Underline</u> the correct words.

1 a borrow = *take* / *give*
  b lend = *take* / *give*
2 a miss = *not win* / *not take*
  b lose = *not win* / *not take*
3 a take = *to here* / *away from here*
  b bring = *to here* / *away from here*
4 a raise = *lift something* / *go up*
  b rise = *lift something* / *go up*
5 a rob = *take from a person or place* / *take something*
  b steal = *take from a person or place* / *take something*
6 a currently = *at the moment* / *in fact*
  b actually = *at the moment* / *in fact*

c Write down three ...

- places that can be robbed.
- things that are difficult to steal.
- things that you would only lend to a good friend.
- things you sometimes borrow.
- things you always take with you when you go out.
- things people often bring back from holiday.

d 💬 Compare your answers for c. Are they the same or different?

↻ REVIEW YOUR PROGRESS

How well did you do in this unit? Write 3, 2 or 1 for each objective.
3 = very well 2 = well 1 = not so well

I CAN ...	
talk about new things it would be good to do	☐
talk about imagined past events	☐
talk about possible problems and reassure someone	☐
write an email with advice.	☐

COMMUNICATION PLUS

1B GRAMMAR Student A

Describe your picture to your partner. Find eight differences between your pictures.

>>> Now go back to p. 13.

5D SPEAKING AND LISTENING

The incorrect statement is number 4: Whales never sleep because they need to breathe.

In fact, whales do sleep. They appear to let the two sides of their brain take turns sleeping. One side of their brain always stays awake so they remember to breathe.

>>> Now go back to p. 64.

Results

Research shows that about 70% of the population are extroverts and about 30% of the population are introverts, but not many people are either extreme introverts or extreme extroverts.

Are you a confident introvert? A shy extrovert? Or something else?

How many 'yes' answers did you have?

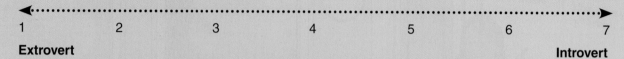

| 1 | 2 | 3 | 4 | 5 | 6 | 7 |

Extrovert   **Introvert**

Introverts don't need much external excitement in order to feel happy. They feel alive when they have time to focus on the thoughts and feelings inside them. If you had four or five 'yes' answers, then you're a sociable introvert. You really enjoy spending time with people, but you always need to balance it with time on your own to recharge your batteries.

Extroverts feel happiest when they have lots of external excitement. They get ideas from any kind of conversation and discussion, and they enjoy having people and activity around them. If you had more 'no' than 'yes' answers, then you're probably a quiet extrovert. You don't always say much when you're around other people, but you love the energy you get from their company.

≫ Now go back to p. 47.

4C SPEAKING Student B

1 Student A wants help buying a new computer. You know a lot about computers and you like helping people. But you have your French class on Tuesdays and Thursdays, so you can't go shopping on those days.

2 You need help moving some furniture and you think that Student A has a big car. You would like to move it on Friday. Ask for Student A's help.

≫ Now go back to p. 51.

5C SPEAKING Student B

1 Student A will tell you about their job. Ask them about what they are going to do.

2 You are going to move to another part of the country. Think about the answers to these questions.
   • Why are you moving?
   • How do you feel about this?

≫ Now go back to p. 63.

1B GRAMMAR Student B

Describe your picture to your partner. Find eight differences between your pictures.

>>> Now go back to p. 13.

6A VOCABULARY Student A

1 Read definitions 1–5 aloud. Student B will match them to compound nouns. Look at the answers in brackets. Tell Student B if their answers are correct.

1 something you need in order to get on a plane (boarding pass)
2 a place you go to stay in a tent (campsite)
3 a system for keeping your room cool (air conditioning)
4 a guided visit to the famous places in a town or city (sightseeing tour)
5 a machine that washes your plates, glasses, knives and forks, etc. (dishwasher)

2 Listen to Student B's definitions. Find matching compound nouns in the box. Choose one word from each column.

street	control
window	bag
bottle	map
passport	opener
sleeping	seat

>>> Now go back to p. 69.

10D READING Student A

✉ ✎ ☆ ⚑   ⊗

Hi Grace,

No wonder you don't want to go straight into an office job next year. Looking after elephants in Thailand sounds much more exciting! I think you should definitely go for it. You don't have much to lose (except a bit of money) and if it doesn't work out, you can always come back. But anyway, I'm fairly sure you'd enjoy it and have a great time – you have always been good with animals. It would definitely look good on your CV, too. It would show that you're an adventurous person and you're interested in different things, not just studying and jobs. It's a pity I've got a job already or I'd come with you! ;-)

Let me know what you decide.

Love,
Amanda

>>> Now go back to p. 125.

6C SPEAKING Student B

1 Your partner will tell you some surprising news. Listen to the news and give some recommendations.
2 You found an old ring in your house. You think it belonged to your great-grandmother, but you aren't sure. You cleaned it and showed it to a friend, who said it was very valuable. Your friend said you could sell it for about £50,000. Tell your partner your news and ask for some recommendations about what to do.

>>> Now go back to p. 75.

8B SPEAKING AND READING

⟫ Now go back to p. 95.

9A GRAMMAR Student B

Audio streaming facts and figures
Audio *has streamed / has been streamed* since 1993. It *started / was started* by an organisation called the Internet Underground Music Archive. Now some of the most popular streaming services that fans *use / are used* are Spotify, Pandora and Apple. The music industry worldwide *has taken / has been taken* over by digital streaming. Today, more than 80% of music revenues *come / is come* from streaming.

⟫ Now go back to p. 106.

9C SPEAKING Student B

You want to arrange an afternoon with Student A.
- You don't really like modern art.
- You are hungry. You've heard about a new café that has good food and great coffee. You can't remember what it is called, but you have the details on your phone.
- There is an exhibition of photography across town, but you don't know where.

⟫ Now go back to p. 111.

10C SPEAKING Student B

You want to talk to Student A about a big presentation you have to do (where? what is it about?).
You're worried because:
- you don't have much time to prepare (when is it?)
- you don't have any experience with public speaking (what problems might you have?)
- you are worried people might ask difficult questions (what might they ask?).

Make notes. Then have the conversation. Reassure Student A about the trip they are going on, but try to bring the conversation back to your presentation.

⟫ Now go back to p. 123.

6A VOCABULARY Student B

1 Listen to Student A's definitions. Find matching compound nouns in the box. Choose one word from each column.

boarding	washer
camp	conditioning
air	tour
sightseeing	site
dish	pass

2 Read definitions 1–5 aloud. Student A will match them to compound nouns. Look at the answers in brackets. Tell Student A if their answers are correct.

1 a plan that shows where things are in a town or city (street map)
2 a place to sit on a plane or train where you can easily look outside (window seat)
3 a gadget for taking the tops off glass bottles (bottle opener)
4 a place where you have to show your identification at an airport (passport control)
5 something you use to keep warm at night when you go camping (sleeping bag)

≫ Now go back to p. 69.

10D READING Student B

✉ ✎ ☆ ⚑   ⊗

Hi Grace,

I'm not sure what I think about your idea of doing a year abroad. I can see that it might be exciting to go off to somewhere like Thailand or Nepal for a year but, if I were you, I'd think very carefully about it before you make a decision.

I think you'd have a good time, but you also need to think about getting a job after you come back. While you're away in Thailand, everyone else will be looking for jobs. Maybe it would be better to do something more closely connected with marketing. I'm not sure experience with elephants would help much in getting you a marketing job!

Anyway, I don't want to sound negative, but I'm just suggesting that you think about it first and make sure it's what you really want to do.

We could meet and talk about it if you like.

Love,
Laura

≫ Now go back to p. 125.

7C SPEAKING Student B

1 Student A is staying in your home. They will ask you for permission to do things. Decide whether or not to give permission.

2 You have started a new job and Student A is your colleague. Ask permission to:
• play music at your desk while you're working
• turn the air conditioning up
• move your desk closer to the window.

≫ Now go back to p. 87.

1A Communication

a **▶ 01.01** Listen to the words in **bold**. What do you think they mean?

1 You **argue** with someone when you *agree / don't agree* about something.
2 You **complain** when you're *happy / not happy* about something.
3 You **encourage** someone when you say *good / bad* things about what they want to do.
4 If you **persuade** someone, you make them *agree / forget* to do something.
5 If you **insist** on something, you say that something *must happen / might happen*.
6 You **greet** someone when they *arrive at / leave* a place.
7 You **admit** something when you tell someone something about yourself that you *want to / don't want to*.
8 You **forgive** someone when you *start / stop* being angry with them because they did something wrong.
9 You **refuse** to do something when you say you *will / will not* do it.
10 You **update** someone when you give them the *most recent / oldest* information.

b **▶ 01.02** Underline the correct words in **a**. Then listen and check.

c 💬 Describe what's happening in pictures 1–4 using the words in **a**.

d 💬 Choose three of these topics to talk about.
  • a time when you complained about something in a shop or restaurant
  • a time when you insisted on doing something
  • a time when you argued about something unimportant
  • a time when you encouraged someone who was having problems
  • a time when someone persuaded you to do something you didn't want to do
  • a time when you admitted something to another person
  • a time when someone updated you on something

e ≫ Now go back to p. 8.

1B Extreme adjectives

a ▶ **01.09** **Pronunciation** Listen to the extreme adjectives in the box. <u>Underline</u> the stressed syllable in each word.

> awful /'ɔːfəl/   boiling /'bɔɪlɪŋ/   brilliant /'brɪlɪənt/   delicious /də'lɪʃəs/   enormous /ɪn'ɔːməs/
> filthy /'fɪlθiː/   freezing /'friːzɪŋ/   furious /'fjuːriəs/   miserable /'mɪzərəbəl/   tiny /'taɪni/

b ▶ **01.10** Complete the sentences with the extreme adjectives in **a**. Then listen and check.
1 Their house is _____! It's got 12 bedrooms.
2 **A** Was it hot?
   B Yes, it was absolutely _____!
3 Why do you look so _____? I've never seen you looking so sad.
4 We had a _____ holiday. The hotel, the weather, the town – it was all really good.
5 The food was absolutely _____ . I'm not going there again!
6 I was _____ when I found out he'd read my private diary!
7 The picture's _____ – I can't see it. Can you make it a bit bigger?
8 **A** It's _____! Why didn't I bring a coat?
   B Here, you can borrow my jacket.
9 Your T-shirt's _____! Put it in the washing machine.
10 That cake is _____! Could I have some more, please?

c 💬 Think of an example of each of the things below. Then work in small groups and compare your answers. Are any of your answers the same?
- someone who earns an enormous amount of money
- something that makes you furious
- a time you felt absolutely miserable
- an awful film or TV programme
- something that tastes delicious
- a brilliant website

d 💬 Use extreme adjectives to describe pictures 1–4.

e ⟫ Now go back to p. 13.

5A Environmental issues

a Match the words in the box with definitions 1–8.

creature /ˈkriːtʃə/   destroy /dɪˈstrɔɪ/   endangered /inˈdeɪndʒəd/   limit /ˈlɪmɪt/
local /ˈləʊkəl/   natural /ˈnætʃrəl/   species /ˈspiːʃiːz/   survive /səˈvaɪv/

1 found in nature and not made by people
2 from a small area, especially of a country
3 to control something so that it doesn't become bigger
4 a type of animal or plant
5 to continue living
6 to damage something so badly that it can't be used
7 anything that lives (but is not a plant)
8 used to describe an animal or plant that might disappear because there are not many alive

b ▶ 05.02 Complete the texts with the correct form of the words in **a**. Sometimes there is more than one possible answer. Then listen and check your answers.

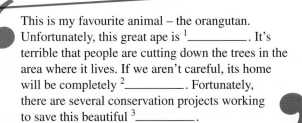

This is my favourite animal – the orangutan. Unfortunately, this great ape is ¹_____. It's terrible that people are cutting down the trees in the area where it lives. If we aren't careful, its home will be completely ²_____. Fortunately, there are several conservation projects working to save this beautiful ³_____.

The ice in the Arctic is melting. Some people say that the melting ice is ⁴_____ – that human beings are not causing climate change. But we need to do something about it, and fast. The weather is getting stranger. Some scientists think that many ⁵_____ will not be able to ⁶_____ if the temperature changes too much.

Pollution is a big problem here. The air is often like a dirty grey fog. You can hardly see what's in front of you! A lot of people are getting ill. The government needs to ⁷_____ the number of cars and factories, but we can't do anything without the support of the ⁸_____ people. The problem is, everyone wants to drive!

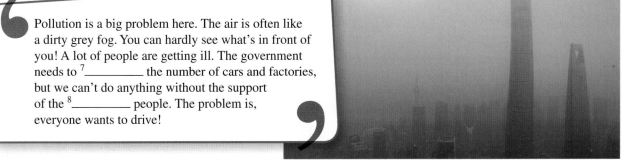

c Write notes about your opinions and feelings about one of these topics.
  • a favourite animal, plant or natural place
  • an environmental problem where you live
  • an environmental problem affecting the planet

d 💬 Take turns talking about your topic.

e ≫ Now go back to p. 56.

5B The natural world

a ▶05.11 Match the words in the box with photos 1–8. Then listen and check.

bay /beɪ/ cave /keɪv/ coast /kəʊst/ desert /ˈdezət/
rainforest /ˈreɪnfɒrɪst/ stream /striːm/ valley /ˈvæli/
waterfall /ˈwɔːtəfɔːl/

b ▶05.12 Underline the correct words. Then listen and check.
1 A *park / national park* is a very large area of natural beauty for use by the public.
2 A *river / stream* is a long (and often large) area of water that flows into the sea.
3 There are five *oceans / seas* in the world: the Pacific, the Atlantic, the Indian, the Arctic and the Southern.
4 A *forest / rainforest* is an area of land in a tropical region, where many trees and plants grow together.
5 A *sea / lake* is a large area of water with land all around it.

c 💬 Take turns to describe the animals or plants you can see in photos 1–6 below. Say where they live.

d ▶ Now go back to p. 61.

136

6B Describing food

a ▶ 06.07 Label the pictures using the pairs of adjectives in the box. Then listen and check.

creamy /'kriːmi/ / crunchy /'krʌntʃi/ fresh /freʃ/ / dried /draɪd/
cooked /kʊkt/ / raw /rɔː/ heavy /'hevi/ / light /laɪt/ sweet /swiːt/ / sour /'saʊə/

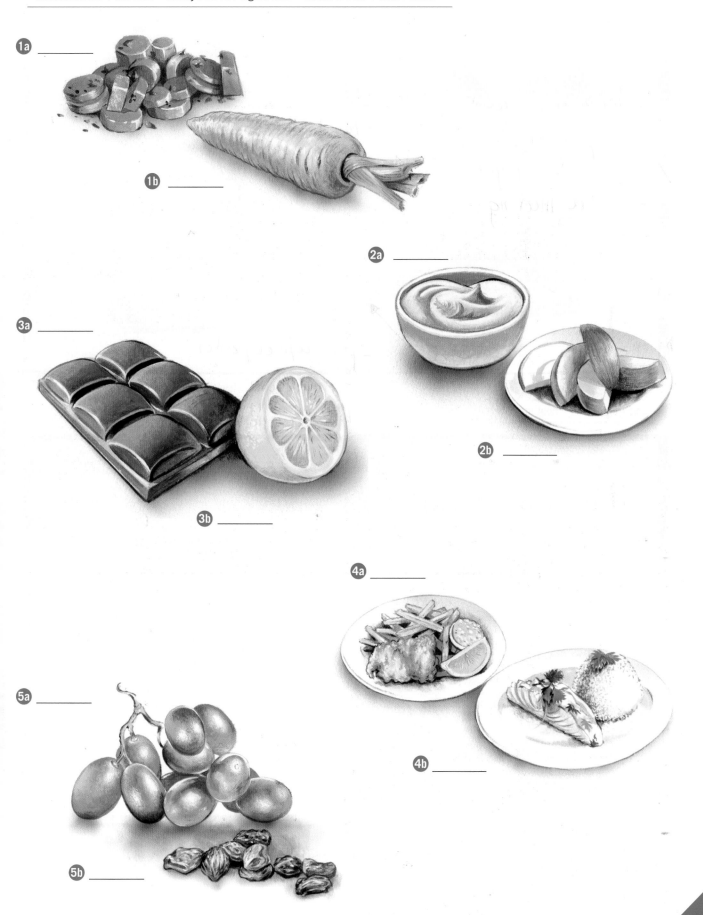

1a _____

1b _____

2a _____

2b _____

3a _____

3b _____

4a _____

4b _____

5a _____

5b _____

b Complete the two recipes with the words in the boxes.

chop mash mix serve squeeze

Guacamole

1 _____ three chillies, three tomatoes, one onion and a bunch of coriander.

2 _____ three avocados in a bowl.

3 _____ all the ingredients together.

4 _____ the juice of half a lime into the mixture.

5 _____ with tortilla chips.

18 • Starters

Starters • 19

add chop fry heat up stir

MEATBALLS
IN TOMATO SAUCE

1 _____ one onion and two cloves of garlic.

2 _____ 500 g minced lamb to the onions and garlic, with salt, pepper and spices. Make the mixture into balls.

3 _____ one tablespoon of olive oil in a pan.

4 _____ the meatballs in the oil.

5 Add two cans of tomatoes and 200 ml of water. Cook for 30 minutes. _____ occasionally.

32 • Pasta

Pasta • 33

c Prepare a simple recipe for a dish you like. Write notes about the ingredients you need and how you make it.

d 💬 Take turns to talk about your recipes. Would you like to eat each other's dishes?

e ≫ Now go back to p. 71.

7A Describing houses and buildings

a ▶07.06 Use the words in the box to label the pictures. Then listen and check.

attic /ˈætɪk/   balcony /ˈbælkəni/   basement /ˈbeɪsmənt/   block /blɒk/ of flats   doorbell /ˈdɔːbel/   first floor /flɔː/
flat /flæt/   front /frʌnt/ door   ground /ɡraʊnd/ floor   landing /ˈlændɪŋ/   lock /lɒk/   steps /steps/   terrace /ˈterəs/

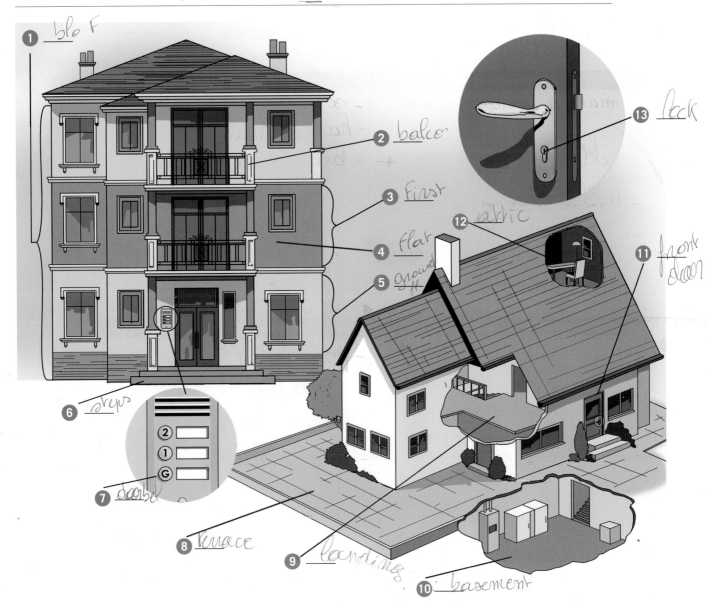

1 _blo F_
2 _balco_
3 _First_
4 _flat_
5 _ground fl_
6 _steps_
7 _doorbel_
8 _terrace_
9 _landing_
10 _basement_
11 _front door_
12 _attic_
13 _lock_

b ▶07.07 Complete the sentences with the words in the box. Then listen and check.

attic   balcony   floor   location   moved house
neighbourhood   rent   view

1 I don't have my own house, so I _rent_ the house I'm living in.
2 I've _____ a lot of times, so I've had lots of different addresses.
3 I live in a very busy _____. There are lots of shops, cafés and cars.
4 We don't have a garden or a terrace, but we do have a _____ where we can sit outside.
5 My home is in a good _____ because it's near the train station.
6 I put all the stuff I don't use in the _____.
7 Our flat is on the third _____ of our building.
8 The _____ from my bedroom is nothing special – just a street and more houses.

c 💬 Discuss the sentences in **b** that are true for you.

> The second sentence isn't true for me. I've only moved house once in my life.

d 💬 Imagine you are going to buy or rent a new home. What kind of house or flat would you choose and why? Which of these things are most important to you?

- price
- views
- location
- number of rooms
- garden
- something else

e ≫ Now go back to p. 81.

8A Sharing information

a Underline the correct verb in the examples. Tick (✓) the two examples where both verbs collocate with the noun.

1 *create / make* a podcast
2 *send / post* a text or email
3 *put up / post* a poster
4 *send / post* on social media

5 *have / hold* a chat or talk with someone
6 *deliver / send* a flyer
7 *create / hold* a meeting
8 *make / brainstorm* ideas

b Put the collocations in the table below. Some can go in more than one category.

Involves talking	Involves writing
– make a podcast	– send a text, email
– deliver a flyer	– have a chat
– hold a meeting	– brainstorm ideas

Involves technology	Doesn't need to involve technology
– post on social media	– put up a poster
	– send a flyer
	– have a chat
	– hold a meeting

c Read sentences 1–3. Match the words in **bold** to definitions a–f.

1 I **subscribe** to podcasts on a lot of ✓ different topics – sports, music, politics and cooking.
2 I found a new **series** of comedy podcasts – each **episode** is absolutely hilarious.
3 I subscribe to this news podcast that's like a kind of **newsfeed** – **items** are **updated** every hour.

a regular delivery of the latest news
b one single programme, e.g., a podcast, from a connected group
c to choose to receive new programmes from someone who creates them on a regular basis
d a number of related programmes that follow one another
e replaced with newer ones
f individual pieces of news

d 💬 Discuss the questions.

1 What are popular topics for podcasts in your country?
2 If you subscribe to any podcasts, what are they about?
   If you don't listen to podcasts, what kind do you think could be interesting?
3 How do most people in your country get news – from the radio, TV, social media or podcasts?

e ≫ Now go back to p. 92.

8B Reporting verbs

a Match the statements with the pictures a–f. Where are the people and what are they doing?

1 'I'll pay for lunch if you like.' _d_ => *offer*
2 'OK, it's true. I wrote all the reviews.' _b_ => *admit*
3 'Don't sit down!' _e_ => *order, warned* *Remind*
4 'Don't forget to read the label.' _a_ => *Remind*
5 'Why don't we ask someone for directions?' _F_ => *suggest*
6 'If I were you, I'd make a formal complaint.' _C_ => *advice*

she remind him to ~~forget to read~~ read the label

He admired ~~the~~ writing the reviews

She advice her to make a formal complait

She suggest to ask someone another directio

She warned him to not sit down here

wallet

not to sit down

don't forget the noun before "to"

b 💬 Write what happened in the situations in **a** using the verbs in the box. Then compare your answers with other students.

| admitted | advised | ~~offered~~ | reminded | suggested | warned |

> We were in a restaurant and he **offered** to pay for lunch.

c 💬 Work with a partner. Student A: Look at the sentences in **a** and write one sentence like these in direct speech. Then read it aloud to your partner. Student B: Summarise what A said using a reporting verb from **b**.

> Don't tell the boss!

> You warned me not to tell the boss.

d ≫ Now go back to p. 97.

a ⏵**10.01** Label the pictures with the words in the box. Then listen and check.

competitor /kɒmˈpetɪtə/   court /kɔːt/   net /net/   opponents /əˈpəʊnənts/   referee /refəˈriː/   track /træk/

① _____

② _____

③ _____

④ _____

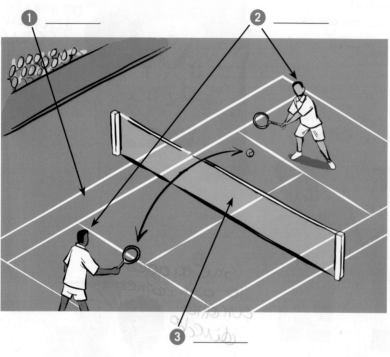

⑤ _____

⑥ _____

b <u>Underline</u> the word in each group that is <u>not</u> possible. You can …
1   *win / lose / beat / score* a point.
2   *beat / attack / score* your opponent.
3   win a *game / point / match / competitor.*
4   *compete for / win / score* a prize.

c 💬 Discuss the questions.
1   When did you last play a game or a sports match? What happened? Did you win?
2   Do you prefer playing in a team or individually?
3   Are you a competitive person?

d Think of a sport and write notes on these questions.
1   Is it a team sport or an individual sport?
2   How do you play it?
3   Do you need a special place or special equipment?
4   Are there any special rules?
5   Is it a popular sport?

e 💬 Describe your sport but do <u>not</u> say its name. Try to guess your partner's sport.

f ⏵⏵ Now go back to p. 117.

10B Expressions with *do*, *make* and *take*

a Write *do*, *make* or *take* for each group of words.
1 _____ money, a decision, a mistake, progress
2 _____ a risk, advantage of something, a chance
3 _____ sense, a difference, the most of something
4 _____ your homework, (some) research
5 _____ well/badly (e.g., in an exam), your best
6 _____ part in something, care of someone, action
7 _____ a break, it easy
8 _____ a phone call, new friends easily

b Complete questions 1–6 using words from **a** or your own ideas.
When was the last time you … ?

1 took _____   4 did _____
2 made _____   5 did _____
3 took _____   6 made _____

c 💬 Ask and answer the questions in **b**.

d ≫ Now go back to p. 121.

GRAMMAR FOCUS

1A Subject and object questions

Most questions in English need an auxiliary verb (e.g., *do*, *be*, *have* or a modal verb) before the subject. Follow this pattern for *Yes / No* and object questions.

▶ 01.03

Question word	Auxiliary verb or *be*	Subject	Main verb	
	Can	I	borrow	your pen?
	Do	you	have	much homework?
Why	were	you		late?
Who	are	you	waiting	for?
How many people	have	you	invited	to the party?

▶ 01.04

When we ask about the subject of the verb, we use the same word order in the question as in the statement (subject – verb – object). Do not add an auxiliary verb to subject questions:

*Who **told you the news**?* (*Stuart **told me the news**.*)
*What **happened yesterday**?* (*Nothing **happened yesterday**.*)

Question word	Verb	
Who	told	you the news?
What	happened	yesterday?
How many people	are coming	to the party?
Which team	won	the match?

In questions with prepositions, the preposition goes at the end of the question:

A ***Who*** *did you go to the cinema **with**?* **B** *My sister.*
A ***What's*** *he talking **about**?* **B** *His job.*

> **Tip**
>
> ***What ... like?*** *and **How ... ?***
> Use *What ... like?* to ask for a description of a person:
> **A** ***What's*** *your teacher **like**?*
> **B** *She's very friendly.*
>
> Use *How ... ?* to ask about a person's health:
> **A** ***How's*** *your sister?*
> **B** *She's very well, thanks.*
>
> You can use *What ... like?* or *How ... ?* to ask for a description of a thing or event:
> **A** ***What*** *was your holiday **like**? / **How** was your holiday?*
> **B** *It was excellent.*

1B Present simple and present continuous

▶ 01.06 **Present simple**
We use the present simple for:
- facts which are true all the time
  *The sun **rises** in the east. The bus **doesn't go** past my house.*
- habits and routines
  *I **study** for about an hour a week. We never **get** much homework.*
- opinions and beliefs.
  *Do you **agree**?   I **don't know** the answer.*

▶ 01.07 **Present continuous**
We use the present continuous for:
- actions that are in progress at the moment of speaking
  *Why **are** you **carrying** an umbrella? It**'s not raining**.*
- actions or situations around the moment of speaking
  *He**'s studying** Russian at university.*
- future arrangements (see 5A p. 152).
  *I**'m meeting** Andrew tonight.*

States and actions
The present continuous is not normally used to describe:
- mental states: *know, agree, understand, believe,* etc.
- likes and preferences: *like, want, love, hate, need, prefer,* etc.
- other states: *be, own, belong, forget, hear, seem, depend,* etc.

Special cases
Some verbs (e.g., *think, see, have*) can be used as states or actions, with different meanings:
State: *I **think** you're wrong.* (= my opinion)
Action: *I**'m thinking** about my birthday.* (= a mental process)
State: *I **see** what you mean.* (= I understand)
Action: *I**'m seeing** the doctor tomorrow.* (= I'm meeting him/her)
State: *I **have** a car / a sister.* (= possession, relationship, etc.)
Action: *I**'m having** a party / dinner.* (= I'm organising)

1A Subject and object questions

a Make questions with the words below.

1 listening / why / me / isn't / to / anybody ?

_____

2 you / question / I / ask / can / a ?

_____

3 borrow / did / book / whose / you ?

_____

4 about / are / worrying / what / you ?

_____

5 has / cake / who / my / eaten ?

_____

b Correct the mistake in each question.

1 What time you will be here? _____

2 Happened what to your leg? _____

3 To what are you listening? _____

4 Which speaker did gave the best presentation?

_____

5 How's your new friend like? _____

c Write a subject and an object question for each statement. The words in **bold** are the answers. Ask about the information in **bold**.

1 **400** people have commented on **your photo**.

How many people have commented on your photo?
What have 400 people commented on?

2 **A fire** damaged **the roof**.

_____

_____

3 **Joanna** is afraid of **spiders**.

_____

_____

4 **His brother** told them a joke about **elephants**.

_____

_____

d ≫ Now go back to p. 9.

1B Present simple and present continuous

a Match the pairs.

1 [b] He drives to work   a at the moment, so he can't answer the phone.
2 [a] He's driving to work   b every day.

3 ☐ He wears a red shirt   c every time he goes to a football match.
4 ☐ He's wearing a red shirt   d so you'll find him easily.

5 ☐ I think   e it's going to be a nice day.
6 ☐ I'm thinking   f about what to do this weekend.

7 ☐ I have dinner   g right now. Can I call you back?
8 ☐ I'm having dinner   h at a restaurant every Saturday.

b Complete the conversation with the present simple or present continuous form of the verbs in brackets.

A What [1] _are you reading_ (you / read)?

B It's an article about learning languages. It's really interesting!

A Really? [2] _____ (it / have) any good advice?

B Yes, it does. The writer [3] _____ (learn) Japanese.
He [4] _____ (want) to learn ten new words a day.
He [5] _____ (always revise) them at the end of each week to check that he [6] _____ (still remember) them.
It [7] _____ (not sound) like much, but after a year, he now [8] _____ (know) over 3,500 new words. That's a lot!

A Wow, yes, I [9] _____ (see) what you mean. So
[10] _____ (you / think) of trying this technique?

B Yes, maybe. I [11] _____ (try) to learn Russian at the moment, but I [12] _____ (not get) any better.

A Really? Why [13] _____ (you / learn) Russian?

B I [14] _____ (think) about going to Moscow next year.

Yes, I'm studying Russian at the moment. I study about an hour a day, but I'm not making much progress,... I don't know why.

c ≫ Now go back to p. 13.

2A Present perfect and past simple

▶ **02.03** **Present perfect**

We use the present perfect to talk about:

- experiences in our lifetime or another unfinished time period
  *She **has worked** in many different countries – France, the USA, Japan …*
  ***Have** you ever **had** a job interview?*
  *I**'ve** never **worked** in an office.*
  We can use adverbs like *ever*, *never* and *three times*.
- news and recent events, often with a present result
  *The interviews **have** already **finished** – you're too late.* (result = You can't have an interview.)
  *We**'ve won** the contract!* (result = Now we have the contract.)
  *She **hasn't called** me back yet.* (result = I'm still waiting to speak to her.)
  We can use adverbs like *already* and *yet*.

▶ **02.04** **Past simple**

We use the past simple for past actions in a completed past time period:
*She **didn't get** the job.*
*The interviews **finished** five minutes ago.*
*Why **did** you **miss** the bus?*
We can use past time phrases like *last week*, *a few days ago*, *when I was a child*.

▶ **02.05** **Present perfect or past simple**

We often introduce a topic with the present perfect and then change to the past simple in the next sentence to talk about the details:
*I**'ve had** lots of job interviews. The last one **was** about three months ago – it **was** terrible.*
*I**'ve lost** my keys. Maybe I **left** them on the bus this morning.*
*He **hasn't worked** here very long. He **started** a few weeks ago.*

Don't use the present perfect when you describe an action that happened at a particular time. Use the past simple instead:
*They **left** yesterday / at four o'clock / ten minutes ago.*

2B Present perfect and present perfect continuous

Unfinished actions and states

To talk about activities or states that started in the past and are still going on:

- We use the present perfect with <u>state</u> verbs:
  *We**'ve had** this car **for** several years and it has never broken down.* (We still have it.)
  *She**'s known** him **since** they were children. They're very good friends.* (They met when they were children – they still know each other.)
- We use the present perfect continuous with <u>activity</u> verbs:
  *How long **have** you **been waiting**?*
  *I**'ve been working** on my essay **since** 6 o'clock.* (I started at six o'clock – I'm still working on it.)
  *He**'s been playing** very well **so far** in this match.* (He's still playing well.)
  With these tenses, we often use a **duration expression** (to show how long): *for*, *since*, *so far*, *How long?*

> **Tip**
>
> Some verbs (e.g., *work*, *live*) can be used as activity verbs or state verbs with no important change of meaning:
> *How long **have** you **worked** here? / How long **have** you **been working** here?*

Recent activities

- We can use the present perfect continuous to talk about an ongoing activity or repeated activity that started recently:
  *I**'ve been exercising** a lot lately.* (I started a few weeks ago.)

*I'm tired. I**'ve been working** on my essay all day.*
A *What **have you been** doing recently?*
B *Nothing much. I've been working a lot. **I haven't been going** out at all.*

With this meaning, we often use time expressions like *lately*, *recently*, *all day*.

▶ **02.08** **Present perfect continuous**

	I / you / we / they	he / she / it
+	I**'ve been using** a new app.	He**'s been using** a new app.
–	I **haven't been sleeping** well.	She **hasn't been sleeping** well.
Y/N?	**Have** they **been living** abroad? Yes, they **have**. / No, they **haven't**.	**Has** she **been living** abroad? Yes, she **has**. / No, she **hasn't**.

2A Present perfect and past simple

a Find and correct the mistakes.

1 **A** Do you ever work in a shop before? **B** No, this is my first time   <u>Have you ever worked</u>
2 I haven't gone to work yesterday – I was ill.   _____
3 **A** We need to email the bank this afternoon.
   B Don't worry – I've done it yet.   _____
4 On her CV she says she's got a lot of experience, but in fact
she hasn't never had a job in her life!   _____
5 I've done various holiday jobs since I've been a student.   _____
6 **A** Have you heard the news? Louise has left her job!
   B Yes, I know. She tells me last week.   _____
7 I'm quite new to the job. I've started in January.   _____

b Complete the conversation with the present perfect or past simple form of the verbs in brackets.

A There's a really good job advert here in the newspaper. [1] <u>Have you seen</u> (you / see) it?
B No, I [2]_____ (not / read) the paper yet. [3]I _____ (only just / get) here. Can you show me?
A It's this one. Senior Marketing Specialist for a bank. I think you should apply for it.
B Er … no, I don't think so. They want someone with a lot of experience in banking, but I [4]_____ (never / work) in a bank.
A No, but you [5]_____ (work) for a lot of marketing companies, and you [6]_____ (do) a lot of projects for banks. Remember? You [7]_____ (work) on a really big banking project about eight years ago. It [8]_____ (be) really good.
B Yes, but eight years is a long time ago. Everything [9]_____ (change) in banking since then. It's a different world now. But what about you? Maybe you should apply. You [10]_____ (tell) me last month that you wanted to try something new.
A Yes, but that [11]_____ (be) last month. I [12]_____ (apply) for a job at a newspaper last week, and they [13]_____ (just / email) me to offer me the job.
B Wow! Congratulations! [14]_____ (you / accept) the offer yet?
A Not yet, no. But I think I will.

c ⟫ Now go back to p. 21.

2B Present perfect and present perfect continuous

a Match the pairs.

1 I've had   <u>b</u>   a tennis lessons for a month.
2 I've been having   <u>a</u>   b swimming lessons a few times.

3 I've read a few sci-fi books. ☐   c I thought they were amazing.
4 I've been reading this book. ☐   d I can't wait to finish it.

5 Have you eaten ☐   e properly recently? You look very thin!
6 Have you been eating ☐   f lunch yet?

b Complete the sentences using the words in brackets and the present perfect continuous.

1 The baby's face is dirty because <u>she's been eating</u> . (she / eat)
2 He's tired because _____ . (he / cut / the grass)
3 They're stressed because _____ . (they / try / to fix the computer)
4 I'm hot because _____ . (I / cook)
5 We're all wet because _____ . (it / rain)
6 They've got muddy shoes because _____ . (they / play / outside)

c <u>Underline</u> the best verb form in each sentence.

1 Amara's on the phone right now – *she's talked / she's been talking* to one of her friends for the last two hours!
2 *I've just bought / I've just been buying* my ticket. I'm so excited about the concert.
3 *I've known / I've been knowing* Jun for about 15 years.
4 I'm so tired. *I've worked / I've been working* since 7 o'clock this morning.
5 I can't drive, but *I've wanted / I've been wanting* to learn for a long time.
6 *They've studied / They've been studying* every night recently because they have an exam next week.

d ⟫ Now go back to p. 25.

3A Narrative tenses

▶ 03.03 Past simple

We use the past simple to describe the main events of a story in the order they happened:

*We **met** a few years ago. He **offered** to help me fix my car. Later, we **became** good friends.*

▶ 03.04 Past continuous

We use the past continuous:

- to describe the situation at the beginning of a story
  *That day, I **was driving** home from university for the summer.*
- for longer actions in comparison with shorter actions in the past simple
  *Where **were** you **going** when I **saw** you by the road?*
  *I **was trying** to get home with some heavy bags when he **stopped** to help me.*
- when actions are interrupted by main events in the past simple.
  *I **was skiing** in the French Alps when I **had** my accident.*

We can connect past simple and past continuous actions with *as*, *while* and *when*:

*Somebody **stole** my bag **when** I **wasn't looking**.*
*Your sister **phoned while** you **were** out **shopping**.*
*He **looked** out of the window **while** the train **was going** through the countryside.*
*The car **broke down** as I **was driving** down the road.*
*We **met** our friends **while** we **were trying** to get home.*

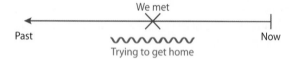

Don't use the past continuous for state verbs. Use the past simple instead:

*We met when I **was** a student.*
NOT ... when I was being a student.

▶ 03.05 Past perfect

We use the past perfect to describe an event that happened before the story started, or earlier in the story than a main event:

*That summer, I **had** just **finished** my second year at university.*
*When we met, my car **had broken** down by the side of the road.*

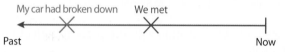

*I **hadn't taken** my phone with me, so I couldn't phone for help.*

> **💬 Tip**
>
> We can use *by* + a time with the past perfect to show what happened sometime before a point in the past:
> *I started reading it on Monday and **by Friday I'd read** the whole book.*
> *They were really late for the party. **By the time they arrived**, everyone else **had gone** home.*

3B used to, usually

▶ 03.09

We use *used to* to describe past habits and states:

*When I was at school, I **used to play** football every Saturday.* (past habit)
*The whole family **used to love** animals. We always had two or three pets in the house.* (past state)

The negative forms are *didn't use to* (NOT *didn't used to*) and *never used to*:

*My parents **didn't use to go** out much, so we spent a lot of time together.*
*We **never used to** understand my dad's jokes.*

There is no present tense of *used to*. Use adverbs of frequency instead:

*They **usually go** out to a restaurant once or twice a week.*
*How many times a month **do** you **usually visit** them?*

You can also use adverbs of frequency with the past simple and a past time phrase (e.g., *when I was a child*, *back then*):

*We **went** abroad for a holiday **quite often back then**.*

We can use the adverbials *not any more* and *not any longer* to say that a past habit or state has now stopped:

*I **don't** play football **any more**. I usually go to the gym instead.*
*They **don't** live in the same house **any longer**.*

We can use the adverb *still* to talk about a past habit or state that has not changed:

*I **still** love board games. I frequently play Chinese Chequers.*
*Do you **still** see him very often?*

Past simple or *used to*

We use *used to* for situations that were true for a long time (e.g., a few months or years). For shorter periods of time, we usually use the past simple:

*When we were on holiday last week, we **went** swimming every day.*
NOT ... we used to go ...

We often use *used to* for situations that aren't true now:

*When I was a child I **used to love** ice cream, but now I don't really like it.*

Use the past simple, not *used to*, to describe something that happened once or a specified number of times:

*I **went** to the USA twice when I was a child.*
NOT I used to go to the USA twice ...

> **💬 Tip**
>
> We often use a mixture of the past simple and *used to* to describe past situations. It sounds unnatural if you use *used to* for every verb.

3A Narrative tenses

a Underline the correct options.

I ¹*meeting / met* my friend Alex while I ²*was fixing / fixed* my bike last year. The wheel ³*fell / had fallen* off and I ⁴*was trying / had tried* to put it back on. Alex ⁵*had walked / was walking* down the street when he ⁶*saw / was seeing* me, and he ⁷*was offering / offered* to help. After that, we ⁸*became / had become* friends.

I ⁹*met / had met* my friend Anna in a hospital. I ¹⁰*was being / was* there because I ¹¹*was falling / had fallen* and ¹²*had broken / was breaking* my arm. Anna ¹³*was / had been* there because she ¹⁴*injured / had injured* her foot. We ¹⁵*started / were starting* talking while we ¹⁶*had waited / were waiting* to see the doctor. By the time the doctor ¹⁷*was arriving / arrived*, we ¹⁸*had become / became* good friends.

b Complete the interview with the correct form of the verbs in brackets. Sometimes there is more than one possible answer.

A When ¹_____*did*_____ the accident _____*happen*_____ (happen)?

B It ²_____ (happen) as I ³_____ (drive) along Main Street last night. I ⁴_____ (see) an old lady. Just as I ⁵_____ (turn) left, she ⁶_____ (fall) over onto the pavement right next to me. I was fairly sure I could see why. A young man ⁷_____ (push) her over. Straight away I ⁸_____ (stop) my car and I ⁹_____ (jump) out. I ¹⁰_____ (run) over to the old lady. She ¹¹_____ (lie) on the ground and she ¹²_____ (cry).

A ¹³_____ (you / notice) anything else?

B Yes … I saw a large flowerpot on the pavement. It ¹⁴_____ (be) broken.

A Where ¹⁵_____ (it / come) from?

B It ¹⁶_____ (fall) from a window above the street. The young man ¹⁷_____ (push) the old lady out of the way. He ¹⁸_____ (save) her life!

c ⫸ Now go back to p. 34.

3B *used to, usually*

a Complete the text with the correct words/phrases.

> didn't use to go   don't go   don't live   live   lived
> used to be   used to enjoy   ~~used to go~~   used to have
> use to have   usually visit   went

When I was a child, I ¹___*used to go*___ to my grandparents' house in the mountains. We ²_____ in a city back then, and we visited them every year. We didn't ³_____ a car at that time, so we travelled by bus. It always took ages! We ⁴_____ in the winter because there was too much snow.

I loved helping my grandfather in his garden (although I usually avoid gardening now!). He never ⁵_____ a lawnmower, so we had to cut the grass by hand. It was hard, but I ⁶_____ it.

I still ⁷_____ in the same city, but I ⁸_____ to the mountains any more. My grandparents ⁹_____ there any longer. They ¹⁰_____ to live in a large town five years ago. Now, I ¹¹_____ them in the summer, but it's not as nice as the mountains ¹²_____ .

b If possible, change the verbs in **bold** to the correct form of *used to*. If it is not possible, put an ✗.

1 I **drank** a lot of cola, but now I don't. ☐ ___*used to drink*___
2 I **celebrated** my birthday with my family last year. ☒
3 She **had** long hair when she was younger. ☐
   _____
4 Where **did** you **live** when you were a child? ☐
   _____
5 I **went** for a run every day last week. ☐
   _____
6 We **didn't wear** matching clothes all the time. ☐
   _____
7 In the past, people **spent** more time at work. ☐
   _____
8 **Did** you **play** with your sister when you were kids? ☐
   _____
9 I **bought** this bag in London – it's my favourite bag. ☐
   _____
10 They **weren't** friends in those days. ☐
   _____

c ⫸ Now go back to p. 37.

4A Modals and phrases of ability

▶ 04.04 General ability

We use *can / could* to talk about general abilities:
*I **can** ski, but I **can't** snowboard.*
*I **couldn't do** maths at school.*

We only use *can* in the present tense and *could* in the past tense, so when we need another form, we use *be able to*.
We use *be able to*:
*   in the present perfect, past perfect and after modal verbs
    *How long **have** you **been able to drive**?*
    *We hope we'**ll be able to come** on Saturday.*
    *Everyone **should be able to swim**.*
*   after other verbs (e.g., *want, need, like*) or prepositions
    (e.g., *of, about*).
    *The person who gets the job **needs to be able to**
    speak English.*
    *I **like being able to visit** my parents regularly.*
    *Don't worry **about not being able to understand**. You'll be fine!*

Specific past achievements

Don't use *could* for specific past achievements:
*When I went to France last year, I **was able to** visit the Louvre.*
NOT *I could visit …*

I couldn't play the piano when I was a child, but I can play very well now.

In negative sentences about specific past events, we use
couldn't or *wasn't able to*:
*I went to France last year, but I **couldn't** remember / **wasn't able**
to remember any words in French.*
We can also use *managed to* for specific past achievements,
especially to show that something was difficult:
*It was hard work, but I **managed to** finish the project.*

4B Articles

▶ 04.06

We use *a/an* and *the* with singular countable nouns. We use *the*
or no article with plural or uncountable nouns. The choice of
article shows:
*   if the topic is new or old
    *I read **a great book** last week.* (= we haven't discussed this
    book before)
    *What was **the book** about?* (= the one we mentioned earlier)
*   if something is the only one
    *Where are **the car keys**?* (= the only car keys we have)
*   if we are talking about things in general or in particular.
    ***Cats** are clever animals.* (= the animal in general)
    ***The cats** are in the garden.* (= our pets)

Other uses of *a/an*

*   We use *a/an* to describe something or say what job someone
    has got:
    *That's **a** beautiful photo. / He's **a** doctor.*
*   We use *a/an* in some frequency expressions:
    *I drink coffee once **a** week / three times **a** day.*

Other uses of *the*

*   We use *the* before a noun that has a defining relative clause:
    *I've just met **the** man who lives next door.* (= one specific man)
*   We use *the* before superlatives:
    *Kyoto is **the** most beautiful city in Japan.*
*   We use *the* with certain countries, oceans, rivers or groups
    of islands:
    *I went to **the** USA / **the** Pacific / **the** Amazon / **the** Bahamas.*
*   We use *the* with some fixed expressions about:
    time: *all **the** time, most of **the** time, at **the** same time*
    places or seasons: *in **the** countryside / city; in **the** summer*
    free-time activities: *go to **the** cinema / **the** gym; listen to*
    ***the** radio (**but** watch TV)*

I've been reading a book.

I've been reading the book you lent me.

Other uses of no article

*   We use no article in phrases about meals:
    *I had **breakfast** / **lunch** / **dinner** at 7 am.*
    NOT *I had a/the breakfast …*
*   We use no article in some fixed phrases about places:
    *I usually **go home** / **go to bed** / **go to work** / **go to school**
    at … o'clock.*
*   We use no article to talk about most countries, continents,
    cities, streets, etc.:
    I went to China / Africa / Paris / Bond Street.

> **💡 Tip**
>
> Don't use *a/an* with uncountable nouns. Instead use no
> article or *some*:
> *We need to buy toothpaste and shampoo.*
> *Can you give me **some** information about the course?*
> We can use *the* with uncountable nouns:
> *Where's **the** shampoo? I need to wash my hair.*
> *I looked at their website. I found **the** information very helpful.*

4A Modals and phrases of ability

a Underline the correct option. If both options are possible, underline both of them.

1 I went to India last year, but I *can't / couldn't* take any pictures because my camera was broken.

2 *He's been able to swim / He can swim* since he was a child.

3 When they were children, they *could / were able to* run really fast.

4 She tried to read *War and Peace*, but she *wasn't able to / didn't manage to* finish it.

5 He *managed to / could* climb trees when he was a boy, but he *can't / couldn't* climb them now.

6 Katya needs to *can / be able to* speak Japanese in her new job.

7 You will *can / be able to* find a new person for the job soon, I'm sure.

8 I'm scared of *not being able to / can't* pass my exam tomorrow.

9 They *couldn't / didn't manage to* find a parking place.

10 I think everyone should *manage to / be able to* drive. It's an important skill.

b Complete the sentences with the phrases in the box.

can swim   could all swim   ~~couldn't swim~~   couldn't walk
didn't manage to   managed to climb   needed to be able
to   be able to   was able to jump   was able to stand

When I was a young child, I [1] ___couldn't swim___ – I only learned to swim when I was about 14. I guess I thought that I didn't need [2] _____ swim because I never went to swimming pools. But one day, I went for a walk on a hill near the sea with my friends – we were about 13 at the time. Part of the path was missing in one place – we [3] _____ along it, so we decided to try to jump across. My friend Andy was quite big, so he [4] _____ across it very easily. But then it was my turn – I was a lot smaller, so I [5] _____ jump across. I fell down the hill and into the sea. My friends [6] _____, so they thought it was really funny to see me in the water, but I was really scared. Luckily, I [7] _____ on a rock under the water and then I [8] _____ out of the water. After that, I knew I [9] _____ to swim, so I started taking swimming lessons every week. And now I [10] _____ really well.

c ⟫ Now go back to p. 46.

4B Articles

a Find the mistakes in these sentences.

1 Do you want to go to a cinema with me?   *Do you want to go to the cinema with me?*
2 I read the very interesting book last weekend.   _____
3 I want to buy new shirt.   _____
4 We had the good time at the beach.   _____
5 They recently moved to a countryside.   _____
6 I like learning the languages.   _____
7 If you have problem, call me.   _____
8 Good night! I'm going to the bed.   _____
9 My brother is engineer.   _____
10 If you go to the shops, can you get me a bread?   _____

b Complete the text with *a/an*, *the* or Ø (no article).

I don't like working in [1] _Ø_ groups because I never know what to say when [2] _____ people talk to me. [3] _____ last year, I joined [4] _____ language class and [5] _____ teacher made [6] _____ students work in [7] _____ groups for [8] _____ most activities. [9] _____ lessons that we had were good, but I wasn't happy about [10] _____ speaking activities. I know practising speaking is probably [11] _____ best way to learn [12] _____ language, but I don't really need to speak in my job. [13] _____ only thing I want is to be able to write [14] _____ good emails without making [15] _____ mistakes. One day, after [16] _____ extremely difficult lesson, I decided to speak to [17] _____ teacher about [18] _____ problem. I explained [19] _____ situation and she listened carefully. She explained [20] _____ purpose of working in [21] _____ groups and said that she needs to find [22] _____ right balance for all of [23] _____ students in [24] _____ class. In [25] _____ end, I agreed to try to speak more, and she agreed to give me [26] _____ more time to work quietly.

c ⟫ Now go back to p. 49.

5A Future forms

▶ 05.04 **Decisions, plans and arrangements**

We use *will* to make a spontaneous decision (= a decision while we are speaking):
OK, I'll come for a run with you.
We use *be going to* to talk about future intentions or plans (= decisions we made earlier):
We're not going to stay at that hotel again.
We use the present continuous to talk about arrangements (= fixed plans, usually involving other people and specific times and places):
She's travelling to Central America on Sunday.

There is not a big difference in meaning between *be going to* and the present continuous to talk about future plans / arrangements. Often both are possible:
I'm visiting / I'm going to visit my sister this weekend.

▶ 05.05 **Offers, promises and suggestions**

We use *will* to make offers and promises:
I'll help you, if you like.
I'll always be here when you need me.

We use *can + I/we* in questions to make offers and *shall + I/we* to make suggestions.
A *Can I carry that for you?*   **B** *Oh, yes, please.*
A *Shall we go swimming on Saturday?*   **B** *That's a good idea.*

▶ 05.06 **Predictions**

We use *will* to make predictions based on our opinions:
I'm sure you'll learn a lot when you go travelling.
Don't put that there! It'll fall off.
We use *be going to* to make predictions based on concrete facts (= things that we can see or information that we have read):
We should leave soon. The roads are going to be busy.
It's not going to rain. There isn't a cloud in the sky.

> 💬 **Tip**
>
> In negative sentences, say *I don't think + will.*
> *I don't think the forest will recover.* NOT *~~I think the forest won't recover.~~*

5B Zero and first conditionals

Conditional sentences have two parts: the *if*-clause describes a possible event and the main clause describes the result of that event. The *if*-clause can come before or after the main clause. When the *if*-clause is first, put a comma between the two parts:
If the lizard gets scared, it hides.
The lizard hides if it gets scared.

▶ 05.08 **Zero conditionals**

Zero conditionals describe events and results that happen regularly or are always true. They are often used to report facts. We use the present tense in both the *if*-clause and the main clause:
If the lizard gets scared, it hides.
If I go to the city centre, I always eat in that restaurant.
Anyone can succeed if they work hard.
Butter doesn't burn in the pan if you add a little oil to it.

▶ 05.09 **First conditionals**

First conditionals describe possible future events and the expected results of those events. We use the present tense in the *if*-clause and a future form in the main clause:
If the scientists succeed, many people will live longer.
If I don't work hard, I won't be successful.
Will you have to commute if you get the job?
He'll cook you an amazing meal if you ask him to. He loves showing off!

Imperative conditionals

We can use imperatives in the main clause. The meaning can be present or future:
If you're tired (now), go to bed (now).
If you're tired when you arrive (this evening), go to bed (then).

Unless

Unless means 'if not'. We can use it in zero or first conditionals and with imperatives:
We play every Saturday unless it rains.
It won't hurt you unless you run away.

> 💬 **Tip**
>
> First conditionals are used to talk about future events where we are unsure if the result will happen.
> *If the government changes the law, this area will become a national park.*
> However, if we are sure the result will happen, we change *if* to *when*:
> *When the government changes the law, this area will become a national park.*

5A Future forms

a Underline the best option in each sentence.

1 **A** It's a bit hot in here.
 B You're right. *I'll / I'm going to* open a window.
2 I'm going to the shops. *Will / Can* I get you anything?
3 **A** Why are you carrying those flowers?
 B Because *I'll / I'm going to* ask Sara to marry me!
4 **A** I'm so tired.
 B *I'll / I shall* make you some coffee, if you want.
5 I've got a bad stomach. I think *I'll / I'm going to* be sick …

b Complete the sentences with *will, can, shall* or *be going to* and the verbs in brackets. Sometimes more than one answer is possible.

1 _Can I carry_ (I / carry) your bag down the stairs?
2 What time _____ (we / meet)?
3 _____ (you / cook) me a nice meal tonight?
4 I _____ (go) to bed when this programme is over – I'm tired.
5 I _____ (come) back one day – I promise.
6 I _____ (have) a steak – no, I _____ (have) fish, please.
7 According to the website, she _____ (talk) about some of her trips.
8 I think you _____ (like) my chocolate cake a lot.
9 Put your money away! _____ (I / get) this.

c Complete the telephone conversation using the verbs in brackets with *will, can, shall, be going to* or the present continuous. Sometimes there is more than one possible answer.

A Hi Dan, it's Tony. Listen, I [1] _'m coming_ (come) to Nottingham for a couple of days next week for a big meeting with a client. I [2] _____ (try) to see some of my old friends while I'm there. Do you want to meet up one evening?
B Sounds good. It [3] _____ (be) good to see you again after all these years.
A Yeah, I know. [4] _____ (we / say) Tuesday evening?
B Er … no, that's not good for me. I [5] _____ (take) the kids to the cinema on Tuesday. We already have tickets.
A OK, no problem. What about Wednesday?
B OK, that's fine. What time do you think [6] _____ (you / be) free?
A The meeting [7] _____ (probably / end) at about 5 o'clock – that's what the client said, anyway.
B OK, so around 7 then? [8] _____ (I / pick) you up at your hotel? Where [9] _____ (you / stay)?
A [10] _____ (I / be) at the King's Hotel. I reserved a room last week.
B Perfect. Listen, I [11] _____ (phone) you before I leave, at about 6.30, to see if you're ready.
A Don't worry – I [12] _____ (be) ready.

d ≫ Now go back to p. 58.

5B Zero and first conditionals

a Match clauses 1–8 and clauses a–h to make sentences.

1 I'll send you a text
2 If a snail is in danger,
3 The animals won't come out
4 If you need some money,
5 If you see a bear in a forest,
6 Snakes don't bite
7 If you go diving,
8 Water freezes at −2°C

a unless we stay quiet.
b don't run!
c I'll lend you some.
d if it contains salt.
e unless they feel scared.
f you'll see lots of different species.
g when Paola arrives.
h it hides in its shell.

b Underline the correct options.

1 If I *eat / will eat* too much, I feel sleepy.
2 If we watch another episode, *I have / I'll have* trouble waking up on time tomorrow morning.
3 *I send / I'll send* you some photos if you give me your email address.
4 If we don't leave now, we *don't / won't* get to the airport on time.
5 If you *go / will go* to Jordan, visit the ancient city of Petra.
6 I go to the cinema every Friday unless *I'm not / I'm* busy.
7 Rua *will speak / won't speak* to Jin-Su unless he apologises.
8 If someone *phones / is going to phone*, don't tell them I'm here.
9 You can do anything *if / unless* you try hard enough.
10 Will I have to bring anything if I *come / will come* to the party?

c Complete the sentences with the verbs in brackets and a conditional form. Use *will* or *'ll* where possible.

1 You ____'ll feel____ (feel) bad if you ____drink____ (drink) too much coffee.
2 If you _____ (not want) to watch the film, we _____ (do) something else instead.
3 He _____ (not make) any money unless he _____ (start) selling more products.
4 If I _____ (listen) to new information and don't read it, I _____ (remember) it more easily.
5 If you _____ (feel) like going out later, _____ (phone) me.
6 Unless it _____ (be) really cold, we _____ (try) to run tomorrow morning.
7 You _____ (not get) there on time if you _____ (not take) the train.
8 If she _____ (study) for more than four hours, she _____ (get) a really bad headache.

d ≫ Now go back to p. 60.

6A Modals of obligation

▶ **06.04** *must*, *have to* and *need to*

We use *have to* or *need to* to say something is necessary:
*You **have to buy** a ticket before you get on the train.*
*We **need to** show our tickets on the train.*

Must is very strong and can be formal or official. We often see *must* in written rules or laws. It is not common in speaking.
*Employees **must** wash their hands.*

There is no past or future form of *must*. When we talk about rules in the past or future, we always use the correct form of *have to* or *need to*:
*When you go to India, you**'ll need to** get a visa.*
*I **had to** wear a uniform at school.*

> **Tip**
>
> Don't use contractions with *have to*:
> *I have to go.* NOT ~~I've to go.~~

> **Tip**
>
> • Often there is not much difference in meaning between *need to* and *have to*.
> • *Have got to* is also used in spoken English and means the same as *have to*.
> • Questions with *must* are very rare.

▶ **06.05** *mustn't*, *can't* and *don't have to*

We use *mustn't* or *can't* to say that something is not allowed. *Can't* is much more common in spoken English. We use *must not* to express strong prohibition or to say something is forbidden.
*Drivers **mustn't** text and drive.*
*We **can't** cross the road yet – the light's still red.*
For things that were not allowed in the past, use *couldn't*:
*I **couldn't** work in Peru because I only had a tourist visa.*

We use *don't have to* or *don't need to* when there is no obligation. It means it is not necessary to do something:
*University students **don't have to wear** a uniform.*
*I **didn't need to** call a taxi. Robert drove me home.*

▶ **06.06** *should* and *ought to*

We use *should* or *ought to* to give advice and recommendations. They have the same meaning, but *ought to* is rarely used in the negative. We use *shouldn't* instead:
*We **should see** as much as possible.*
*We **shouldn't waste** time.*
*We **ought to see** as much as possible.*

Next we need to make the sandwiches. We don't have to make a cake because Francesca bought one.

6B Comparatives and superlatives

		Adjectives	Adverbs
One syllable		*rich* → *rich**er**, the rich**est***	*fast* → *fast**er**, the fast**est***
Two or more syllables*	**Ending in -y:** *easy* → *eas**ier**, the eas**iest*** *friendly* → *friendl**ier**, the friendl**iest***	**All:** *often* → **more** *often, the* **most** *often* *carefully* →	
	Other: *careful* → **more** *careful, the* **most** *careful*	**more** *carefully,* **the most** *carefully*	
Exceptions	*good* → **better, the best** *bad* → **worse, the worst** *far* → **further, the furthest** **more / the most** *bored / tired*	*well* → **better, the best** *badly* → **worse, the worst** *far* → **further, the furthest** *early* → **earlier, the earliest**	

*Some two-syllable adjectives can follow the rules for one-syllable adjectives: *narrow, shallow, quiet, simple.*

▶ **06.11** **Comparison**

We can use comparative adjectives and adverbs to compare two things, situations, times, actions, etc., usually with *than*. We can change the degree of comparison with words like *a lot, much, far, even, slightly, a bit, a little*:
*Life's **a lot more interesting than** before.*
*She's **a bit happier than** she used to be.*
*He's speaking **much more slowly than** usual today.*

The opposite of *more* is *less*. We can use it with all adjectives and adverbs:
*The car's **slightly less clean than** it was.*
*I drive **less quickly than** he does.*

as + adjective/adverb + *as* shows that two things are equal; *not as … as* means *less than*:
*They're **as wealthy as** the royal family.*
*She does**n't listen as carefully as** she should.*

Some common adverbs can change the degree of the comparison:
*You're **just** as pretty as your sister!* (= exactly equal)
*My brother isn't **nearly** as hard-working as me.* (= very different)
*She doesn't sleep **quite** as well as I do.* (= slightly different)

Extremes

We use superlative adjectives and adverbs to talk about extremes:
*It's **the worst** hotel in the world!*
*I got **the lowest** score possible.*

We often use the present perfect with *ever* with superlatives:
*This is **the best** meal I**'ve ever eaten**.*
*It was **the least interesting** film I**'ve ever seen**.*

We can use the expressions *by far* and *easily* to say an extreme is very different from all others:
*That's **by far the highest** mountain I've ever climbed.*

6A Modals of obligation

a Complete the sentences with the correct form of *have to*, *need to* or *must*. Sometimes more than one answer is possible.

1 In my country, you ___*have to*___ cross the road at a pedestrian crossing – it's illegal to cross anywhere else.
2 When I lived in Moscow, I _____ leave home two hours before work because the rush hour traffic was so bad.
3 _____ Alex _____ wear a tie to work?
4 I'll tell you a secret, but you _____ tell anyone. I don't want anyone else to know.
5 We took plenty of money, but in the end, we _____ pay – everything was free.
6 All visitors _____ (have to / must) report to reception.
7 If you want to be there on time, you'll _____ leave here very soon.
8 Your brother can borrow my books tonight, but he _____ forget to bring them back tomorrow. I need them for my class.

b Look at the signs. Then complete the advice using the verbs in brackets and a modal verb. Sometimes more than one form is possible.

NO PARKING	FREE BUS TO SHOPPING CENTRE	WARNING! Car thieves in this area. LOCK YOUR CAR	Fire exit Emergency only	USE OFFICIAL TAXIS ONLY

You ¹ ___*mustn't /*___ ___*can't park*___ (park) here.

You ² _____ (pay) for the bus to the shopping centre.

You ³ _____ (leave) your car unlocked. It might get stolen.

You ⁴ _____ (use) that door – it's for emergencies only.

You ⁵ _____ (only use) the official taxis.

c ≫ Now go back to p. 70.

6B Comparatives and superlatives

a Complete the sentences with the comparative or superlative form of the words in brackets. Add *than* or *the* where necessary.

1 Indian food is ___*spicier than*___ French food. (spicy)
2 This is _____ meal I've ever eaten. (delicious)
3 The weather was _____ I expected. (hot)
4 She's a _____ driver _____ I am. (slow)
5 Are you _____ person in your class? (clever)
6 I didn't have a good holiday. The _____ thing was the hotel. It was terrible. (bad)
7 Your English is _____ mine. (good)
8 I'm sorry, I can't come on Friday. That's my _____ day. (busy)

b Complete the sentences so that they mean the same as the sentences in **a**. Use two to five words.

1 French food isn't ___*as spicy as Indian food*___.
2 I've never eaten a _____ meal than this.
3 I didn't expect the weather to be _____ it was.
4 She drives _____ I do.
5 Is anybody in your class _____ you?
6 I didn't have a good holiday. The hotel was _____ everything else.
7 I don't speak English _____ you do.
8 I'm sorry, I can't come on Friday. It's _____ the other days.

c Complete the sentences with one word from the box in each space. Use each word once only.

a̶	as	bit	by	ever	just	m̶o̶r̶e̶
most	nearly	one	slightly	than	the	

1 Today's lesson was ___*a*___ lot ___*more*___ interesting than usual – it was excellent.
2 That's _____ worst joke I've _____ heard!
3 The exam went really well. It wasn't _____ as difficult as I expected.
4 I think she's _____ of the _____ innovative designers in the world.
5 Our holiday was a _____ more expensive _____ we thought, but it was still good value.
6 They started _____ later than usual, but they still finished on time.
7 _____ far the oldest person in my family is my great-grandmother.
8 Our new TV is fantastic – the picture quality is _____ as good _____ in the cinema, or maybe even better.

d ≫ Now go back to p. 72.

7A Modals of deduction

We can use modal verbs to show that we are making a deduction using evidence, not stating a fact:

▶07.03

We **must be** early. Nobody else has arrived yet.
They work at the same office, so they **may know** each other.
She **might not be** in. The lights are all out.
That **can't be** Mark's car. He told me it was in the garage.

Different modal verbs tell us how sure about a deduction we are:

It's cold in that house.	Fact: I **know** it is.
It **must** be cold in that house.	Deduction: I'm **sure** it is.
It **may / might / could** be cold in that house.	Deduction: It's **possible** that it is.
It **may / might not** be cold in that house.	Deduction: It's **possible** that it isn't.
It **can't** be cold in that house.	Deduction: I'm **sure** it isn't.
It isn't cold in that house.	Fact: I **know** it isn't.

- The opposite of *must* for deductions is *can't*. Don't use *must not / mustn't*, *can* or *couldn't* for deductions:
  This bill **can't** be right. I only ordered a salad.
  NOT ~~This bill couldn't / must not / mustn't be right.~~
  There **must** be a mistake.
  NOT ~~There can be a mistake.~~
- There is almost no difference between *may*, *might* and *could*. All three mean that something is possible.
- To make deductions about actions happening now, use a modal + *be* + verb + *-ing*:
  She isn't answering the phone. She **might be listening** to music.

7B Quantifiers

▶07.10 *some*, *any* and *no*

We usually use *some* in positive statements and in questions that are offers. We use *any* in negative statements and other questions:
There are **some** nice views from the hotel.
Would you like **some** coffee?
He does**n't** have **any** good music.
Do you have **any** local currency?

We can use *no* in positive sentences to talk about zero quantity:
There's **no** crime around here.

To talk about zero quantity, we can also use *none of* + plural / uncountable or *none*:
None of my friends could help.
A How many holidays have you been on this year?
B **None** at all.

▶07.11 Large quantities

We use *a lot of / lots of* in positive sentences, *not many / not much / not a lot of* in negative sentences and *many / much / a lot of* in questions:
There are quite **a lot of** cars on the roads today.
I have**n't** got **much** money with me.
Did **many** people come to the concert?
We do**n't** need **a lot of** time to finish this work.

In positive sentences, we can use *plenty of* to show we are happy with the amount:
Don't worry – we've got **plenty of** food.

▶07.12 Small quantities

We use *a few / a little* to talk about an amount. We use *few / little* to talk about a negative amount (i.e., there is not a lot):
We have **a little** time before the show starts.
There are **a few** things I need from the shops.
I have **very little** time to finish this work.
This dish has **very few** ingredients.

We can say *quite a few / very few / very little* to increase / decrease the amount.

▶07.13 *too / not enough*

We use *too much / too many* + noun to say there is more than the right amount. We use *not enough* to say there is less than the right amount:
I have **too much furniture**. There is**n't enough room** for all of it!
I couldn't move at the concert because there were **too many people**.

We also use *too* + adjective/adverb and *not* + adjective/adverb *enough*:
This suitcase is **too heavy**. They won't let you on the plane.
You're walking **too quickly**. I can't keep up!
The meeting room is**n't big enough** for all of us. There are**n't enough** chairs.
You're **not** walking **fast enough**. Hurry up!

We often use different quantifiers with **uncountable** nouns and with **plural countable** nouns.

quantifier + uncountable noun	quantifier + countable noun
lots of time/tourists	
plenty of time/tourists	
not much time	not many tourists
how much time?	how many tourists?
too much time	too many tourists
not enough time/tourists	
a little time	a few tourists
very little time	very few tourists

Marta invited **a few** friends to her party.
We only had **a little** money left at the end of our holiday.
I've eaten **too many** biscuits.
Don't give the children **too much** lemonade.

7A Modals of deduction

a Match the deductions 1–8 with the best sentences a–h.

1 ☐ f That man must be a doctor.
2 ☐ That man might be a doctor.
3 ☐ That man might not be a doctor.
4 ☐ That man can't be a doctor.
5 ☐ They must be eating dinner now.
6 ☐ They could be eating dinner now.
7 ☐ They may not be eating dinner now.
8 ☐ They can't be eating dinner now.

a He doesn't know anything about medicine.
b They finished their dinner an hour ago.
c He's wearing a white coat.
d I remember they booked a table at a restaurant for this time.
e Perhaps they've finished.
f Look – he's listening to that man's heart.
g They usually eat around this time.
h It's possible that he's a nurse.

b Complete the sentences using an appropriate modal of deduction. Sometimes more than one modal is possible.

1 It's impossible that she's in the office – she flew to Beijing yesterday.
She _can't be in the office – she flew to Beijing yesterday._

2 I'm sure you're right.
You _____

3 It's possible that they want to sell their flat.
They _____

4 I'm sure he isn't speaking Russian – it sounds more like Spanish to me.
He _____ – it sounds more like Spanish to me.

5 It's possible that you're the perfect person for the job.
You _____

6 There's a possibility that he doesn't know the answer.
He _____

7 I'm sure you don't need that coat today – it's 30°C!
It's 30°C! You _____

8 They're probably building a new shopping centre.
They _____

c ⟫ Now go back to p. 80.

7B Quantifiers

a Underline the correct quantifier in each sentence.

1 We had *any* / *no* / *none* problems.
2 My parents read *a lot* / *a lot of* / *much* books.
3 I'm not tall *enough* / *too* / *plenty* to be a police officer.
4 There's too *little* / *many* / *much* noise in my neighbourhood. I can't sleep.
5 You don't go out *little* / *many* / *enough*. You should go out more.
6 I watch *much* / *many* / *a lot of* television.
7 **A** Did you get much work done?
   B Yes, I got *a lot of* / *a lot* / *none* done.
8 **A** Have you got any potatoes?
   B No, I haven't got *some* / *any* / *none*.
9 I've been to quite *many* / *few* / *a few* countries.
10 It's *too much* / *too* / *enough* hot in here. Can I open a window?

b Complete the second sentence so that it means the same as the first sentence.

1 **a** I want no visitors for the next 30 minutes.
   b I don't _want any visitors for the next 30 minutes._
2 **a** There aren't enough chairs for everyone.
   b There are too _few chairs_
3 **a** I wanted a biscuit, but there weren't any left.
   b I wanted a biscuit, but there were _none left_
4 **a** Make sure you take plenty of money.
   b Make sure you take a _lot of money_
5 **a** They gave us too little information.
   b They didn't _gave us enought_
6 **a** I didn't see many people.
   b I saw very _few people_
7 **a** We didn't have any money.
   b We had _no money_
8 **a** She has plenty of time tomorrow.
   b She has a _lot of time_

c ⟫ Now go back to p. 85.

8A Reported speech

Reported speech and direct speech
When we talk about what somebody said or thought, we can use direct speech or reported speech:
- *Direct speech:* He said, 'I don't want to talk to you.'
- *Reported speech:* He said he didn't want to talk to me.

▶ 08.04

Direct speech		Reported speech
'I **don't want** to talk to you.'	→	He said he **didn't want** to talk to me.
'I'm **planning** to resign.'	→	She said she **was planning** to resign.
'I've already **told** you.'	→	He said **he had** already **told** me.
'I **saw** you break it.'	→	I told him I **had seen** him break it.
'I'm **going to** cook tonight.'	→	You said you **were going to** cook tonight.
'I'll **see** you soon.'	→	He said he **would** see me soon.
'I **can't** hear you.'	→	She said she **couldn't** hear me.
'You **may** be right.'	→	He said I **might** be right.

Some modal verbs (*would, could, should, might*) stay the same in reported speech:
'I'd like to go.' → He said he'**d** like to go.
'It **might** be difficult.' → She said it **might** be difficult.

When I asked him if he **was** going to resign, he said he **didn't want** to talk to me.

EXIT

TV

▶ 08.05 Reported questions
When you report a *Wh-* question, put the subject before the verb. Don't use the auxiliary *do / does / did*:
'Where **are you** from?' → She asked me where **I was** from.
'Why **did she say** that?' → He asked me why **she had said** that.
For *Yes/No* questions, use *if/whether*. *Whether* is more formal than *if*:
'Are you going to help?' → We asked them **if** they were going to help.
'Did you visit the London Eye?' → She asked us **whether** we had visited the London Eye.

Other changes
When we report speech, we usually need to change the pronouns (e.g., *I, he*) and possessives (e.g., *my*), depending on who is talking to whom. Time and place words may also need to change:
'I want **you** to give **this** message to **your** boss **tonight**.'
→ She said **she** wanted **me** to give **a/the** message to **my** boss **that night**.

> **Tip**
> You don't need to change the tense when you want to show that the speaker's words are still true now:
> I **told** you yesterday that I **don't** want to talk to you.
> (= I still don't want to talk to you today.)

Say and *tell* have different patterns. Always use a person or pronoun after *tell*:
Tom **said** he had a new car. NOT ~~Tom said me he had a new car.~~
Tom **told me** he had a new car. NOT ~~Tom told he had a new car.~~

8B Verb patterns

▶ 08.06 verb + -ing or infinitive
- Some verbs (e.g., *enjoy, mind, keep, admit, recommend, suggest*) are followed by a verb + *-ing*:
  She **didn't mind working** late.
  The negative form is *not* + verb + *-ing*:
  I **enjoyed not cooking** for a change.
- Other verbs (e.g., *want, hope, agree, offer, promise, refuse, threaten, plan*) are followed by *to* + infinitive:
  They **threatened to tell** the police.
  The negative form is *not* + *to* + infinitive:
  I **promise not to break** anything.
- Some verbs (e.g., *start, begin, continue*) can be followed by both patterns, with no change of meaning:
  People **started arriving** an hour ago.
  He **started to feel** angry.
- Some verbs (e.g., *try, forget, remember*) can be followed by both patterns, but the meaning changes:
  I **tried reading** some reviews online, but they didn't help much. (= I read them as an experiment)
  I **tried to read** some reviews online, but my Internet connection wasn't working. (= I attempted to read them)
  I **remember going** there for the first time. (= I'm looking back at an earlier experience)
  Please **remember to book** a table. (= keep the plan in your memory)

- Some verbs (e.g., *advise, ask, invite, remind, tell, warn*) need an object before *to* + infinitive:
  They **warned** me not **to tell** anyone.
  I've **invited** your parents **to visit** us.
  Make (= force) and *let* (= allow) are followed by an object and an infinitive:
  My boss **made me work** late.
  He **let me drive** his car.

Other uses of verb + -ing
- When a verb comes after a preposition (e.g., *about, of, by*), the verb is always in the *-ing* form:
  I'm worried **about** not be**ing** good enough.
  They escaped **by** breaking a window.
- When a verb is the subject of a sentence, it is usually in the *-ing* form:
  Eating in a restaurant is more expensive than eating at home.

Other uses of to + infinitive
- Infinitive of purpose:
  I went online **to read** the news.
- adjective + *to* + infinitive:
  I was relieved **to see** I wasn't late.
- verb + question word + *to* + infinitive:
  I don't know where **to go** or who **to ask**.

8A Reported speech

a Complete the reported speech with the correct verb form. Change the tense where possible.

1 'It's going to be a beautiful day.'   He said it _____was going to be_____ a beautiful day.
2 'I don't want to go out this evening.'   She told me she _didn't want to go_ that evening.
3 'We're waiting for you.'   They said they _were waiting_ for us.
4 'My sister can't drive.'   She said her sister _couldn't drive_.
5 'I've lost my car keys.'   She told me she _had lost_ her car keys.
6 'Mei might have a new job.'   He said Mei _might have_ a new job.
7 'I'll help you with those bags.'   He said he _would help_ me with my bags.
8 'Marco bought a new car.'   You told me that Marco _had bought_ a new car.

b Read Harry's conversation with Ali. Then choose the best word or phrase to complete Ali's conversation with Harry's sister, Lucy.

> **HARRY** I'm trying to buy a book for my sister, Lucy. It's her birthday tomorrow.
> **ALI** What kinds of books does she like?
> **HARRY** I'm not sure. She likes reading about history.
> **ALI** This is really good, *A Short History of the World*. I read it a few months ago.
> **HARRY** No, I think she's already read that. She didn't like it. No, I'm going to get her this one, *A History of Amazing Buildings*. I think she'll love it.
>
> *Two days later, Ali sees Lucy in the street …*
>
> **ALI** Hi, Lucy. I saw your brother a couple of days ago – he said it was ¹*my / your / her* birthday ²*tomorrow / the previous day / yesterday.*
> **LUCY** Yes, that's right. Where did you see him?
> **ALI** At the bookshop. When I asked him what he was doing ³*here / there / near*, he said ⁴*he was / he's / I'm* looking for a present for ⁵*me / you / her.*
> **LUCY** Really?
> **ALI** Yes. I asked him what books ⁶*you liked / do you like / does she like*, and he said he wasn't sure. He said ⁷*she reads / you read / I read* history books. So I showed him *A Short History of the World* – I said it was really good. I told him ⁸*you've / I've / I'd* read it a few months ⁹*earlier / ago / later*. But he said ¹⁰*you'd / she's / I'd* already read it, and you hadn't liked it.
> **LUCY** What? I thought it was wonderful!
> **ALI** Yeah. Anyway, he said ¹¹*I'm / he's / he was* going to get *A History of Amazing Buildings*.
> **LUCY** Yes – and he did. It's really cool.
> **ALI** Great – he said ¹²*you'd love it / she'll love that / you'll love that.*

=> ago = specifique

c ⟫ Now go back to p. 94.

8B Verb patterns

a Underline the correct option.

1 I agreed *going / to go* to the hospital.
2 He admitted *to take / taking* the money.
3 Remember *to pick up / picking up* the dry cleaning on your way home.
4 We tried *making / to make* a cake, but the oven wasn't working.
5 I made the dog *sit / sitting* down.
6 Maria refused *watching / to watch* the scary film.
7 It's important *making / to make* a reservation in advance.
8 They don't *mind* *walking / to walk* home tonight.
9 We advised *to take / them to take* a short holiday.
10 When I was little, my mum always let me *stay / to stay* up late.

b Complete the conversation.

A I want ¹ _to get_ (get) my laptop fixed. I don't know where ² _to go_ (go).
B Have you tried ³ _to look_ (look) online? It's easy ⁴ _to find_ (find) repair shops, and you can read reviews ⁵ _to see_ (see) if they're good.
A Er … no. ⁶ _Checking_ (check) the Internet is going to be quite difficult because my computer's broken.
B Oh, right, sorry, I keep ⁷ _forgetting_ (forget). Listen, I think I know who ⁸ _to ask_ (ask). My neighbour's a computer engineer. I'll phone him now ⁹ _to ask_ (ask) him what ¹⁰ _to do_ (do).

Five minutes later …
B OK, so he says he doesn't mind ¹¹ _helping_ (help), but he's a bit busy. He suggests ¹² _turning_ (turn) it off and back on again ¹³ _to see_ (see) what happens. He says that usually works.
A Yes, I remember ¹⁴ _doing_ (do) that the last time I had a problem, and it did work. But now my computer just refuses ¹⁵ _to start_ (start) up.
B Hmm. I think I know how ¹⁶ _to fix_ (fix) it, but I need ¹⁷ _to take_ (take) the back off. I promise not ¹⁸ _to break_ (break) it …

c ⟫ Now go back to p. 96.

9A The passive

We form the passive using a form of *be* + past participle.

Active	09.03 Passive
They **make** a lot of films in Hollywood.	A lot of films **are made** in Hollywood.
The scriptwriters **are writing** a new script this week.	A new script **is being written** this week.
The estate agent **has sold** the house for £1 million.	The house **has been sold** for £1 million.
There was an accident while they **were building** the bridge.	There was an accident while the bridge **was being built**.
A film studio **will make** a film from the book.	A film **will be made** from the book.
Somebody **stole** our car in the night.	Our car **was stolen** in the night.
An expert **should do** the work.	The work **should be done** by an expert.

We use passive verb forms:
- when the main thing we are talking about is the object of the verb
  A film **will be made** from the book.
  The work **should be done** by an expert. (We are talking about the work, not the expert.)

- when the agent (the doer) isn't important
  The house **has been sold** for £1 million. (We're not interested in the estate agent.)
- when the agent (the doer) is very obvious
  A new script **is being written** this week. (by scriptwriters)
- when we don't know who did something / what caused something.
  Our car **was stolen** in the night.

Negatives and questions are made in the same way as other uses of *be*:
*Films **aren't** made here.*
***Is** a film **being** made here?*

We use *by* to introduce the person or thing that did the action (the agent):
*This frame was drawn **by** one of the animators.*
We usually use *with* to introduce a tool, instrument or technique that was used by the agent:
*The pirate's beard was controlled **with** a wire.*

> **Tip**
> We can say something was made by hand or by machine:
> *This jumper was made **by hand** in Scotland.*

9B Defining and non-defining relative clauses

09.07 Defining and non-defining relative clauses

Defining relative clauses define a noun or make it more specific. They tell us which particular thing or what kind of thing. In defining relative clauses, we can use *that*, *which* or *who*:
*I love music **that/which makes people dance**.*
*I hate books **that/which don't have happy endings**.*
*My dad met the woman **who reads the news on TV** yesterday!*

Non-defining relative clauses often start with *which* or *who*. They give extra information about a noun, but they are not necessary for the sentence to make sense:
The DJ was playing hip-hop. (This sentence is complete.)
*The DJ was playing hip-hop, **which is my favourite kind of music**.* (This relative clause adds more information.)
My parents are from Turkey. (This sentence is complete.)
*My parents, **who came to the UK 20 years ago**, are from Turkey.* (This relative clause adds more information.)

In writing, we need a comma before and after a non-defining relative clause. Don't use commas in defining relative clauses:
*We visited the market on a **Sunday, when they sell clothes and jewellery**.*
*I met **Lucy, who was staying with relatives nearby**, for a coffee.*

In both types of relative clause, we can use *who*, *which*, *whose*, *where* and *when*. Don't use *that* in a non-defining relative clause.
*Have you been to **that restaurant where you cook your own food at the table**?*
*Did you meet **the girl whose father climbed Mount Everest**?*

After *where*, we need to add a new subject to the relative clause. Compare:
*That's the shop **which sells** dictionaries.* (*which* is the subject of the relative clause)
*That's the shop **where you can buy** dictionaries.* (the relative clause has a new subject: you)

Omitting relative pronouns

We can often leave out *who/which/that* or *when* from defining relative clauses:
*He likes the cheese (**which/that**) I bought.*
(I bought the cheese. *cheese* = object)

Don't leave out the relative pronoun if it's the subject of the relative clause (*who*, *which* or *that*):
*He likes the cheese **that** comes from Turkey.* (The cheese comes from Turkey. *cheese* = subject)

Never leave out the relative pronoun from a non-defining relative clause:
*This cheese, **which** Greg really likes, comes from Turkey.*
NOT *This cheese, Greg really likes, ...*

I think we should buy the chair you are sitting in.

9A The passive

a Complete the passive sentences. Don't include any agents that are in brackets.

1. Ryan Coogler directed *Black Panther*.
2. (People) still make these shoes by hand.
3. (They) will build a new bridge next year.
4. My grandfather gave me this watch.
5. (We)'ve told everybody to be here on time.
6. (People) will laugh at you if you wear that hat.
7. A computer program creates the special effects.
8. My parents are looking after our dog this week.
9. (They) offered me £1,000 for my painting.
10. (Somebody) was repairing my car at the time.

Black Panther _____ was directed by Ryan Coogler.
These shoes _____ are still made by hand.
A new _____
I _____
Everybody _____
You _____
The special effects _____
Our dog _____
I _____
My car _____

b Rewrite the sentences as either *Yes/No* questions (?) or negatives (–).

1. We were picked up at the airport.
2. The painting's already been sold.
3. The work will be finished by Saturday.
4. The film's being made in Brazil.
5. Tomatoes are grown in Spain.
6. The car was being driven too fast.
7. The costumes were made by hand.
8. The sculpture has been taken to the museum.

(–) _____ We weren't picked up at the airport.
(?) _____ Has the painting already been sold?
(–) _____
(?) _____
(?) _____
(–) _____
(?) _____
(–) _____

c ≫ Now go back to p. 106.

9B Defining and non-defining relative clauses

a Complete the sentences with a word from the box. Sometimes more than one answer is possible. You will use some words more than once. Which sentence is also correct without a relative pronoun?

that when where which who whose

1. I love people _____ can make me laugh.
2. I told Paula my secret, _____ she then told everyone!
3. The film _____ I saw was really good.
4. Yesterday was the day _____ everything went wrong.
5. This album, _____ came out in 1995, has some great songs.
6. Mark is the person _____ father used to be a singer.
7. The shop _____ I bought this T-shirt has closed now.
8. I met Sara, _____ husband I work with, yesterday.

b Rewrite the sentences, adding the information in brackets as a non-defining relative clause. Use relative pronouns that refer to the underlined words.

1. Ariana Grande performed <u>*No Tears Left to Cry*</u>. (She recorded it in 2018.)
   Ariana Grande performed No Tears Left to Cry, which she recorded in 2018.
2. <u>*Auld Lang Syne*</u> is sung around the world on New Year's Day. (It was written by the poet Robert Burns.)

3. We're going to <u>Cuba</u>. (Mambo music comes from there.)

4. <u>The Glastonbury Festival</u> also has theatre, comedy and circus performances. (It's most famous as a music festival.)

5. My favourite singer is <u>Beyoncé</u>. (Her album *Lemonade* was released in 2016.)

6. The best day of the festival is the <u>last day</u>. (There's a big fireworks display then.)

c Rewrite the sentences, adding the information in brackets as a defining relative clause. Leave out *who*, *which* or *that* if possible.

1. I like the tune. (You were singing it.)
   I like the tune you were singing.
2. That's the DJ. (He was here two weeks ago.)

3. We need music. (It makes you want to dance.)

4. That's the stage. (We're going to perform there.)

5. I downloaded a new song. (You'll like it.)

6. What did you think of the music? (I chose it.)

7. What's the name of your friend? (You borrowed his earbuds.)

8. The song changed my life. (It's playing on the radio.)

d Are the sentences below correct (✓) or incorrect (✗)? Sometimes both sentences in a pair are correct.

1. a I like music which makes me dance. ✓
   b I like music makes me dance. ✗
2. a It's a drum that you play with your hands.
   b It's a drum you play with your hands.
3. a My father, that is a dentist, looks after my teeth.
   b My father, who is a dentist, looks after my teeth.
4. a This album, I bought last week, is really good.
   b This album, which I bought last week, is really good.

e ≫ Now go back to p. 108.

10A Second conditional

We use the second conditional to talk about imagined events or states and their consequences. They can be about the unreal present or the unlikely future.

Real present		10.04 Unreal present and consequence
I don't know the answer.	→	*If I **knew** the answer, I'**d tell** you.*
Likely future		**Unlikely/imagined future and consequence**
She won't find out that you lied.	→	*She **would be** angry if she **found** out you had lied.*

We usually use the past simple in the *if*-clause and *would* in the main clause.
We can use *could* or *might* instead of *would* to say that something is less likely:
*You **could afford** to go on holiday if you **were** more careful with your money.*
*If you **tried** harder, you **might win** a medal.*

In the *if*-clause, it is possible to use *were* for all persons (*if I were, if you were, if she were*, etc.). We can still use *was* with *I*, *she* and *he* (*If I was, If he/she was*):
*If **I were** taller, I'd be better at basketball.*

We use the phrase *If I were you* to give advice:
If I were you, *I wouldn't eat that fish. It doesn't smell fresh.*

We don't always need to include the *if*-clause if the meaning is clear:
*Look at that house! That **would** be a great place to live.* (... if I moved there)
*I'm sure Jack **would** help you.* (... if you asked)

> **Tip**
>
> When talking about the future, you can usually choose between the first and second conditional. Use the first conditional if you think a future event is likely; use the second conditional if you think it is unlikely.
> - *If we **score** one more point, we'**ll** win.*
>   (I think there's a good chance of this.)
> - *If we **scored** four more points, we'**d** win* (but we probably won't).

> **Tip**
>
> The contracted form of *would* (*'d*) is the same as the contracted form of *had*.
> You can tell the difference by looking at the verb that comes next.
> - *'d* + past participle: *He'**d won** (= had won) the match.*
> - *'d* + infinitive: *He'**d win** (= would win) the match.*

10B Third conditional

 10.08

We use the third conditional to talk about imagined past events or states and their consequences:
*If you'**d told** me about your birthday, I **would have** bought you a present.*

We use the past perfect in the *if*-clause and *would have* + past participle in the main clause.

Real past		Unreal past and consequence
I didn't know the answer.	→	*If I'**d known** the answer, I'**d have done better** in the exam.*
Lou didn't work hard.	→	*If Lou **had worked** harder, he **would have earned** more money.*

We can also use *could have* or *might have* instead of *would have*:
*We **could have saved** some money if we'**d known** about the offer.*
*If I **had done** more work, I **might have passed** the exam.*

Common uses of the third conditional

1 Regrets about things that happened or didn't happen in the past:
   *If I'**d sold** my house two years ago, I'**d have made** a fortune.*
2 Relief about avoiding a past problem:
   *I **might have missed** the flight if you **hadn't woken** me up.*
3 Surprise about how things were different from expected:
   *If you'**d told** me five years ago I'd have my own company one day, I **wouldn't have believed** you.*

> **Tip**
>
> Be especially careful with the contraction *'d*. In the *if*-clause, it's a contraction of *had*. In the main clause, it's a contraction of *would*.

If you'd told me about your birthday, I'd have bought you a present.

10A Second conditional

a Match the sentence beginnings 1–8 with the most logical endings a–h.

1 If I had more money,   `c`
2 I'd be grateful   ☐
3 If I were you,   ☐
4 If you asked her again nicely,   ☐
5 I wouldn't be so relaxed   ☐
6 If he weren't so rude,   ☐
7 I could get a better job   ☐
8 Angela would be really sad   ☐

a she might change her mind.
b more people would like him.
c I could eat in restaurants more often.
d if I spoke better English.
e if we didn't invite her.
f I'd complain to your boss.
g if you didn't tell anybody my secret.
h if I had an exam tomorrow!

b Underline the correct options.

1 *I'd go* / *I went* swimming more if *I'd have* / *I had* time.
2 If *I'd know* / *I knew* his number, *I'd call* / *I called* him.
3 *Would* / *Did* you mind if *I'd ask* / *I asked* you a question?
4 If you *wouldn't* / *didn't* have a car, how *would* / *did* you get around?
5 *You'd be* / *You were* a lot healthier if you *wouldn't* / *didn't* eat so much.
6 If *I'd be* / *I were* you, *I'd get* / *I got* some new shoes.
7 What *would* / *did* you do if *you'd see* / *you saw* a fire?
8 If someone *would treat* / *treated* you like that, how *would* / *did* you feel?

c Decide if the first or second conditional is more appropriate for each situation. Then complete the sentences with the correct form of the verbs in brackets.

1 I think I'll probably leave my job soon. But if I _____leave_____ (leave) my job, it _____'ll be_____ (be) difficult to get a new one.
2 I think it's going to be a nice day. We _____ (can) have a picnic if the weather _____ (stay) nice.
3 I'm not very good at football. If I _____ (can) play better, I _____ (join) a football team.
4 If I _____ (win) the lottery, I _____ (buy) a new house. But I know it's never going to happen.
5 I think we're the best team. If we _____ (win) the competition, I _____ (not be) surprised.
6 You drink too much coffee. If you _____ (not drink) so much, you _____ (not be) so stressed.
7 She goes shopping all the time! She _____ (not have) any money left if she _____ (not stop) spending it!
8 I don't like my house in the city. If I _____ (live) in the countryside, I _____ (be) much happier.

d ≫ Now go back to p. 117.

10B Third conditional

a What does *'d* mean in each sentence? Write *had* or *would*.

1 If you'd (_had_) told me earlier, we'd (_would_) have saved a lot of time.
2 I don't know what I'd (_____) have done if you hadn't helped me.
3 We might have been seriously hurt if you'd (_____) crashed.
4 She'd (_____) have got the job if she'd (_____) applied for it.
5 I'd (_____) have loved to go to the party, but I wasn't invited.

b Write third conditional sentences about the situations.

1 Real past: I didn't win the competition because I made a stupid mistake.
   Unreal past: If _I hadn't made a stupid mistake, I would have won the competition._
2 Real past: He went to live in Japan. While he was there, he met his wife.
   Unreal past: If he _____
3 Real past: The car broke down, so we couldn't go to the concert.
   Unreal past: We _____
4 Real past: I didn't go to see the film because I didn't know it was so good.
   Unreal past: I _____
5 Real past: You didn't take my advice, so you got lost.
   Unreal past: If _____
6 Real past: You helped me so much. That's why I was so successful.
   Unreal past: I wouldn't _____

c Find and correct the mistakes.

1 If you'd been there too, you ~~would enjoy~~ yourself.
   _____would have enjoyed_____
2 We couldn't have bought the house if they wouldn't have lent us the money.
   _____
3 If they hadn't noticed the fire, the whole house could burned down.
   _____
4 If I know it was dangerous, I'd never have gone there.
   _____
5 What you would have done if I hadn't helped you?
   _____
6 He could have been an opera singer if he'd have some training.
   _____
7 If they'd arrive a few minutes later, they might have missed you.
   _____

d ≫ Now go back to p. 121.

Phonemic symbols

Vowel sounds

Short

/ə/ teach**er**	/æ/ m**a**n	/ʊ/ p**u**t	/ɒ/ g**o**t
/ɪ/ ch**i**p	/i/ happ**y**	/e/ m**e**n	/ʌ/ b**u**t

Long

/ɜː/ sh**ir**t	/ɑː/ p**ar**t	/uː/ wh**o**	/ɔː/ w**a**lk	/iː/ ch**ea**p

Diphthongs (two vowel sounds)

/eə/ h**air**	/ɪə/ n**ear**	/ʊə/ t**our**	/ɔɪ/ b**oy**	/aɪ/ f**ine**	/eɪ/ l**a**te	/əʊ/ wind**ow**	/aʊ/ n**ow**

Consonants

/p/ **p**icnic	/b/ **b**ook	/f/ **f**ace	/v/ **v**ery	/t/ **t**ime	/d/ **d**og	/k/ **c**old	/g/ **g**o	/θ/ **th**ink	/ð/ **th**e	/tʃ/ **ch**air	/dʒ/ **j**ob
/s/ **s**ea	/z/ **z**oo	/ʃ/ **sh**oe	/ʒ/ televi**si**on	/m/ **m**e	/n/ **n**ow	/ŋ/ si**ng**	/h/ **h**ot	/l/ **l**ate	/r/ **r**ed	/w/ **w**ent	/j/ **y**es

Irregular verbs

Infinitive	Past simple	Past participle
be	was /wɒz/ / were /wɜː/	been
become	became	become
begin	began	begun
blow	blew /bluː/	blown /bləʊn/
break /breɪk/	broke /brəʊk/	broken /ˈbrəʊkən/
bring /brɪŋ/	brought /brɔːt/	brought /brɔːt/
build /bɪld/	built /bɪlt/	built /bɪlt/
buy /baɪ/	bought /bɔːt/	bought /bɔːt/
catch /kætʃ/	caught /kɔːt/	caught /kɔːt/
choose /tʃuːz/	chose /tʃəʊz/	chosen /ˈtʃəʊzən/
come	came	come
cost	cost	cost
cut	cut	cut
deal /dɪəl/	dealt /delt/	dealt /delt/
do	did	done /dʌn/
draw /drɔː/	drew /druː/	drawn /drɔːn/
drink	drank	drunk
drive /draɪv/	drove /drəʊv/	driven /ˈdrɪvən/
eat /iːt/	ate /et/	eaten /ˈiːtən/
fall	fell	fallen
feel	felt	felt
find /faɪnd/	found /faʊnd/	found /faʊnd/
fly /flaɪ/	flew /fluː/	flown /fləʊn/
forget	forgot	forgotten
get	got	got
give /gɪv/	gave /geɪv/	given /ˈgɪvən/
go	went	gone /gɒn/
grow	grew /gruː/	grown /grəʊn/
have /hæv/	had /hæd/	had /hæd/
hear /hɪə/	heard /hɜːd/	heard /hɜːd/
hit	hit	hit
hold /həʊld/	held	held
keep	kept	kept
know /nəʊ/	knew /njuː/	known /nəʊn/

Infinitive	Past simple	Past participle
leave /liːv/	left	left
lend	lent	lent
let	let	let
lose /luːz/	lost	lost
make	made	made
meet	met	met
pay /peɪ/	paid /peɪd/	paid /peɪd/
put	put	put
read /riːd/	read /red/	read /red/
ride /raɪd/	rode /rəʊd/	ridden /ˈrɪdən/
ring	rang	rung
run	ran	run
say /seɪ/	said /sed/	said /sed/
see	saw /sɔː/	seen
sell	sold /səʊld/	sold /səʊld/
send	sent	sent
set	set	set
sing	sang	sung
sit	sat	sat
sleep	slept	slept
speak /spiːk/	spoke /spəʊk/	spoken /ˈspəʊkən/
spend	spent	spent
stand	stood /stʊd/	stood /stʊd/
steal /stiːl/	stole /stəʊl/	stolen /ˈstəʊlən/
swim /swɪm/	swam /swæm/	swum /swʌm/
take /teɪk/	took /tʊk/	taken /ˈteɪkən/
teach /tiːtʃ/	taught /tɔːt/	taught /tɔːt/
tell	told /təʊld/	told /təʊld/
think	thought /θɔːt/	thought /θɔːt/
throw /θrəʊ/	threw /θruː/	thrown /θrəʊn/
understand	understood /ʌndəˈstʊd/	understood /ʌndəˈstʊd/
wake /weɪk/	woke /wəʊk/	woken /ˈwəʊkən/
wear /weə/	wore /wɔː/	worn /wɔːn/
win	won	won
write /raɪt/	wrote /rəʊt/	written /ˈrɪtən/

Acknowledgments

The authors and publishers acknowledge the following sources of copyright material and are grateful for the permissions granted. While every effort has been made, it has not always been possible to identify the sources of all the material used, or to trace all copyright holders. If any omissions are brought to our notice, we will be happy to include the appropriate acknowledgements on reprinting and in the next update to the digital edition, as applicable.

Key:
U = Unit, V = Vocabulary, C = Communication Plus

Text
U1: Guardian News & Media Limited for the adapted text from 'How I learned a language in 22 hours' by Joshua Foer, *The Guardian* 09.11.2012. Copyright © The Guardian. Reproduced with permission; **U4:** Guardian News & Media Limited for the adapted text from 'Are you an introvert? Take our quiz', *The Guardian* 2012. Copyright © The Guardian. Reproduced with permission.

Photographs:
The following photographs are sourced from Getty Images.

U1: Stuart Fox; Moyo Studio/E+; LeoPatrizi/E+; RyanJLane/E+; Geber86/E+; PeopleImages/E+; Dougal Waters/DigitalVision; Eclipse_images/E+; Ferrantraite/E+; CarmenMurillo/iStock; Martinedoucet/E+; Matthias Ritzmann/The Image Bank; **U2:** Frank van Delft/Cultura; Skynesher/E+; MangoStar_Studio/iStock; Svetikd/E+; Kupicoo/E+; Filistimlyanin/iStock; Nomad/E+; Tinpixels/E+; Jacoblund/iStock; ljubaphoto/E+; IakovKalinin/iStock; D3sign/Moment; Westend61; Owngarden/Moment; TONNAJA/Moment; **U3:** Erik Dreyer/Stone; SeanShot/iStock Unreleased; Betsie Van der Meer/DigitalVision; XiFotos/E+; Lisa Stirling/Photographer's Choice RF; Louise Morgan/Moment; Martin-dm/E+; Jeff Kravitz/FilmMagic, Inc; Vera Anderson/WireImage; Allen Berezovsky/WireImage; Pixelfit/E+; Filadendron/E+; Westend61; George Marks/Retrofile RF; George Marks/Retrofile RF; **U4:** Ghislain & Marie David de Lossy/Cultura; Sean Gallup/Getty Images Entertainment; Pablo Morano/MB Media/Getty Images Sport; Pierre Suu/Getty Images Entertainment; James Devaney/WireImage; Kali9/E+; Fizkes/iStock; Urbazon/iStock; Bettmann; Steven Ferdman/Getty Images Entertainment; William Philpott/Hulton Archive; Dia Dipasupil/Getty Images Entertainment; Dougal Waters/DigitalVision; SDI Productions/E+; Tim Graham/Getty Images News; Jacob Wackerhausen/E+; **U5:** Ken Kiefer 2/Image Source; Hanohiki/iStock Editorial; Suzanne Dehne/Moment; Gabrielle Therin-Weise/Photographer's Choice RF; Sergio Saavedra Ruiz/iStock; Ben Cranke/The Image Bank; Plume Creative/DigitalVision; Kevin Wells/iStock; JHVEPhoto/iStock; Scacciamosche/E+; Stocksnapper/iStock; SergeyChayko/iStock; FiledIMAGE/iStock; Luc Pouliot/iStock; P A Thompson/The Image Bank; Siraphol/iStock; Mark Ralston/AFP; Stephen Frink/The Image Bank; Merethe Svarstad Eeg/EyeEm; Micheldenijs/E+; Stefan Wackerhagen; Paul Carpenter/iStock; Wrangel/iStock; Marzolino/iStock; Adisak Mitrprayoon/iStock; Guenter Fischer; Davidhoffmannphotography/iStock; Greg Wood/AFP; CnOra/iStock Editorial; **U6:** Matteo Colombo/Moment; Deimagine/E+; Imtmphoto/iStock; Javier Sánchez Mingorance/EyeEm; Olga Mazyarkina/iStock; Mariha-kitchen/iStock; Teen00000/iStock; Mizina/iStock; Sheri L Giblin/Photolibrary; Nick Dolding/Stone; Mukesh-kumar/iStock; Calvin Chan Wai Meng/Moment; John Seaton Callahan/Moment; Fazeful/iStock; luchezar/E+; Enes Evren/E+; Bruno De Hogues/Photographer's Choice; Keipher McKennie/WireImage; JazzIRT/E+; **U7:** Ed Freeman/Stone; Maica/iStock; Future Publishing; Wibowo Rusli/Lonely Planet Images; Vostok/Moment; Canopy; ivo Gretener/iStock; Kartik Sewani/iStock Editorial; ArabianEye; Thomas Roche/

Moment Open; Lonely Planet Images; Golibo/iStock; Jenny Jones/Lonely Planet Images; Roberto Machado Noa/Moment Unreleased; Eduardo Fonseca Arraes/Moment; Sergio Formoso/Moment; Jekaterina Nikitina/Stone; Tim Robberts/DigitalVision; Mitchell Funk/Photographer's Choice; Photographer's Choice; BRUCE WEAVER/AFP; Nisian Hughes/Stone; **U8:** Andre Ringuette/National Hockey League; Cavan Images; MEHDI FEDOUACH/AFP; 10'000 Hours/DigitalVision; Pekic/E+; Mixetto/E+; MStudioImages/E+; Eva-Katalin/E+; Liesel Bockl; FangXiaNuo/E+; FG Trade/E+; Santiago Urquijo/Moment; AzmanL/E+; Stock4Bcreative; **U9:** Perboge/iStock Editorial; Westend61; Yiu Yu Hoi/The Image Bank; Erik Dreyer/Stone; PeopleImages/E+; Ivan Jones/Stone; David Redfern/Hulton Archive; Hiroyuki Ito/Hulton Archive; Kevin Mazur/Getty Images Entertainment; Chris Mouyiaris/Robertharding; Kiyoshi Ota/Getty Images Entertainment; Richard Newstead/The Image Bank; Wayne Eastep/The Image Bank; Frank van Delft/Cultura; Mark Andersen; Jeff Kravitz/FilmMagic, Inc; Hiroyuki Ito/Hulton Archive; **U10:** PeopleImages/E+; Technotr/E+; CHRISTOF STACHE/AFP; Bacalao64/iStock; Anadolu Agency; Frederic Pacorel/Photographer's Choice; Mint Images-Steve Prezant; Trevor Williams/Photographer's Choice; Lorado/E+; Tom And Steve/Photographer's Choice; FG Trade/E+; NDStock/iStock; Fizkes/iStock; Neale Clark/robertharding; miodrag ignjatovic/E+; Kupicoo/E+; Westend61; Morsa Images/DigitalVision; Jamie Grill; Kieran Stone/Moment; SimonSkafar/E+; Peter Griffith/Stone; **V:** Herianus Herianus/EyeEm; MB Photography/Moment; Yaorusheng/Moment; FEBRUARY/Moment; Boonchai wedmakawand/Moment; Didier Marti/Moment; Alison Taylor Photograpy/iStock; FG Trade/iStock; Michael Gebicki/Lonely Planet Images; Robert Kneschke/EyeEm; Westend61; Paul Starosta/Stone; Ugurhan/E+; JillianSuzanne/iStock; Mathieu/500px; MirasWonderland/iStock; Christopher Furlong/Getty Images News.

The following photographs are sourced from other sources/libraries.

U1: © Cambridge University Press; **U3:** Topfoto/Topfoto.co.uk; © Rachel Hojnson; **U5:** © Whitley Fund For Nature; © Alexander Blanco; **U6:** Lucas Vallecillos/Alamy Stock Photo; © Dee and John Lee; **U8:** © Chris Bethell; **C:** © Chris Bethell; © Theo C. McInnes.

Cover photography by Thomas Barwick/DigitalVision/Getty Images.

Commissioned photography by Gareth Boden: **U1** & **U10**.

Commissioned video stills by Rob Maidment and Sharp Focus Productions: **U1 – U10**.

Illustrations:
QBS Learning; Beatrice Bencivenni; Mark Bird; Mark Duffin; Jo Goodberry; Mark (KJA Artists); Jerome Mireault; Gavin Reece; Gregory Roberts; Sean (KJA Artists); David Semple; Sean Sims; Marie-Eve-Tremblay.

Audio production by Leon Chambers and by Creative Listening.

Typeset by QBS Learning.

Corpus

Development of this publication has made use of the Cambridge English Corpus (CEC). The CEC is a computer database of contemporary spoken and written English, which currently stands at over one billion words. It includes British English, American English and other varieties of English. It also includes the Cambridge Learner Corpus, developed in collaboration with the University of Cambridge ESOL Examinations. Cambridge University Press has built up the CEC to provide evidence about language use that helps us to produce better language teaching materials.

English Profile

This product is informed by English Vocabulary Profile, built as part of English Profile, a collaborative programme designed to enhance the learning, teaching and assessment of English worldwide. Its main funding partners are Cambridge University Press and Cambridge Assessment English and its aim is to create a 'profile' for English, linked to the Common European Framework of Reference for Languages (CEFR). English Profile outcomes, such as the English Vocabulary Profile, will provide detailed information about the language that learners can be expected to demonstrate at each CEFR level, offering a clear benchmark for learners' proficiency. For more information, please visit www.englishprofile.org.

CALD

The Cambridge Advanced Learner's Dictionary is the world's most widely used dictionary for learners of English. Including all the words and phrases that learners are likely to come across, it also has easy-to-understand definitions and example sentences to show how the word is used in context. The Cambridge Advanced Learner's Dictionary is available online at dictionary.cambridge.org.

Shaftesbury Road, Cambridge CB2 8EA, United Kingdom

One Liberty Plaza, 20th Floor, New York, NY 10006, USA

477 Williamstown Road, Port Melbourne, VIC 3207, Australia

314–321, 3rd Floor, Plot 3, Splendor Forum, Jasola District Centre, New Delhi – 110025, India

103 Penang Road, #05–06/07, Visioncrest Commercial, Singapore 238467

Cambridge University Press & Assessment is a department of the University of Cambridge.

We share the University's mission to contribute to society through the pursuit of education, learning and research at the highest international levels of excellence.

www.cambridge.org
Information on this title: cambridge.org/9781108959575

First published 2022
20 19 18 17 16 15 14 13 12 11 10 9 8 7 6

Printed in Malaysia by Vivar Printing

A catalogue record for this publication is available from the British Library

ISBN 978-1-108-95957-5 Intermediate Student's Book with eBook
ISBN 978-1-108-96149-3 Intermediate Student's Book with Digital Pack
ISBN 978-1-108-96153-0 Intermediate Workbook with Answers
ISBN 978-1-108-96178-3 Intermediate Workbook without Answers
ISBN 978-1-108-96151-6 Intermediate Combo A with Digital Pack
ISBN 978-1-108-96152-3 Intermediate Combo B with Digital Pack
ISBN 978-1-108-96179-0 Intermediate Teacher's Book with Digital Pack
ISBN 978-1-108-95973-5 Intermediate Presentation Plus
ISBN 978-1-108-96150-9 Intermediate Student's Book with Digital Pack, Academic Skills and Reading Plus

Additional resources for this publication at cambridge.org/empower

This page is intentionally left blank.

This page is intentionally left blank.

This page is intentionally left blank.